Unveiling Traditions

Anouar Majid

Unveiling Traditions

Postcolonial Islam in a Polycentric World

Duke University Press   Durham & London   2000

Printed in the United States of America
on acid-free paper ∞
Designed by C. H. Westmoreland
Typeset in Minion
by Keystone Typesetting, Inc.
Library of Congress Cataloging-in-Publication
Data appear on the last printed page of this book.

Chapter 1 is a modified version of the article
"Can the Postcolonial Critic Speak? Orientalism
and the Rushdie Affair" *Cultural Critique* (winter 1995–96). Chapter 4 (Women's Freedom in
Muslim Spaces) is also a slightly modified version of an article that appeared in *Signs: Journal
of Women in Culture and Society* 23 (winter 1998)
under the title "The Politics of Feminism in Islam" by the University of Chicago. The editors
of *Signs* published two comments on that article, to which the author responded. Some of
the information in the *Signs* article and reply
("Reply to Joseph and Mayer: Critique as a De-
hegemonizing Practice" 23 [winter 1998] by the
University of Chicago) may be found in notes
and other parts of this book. The author is
grateful to the University of Minnesota Press
and the University of Chicago Press for allowing
him to reprint his articles in this book.

Contents

Preface

Unveiling Traditions was conceived as a project to examine the extent to which Islam shapes intellectual practice in primarily Muslim societies and to give Islamic cultures a more prominent role in postcolonial and multicultural theories. The global furor over the Rushdie affair did more than any recent event to bring postcolonial fiction into the mainstream; yet, with very few exceptions, postcolonial critics never seriously examined the place of Islam in debates of multiculturalism. The challenge of including Islamic subjectivities and cultural epistemologies into a world of equal differences has been left untheorized, probably because the religious imaginary is dismissed ahead of time as either conservative or unredeemable. Yet I don't think people can step out of their cultures (notwithstanding the much vaunted hybridizing effects of the market place) and reconstitute themselves in an entirely new vocabulary. My defense of Muslims' rights to their identities and memories is motivated exclusively by my strong belief that only secure, progressive, indigenous traditions, cultivated over long spans of time, can sustain meaningful global diversities and create effective alternatives to the deculturing effects of capitalism. I chose Islam because it is the religion and culture I am most familiar with. I would have done the same with America's native populations, or any other cultural community (including Euro-American ones) whose identity springs from a pre- or noncapitalist cosmology, had I been confident in my ability to capture the histories and spirit of those traditions. In any case, I have always believed that revitalizing traditions from within is preferable to adopting new ideologies and worldviews.

Working with concepts such as Islam, capitalism, the West, and other charged terms turned out to be emotionally draining at times. My call for a progressive Islam and my critique of capitalism are inspired by the vision for a more humane global civilization; they are not expressions of my own personal practices, devotions, or pieties. It is needless to state (except for those who genuinely believe in super-human wills) that I am as captured by the pervasive networks of capitalist culture as anyone who celebrates the free-market ideology as a liberating economic force. Though there is no doubt at all that I blame capitalism for the imbalances of our era, I don't extend the blame to the people who participate in that system (whether actively or not), for nothing is more natural than to adhere to the social rules that existing (bourgeois) systems make available to us. It would be utterly unrealistic—if not quite infantile—to expect a parent not to work as a stockbroker or a banker and let one's children starve or suffer need-lessly because of strong objections to or reservations about capitalism. Since participation in the capitalist system has become unavoidable for most people (especially those who live in urban centers and indus-trialized nations), my critique entails a call for changing the rules that frame our thoughts and behaviors; it suggests—without articulating any blueprints or outlining any utopian visions—a proposal for con-sidering alternative regulatory social mechanisms, venues that allow people to satisfy basic human needs and communal obligations with-out imperiling our human, social, and environmental fabrics.

While I make no claim to transcending the immediate realities of capitalist relations, my argument in favor of a progressive Islam is also a proposal that says nothing at all about my own religious prac-tices. In this book I speak as a layperson born into the Muslim faith, the traditional liberal variety of Moroccan Islam. More than that, my intellectual outlook was forged in the city of Tangier, whose notori-ously jaded cosmopolitanism and "carnal stereophony" (in the words of the great semiotician, Roland Barthes) perpetually subvert the "power of [syntactic] completion" and invariably work against the crystallization of ideas into hard, inflexible certainties.[1] My identity was nurtured in the aporetic linguistic spaces of Tangier's streets and

cafes, places where virtue has always been measured by one's ability
to propose narratives of hope while maintaining that such hope must
forever remain a procrastinated reality. For in Tangier only fools
seriously think that they will some day inhabit the gilded quarters of
their enchanting fables.

Still, regardless of the lacunas that polarize intentions and material
life into what are often irreconcilable spheres, we need the tensions
that narratives of hope generate if only to reach beyond our mundane captivities. Like any storyteller, an academic's vocation is to
imagine a bright future for her students and audiences, to believe
(however quixotically) in the possibility of a miraculous feat, a collective human enterprise that is capable of sustaining a civilization of
rich and enriching diversities. Such hope invites the scholar to participate in a process of critical engagements designed to foster and
cultivate a non-rancorous democratic spirit of meaningful dialogue.
Michel Foucault, who had at one time despaired of ever encountering real intellectuals, said that the intellectual's duty is "to question
over and over again what is postulated as self-evident, to disturb
people's mental habits, the way they do and think things, to dissipate
what is familiar and accepted, to reexamine rules and institutions and
on the basis of this reproblematization (in which he carries out his
specific task as an intellectual) to participate in the formation of a
political will (in which he has his role as citizen to play)."[2] Such
Nietzschean moves could be quite invigorating if master narratives of
hope are maintained as guiding principles.

While I worked on this project for the better part of a decade,
rarely reaching beyond the confines of my home institution, I was
sustained by the friendship of my colleague and formidable interlocutor, Jacques Downs. Jacques's Franklinian interests, wide-
ranging historical views, and ability to maintain the longue durée
firmly in mind even while he addresses transient and seemingly
mundane issues have convinced me that Foucault's pessimism is still
not fully justified. Committed to global education, he introduced me
to Mexico at a critical moment in that great country's history and
thus added a whole new world to my small cultural repertoire. I am
also grateful to my comrade Michael Morris for his constant support
and for inviting me to an inspiring Zuni ceremonial dance and din-

ner that have allowed me to feel the resiliently vibrant but embattled pulse of native American traditions. As I stood surrounded by sunset-tinted New Mexico mesas watching "mudheads" and Kachinas perform their mirthful dance on a cold winter evening, I was able to trace—albeit fleetingly—the course of modern history, with both its well-known tragic consequences and its glimpses of hope. Other colleagues at the University of New England—too special to name casually—have been equally generous with their books, time, and encouragement. I seriously doubt whether I could have written this book, or even started it, had I been at a more traditional academic setting in which the rigid and unexamined boundaries of disciplines still shape intellectual pursuits.

This book benefited from the insightful critiques and supportive comments of Leila Ahmed and Abdul JanMohamed. Ahmed's seminal work on gender, identity, and Islam has inspired my project in several ways, while JanMohamed's engaging questions have pushed me to polish my argument and think harder about some issues. I feel particularly honored that my work has been read by these two distinguished scholars. I am also grateful to J. Reynolds Smith whose editorial judgment confirmed to me that the book was worth writing in the first place. Paula Dragosh's careful reading and astonishing eye for detail turned the manuscript into a more polished text, while Carol Roberts's meticulous indexing skills added a useful section at the end of this book. Sharon Parks Torian's good-humored encouragement and Rebecca Johns-Danes's diligent oversight over the production process made the long publication wait easier to bear.

When I survey the vast field of people and institutions who have been kind and generous to me, I feel compelled to single out a whole succession of teachers and professors in Tangier and Fez as the ones who were ultimately responsible for instilling in me a passion for critical textual analysis. Since that formative period, my intellectual engagements have always been based on textual production (broadly defined to include ideologies), never with speakers, writers, or ideologues. The difference is crucial, since texts allow readers to critique and disagree with one another while asserting and defending the human dignity of their interlocutors. I only hope that the following argument does justice to my old masters' tradition.

The question returns. What shall we do? I confess, all attempts to project and establish a Cultus with new rites and forms seem to me vain. Faith makes us, and not we it, and faith makes its own forms. All attempts to contrive a system, are as cold as the new worship introduced by the French to the goddess of Reason—today, pasteboard and fillagree, and ending to-morrow in madness and murder. Rather let the breath of new life be breathed by you through the forms already existing.

—Ralph Waldo Emerson,
"The Divinity School Address" (1838)

Introduction

Villainies Veiled and Unveiled

Was our society, which had always been so assured of its superiority
and rectitude, so confident of its unexamined premises, assembled
round anything more permanent than a congeries of banks,
insurance companies and industries, and had it any beliefs more
essential than a belief in compound interest and the maintenance of
dividends? Such thoughts as these formed the starting point, and
must remain the excuse, for saying what I have to say.
—T.S. Eliot, *The Idea of a Christian Society*

On August 11, 1999, the *Wall Street Journal* published a long article
detailing the power struggle in Iran between "leftist mullahs" who
support the reform policies of the popularly elected president and
conservative, right-wing clerics who are fiercely opposing these reforms. The article clearly showed that while the Islamic regime was
no longer seriously questioned, Islam is expansive enough to allow
for different interpretations and genuine democratic contestations.
What is interesting about this article, though, is that after devoting
considerable space to explaining that the Iranian reformists who
champion President Khatami, favor and defend an open press, and
even daringly advocate the separation of religion and state are as
religious as the conservatives they oppose, the author relied so thoroughly on European political categories that he opened his article

by stating, mistakenly, that the struggle in Iran is "between Islamic clerics and secular reformers." This syntactic slippage was noted by a reader who promptly wrote to the editor to comment on the use of the term *secular.* "Those, such as myself, who oppose the undemocratic elements in the Iranian regime," the reader explained, "are not secular at all. We believe the Republic should be run according to Islamic principles of justice and equality. That we are striving for increased transparency and democracy in Iran doesn't make us 'secular.'" A Muslim, the reader wanted to emphasize, doesn't have to be "secular" to believe in the universal virtues of social justice and the inviolability of human dignity.[1]

I want to present this view not because Islam's capacious inclusiveness needs defending but because a progressive multicultural world of linked but irreducible cultural singularities (perhaps a sort of noncapitalist heterotopia)[2] has become a historic necessity. The *Wall Street Journal* article shows how local ideological assumptions permeate Western discourses and how the reporter's entrapment in a (often unexamined or ambiguous) Eurocentric vocabulary is remarkably common and transcends most ideological boundaries.[3] Like *Orientalism,*[4] *Islam,* and other highly charged terms examined in this book, the term *secularism* cannot avoid its unmistakable cultural origins. The secular worldview that emanated from the late eighteenth century and the first few decades of the nineteenth was the product of Enlightenment thought and a classical liberal philosophy whose goal was nothing less than the recalibration and redefinition of human morality to adjust it to a new social calculus that excluded traditional religious commitments (irrational as these might have been). Endowed with "natural rights" that extended into the ownership of private property, individuals were sent into the world to maximize their self-interest and enter into all sorts of "contracts," whether with business partners, workers, or states. In this new order, the well-being of society, Eric Hobsbawm suggests, was measured by "the arithmetical sum of individual aims." Such a view also assumed that "progress" is as natural as capitalism, for almost all the great political economists of the period genuinely believed that the "invisible hand" of the market was eventually destined to enrich everyone and, in the process, substantially expand the scope of human freedom and happiness. But capitalism hasn't proffered its graces equally on all peoples, which is why the Marxist and socialist movements of the nineteenth century (secular and steeped in the same classical liberalism that led the philosophers of free markets to wrap economic interest and liberty into one ideological package) emerged to correct and contest the exuberant confidence of the earlier political economists.[5]

However, the tone of "reasonableness" and the exalted virtues of scholarly *sang froid* and emotional detachment that the secular attitude embodies often hide the controversial origins of the secularization process and its inextricable connection to a wider body of thought that continues to assume the naturalness of bourgeois social and political organization. Secularization theory, Nikki Keddie wrote in a recent article, "shares the linear-progressive viewpoint of modernization theory, and is really a sub-category of that theoretical approach." After noting that the "state today is entirely secular or entirely non-secular," Keddie supports John Ruedy's view in his edited volume on *Islamism and Secularism in North Africa* (1994) that the boundaries of the two spheres (secularism and religion) are characterized by a tension that has so far been unsettled. Keddie's article reiterates that secularization has been mostly imposed by the state, not only in Islamic nations but also in the West itself.[6]

The secular premises of scholarship have thus increased the remoteness of Islam; they thickened and intensified the opaqueness of a Muslim subjectivity shrouded in a different "regime of truth," as Foucault suggested in an interview following the Islamic revolution in Iran.[7] These premises have imposed serious limitations on progressive theories of inclusion (since the model of change envisioned, or rather vaguely suggested, in prevailing postcolonial discourses is heavily colored by Eurocentric biases) and have prolonged the false belief that global harmonies remain elusive because of cultural conflicts, not because human cultures are being constantly battered by the capitalist system.

I am not denying that talking about cultures, at least in their epistemological sense, can be fraught with misunderstandings; at some level, I do agree with the culturalists who insist that people ought to preserve and nourish their own traditions and resist the tempting illusion of melting into an alienating cosmopolitanism. In Geoffrey H. Hartman's theoretical meditation on the complexity of the term, culture, cleansed from nationalist pathologies and political manipulations, appears as an indispensable, long-term solution to the generalized and perhaps fundamental human crises of "ghostliness" and alienation. Cultures, in this sense, answer the primordial need for belonging or "reembodiment"; they "convert longing into belonging" while distancing themselves from and even affirming themselves as antidotes to the political. "The aspiration to totality on the part of both religious and postreligious cultures is," Hartman speculates, "a reaction to an intolerable sense of decadence, or ghostliness, or alienation from the sources of life." When Hartman wonders, at the end of his book, whether "an idea of culture can be formulated that remains generous, that is not the pawn of politics and does not rationalize suicidal acts of collective self-differentiation,"[8] he raises a question that has motivated the writing of this book, a question that I hope I can address (however tangentially, for this project still needs to be more fully elaborated) without being inscribed into the ideological straightjackets that await anyone who tackles the treacherous subjects of capitalism and Islam.

Using Islam for illustrative purposes, I argue that Hartman's Schillerian proposal for a nonviolent and less traumatic transition into a different future is an indispensable one, but only if the notion of culture itself is not totally disembodied from the economic, or if reimagining progressive cultures does not suicidally avoid theorizing the serious threats generated by the capitalist mode of production. Although my theoretical approach and critical engagements are motivated by a spirit of inquiry that implicitly expresses a profound respect for the authors and theories I contest (the prevalence of nondialogic, uncritical scholarship may indicate that the democratic spirit is still woefully fragile in academia and cannot manifest itself without leading to excess), I also start from the conviction that human solidarities (not human or cultural hegemonies) are the only legitimating factor in this intellectual project. To think (*penser*) a polycentric world (to borrow Samir Amin's useful expression)—a mosaic of cultures and traditions, sharing the same planet and implementing progressive visions to mend injuries and unveil the political economy of prejudice and hatred—is the only alternative I see for the future of human civilizations and for reinvesting academic studies with a much-needed relevance. But to dismiss once dynamic cultural legacies as outdated, as no longer suitable, is, in effect, to accept a linear view of history that ends with Western capitalist civilization (for the rise of the modern West is coterminous with the rise of capitalism), and this prospect, I argue, augurs ill for all human communities, winners and losers alike. It needs to be emphasized (if only because I myself am profoundly shaped by Western intellectual traditions) that questioning deeply held Eurocentric assumptions in order to diminish their hegemony and open up meaningful spaces for other expressions is not intended to downplay the historic contributions of the Euro-American cultures in the struggle to bring forth a better world for all.

The persistent triumph of the irrational forces of narrowly defined identities (whether religious, cultural, or national) over the embattled and eclipsed voice of human solidarity increasingly appears as a deliberately crafted ideology whose main purpose is to cast a blanket of silence over the real forces threatening the viability of all human cultures. The unexamined celebration of the rich heritages of Islam and the West leads to theoretical and political excesses and, at the same time, successfully veils the corrosive processes of existing capitalism, an economic system that is forever postponing the proclaimed goal of cultural dialogue and, to risk a suspiciously utopian wish, a better world for humanity.[9] Yet to examine how capitalism obstructs the long-awaited emancipation of human cultures leads one treacherously close to the equally vilified corridors of Marxism and socialism, legacies long repudiated in the United States as decidedly un-American. Hence the examination of the all-pervasive context of a free-market capitalism uncritically assumed to be an indissociable part of the freedom package that, for better or worse, is an exclusive product of Western civilization is simply avoided for the safer pursuit of antihistorical cultural essentialisms. If Muslims are hopelessly mired in a host of social ills, the cause is attributable to an unusable tradition. Muslims are exotically colorful and charming in their immutability; but, as Muslims, they do not—cannot—change from within. Thus Muslims continue to be represented as noble Bedouins, decadent court officials, turbaned fanatics, or oppressively shrouded women; in any case, they remain the villainous Other, incapable of comprehending the enlightening forces of history, the changes so felicitously extended by a dynamic European culture. Attached to their archaic religion, Muslims simply do not understand the West and its heritage.

There are a few compelling reasons for defenders of the West to insist on the incompatibility of civilizations. The successful and mass-based Islamic revolution in Iran has turned out to be more durable than expected and is probably the first major revolution to depart from the secular vocabulary of the Western tradition since 1789.[10] The publication of Salman Rushdie's *The Satanic Verses* in the late 1980s strained relations between Islam and the West for the remainder of the twentieth century. The West was seen as irreconcilably clashing with a medieval Islam unable to appreciate the loftier principles of freedom of expression and international civility. While the novel remained unread, or read with the simple intention of studying the blasphemous or injurious passages that ignited the global uproar, it nevertheless symbolized the gulf that divides Islam from the Western world. The vast majority of Muslims, caught between secular and Islamic fundamentalisms, became the "people" whose faceless existence was opportunistically exploited by the contending parties. Although many scholars are eager to preserve and differentiate the world's various cultural legacies, they often do not question the foundations of the economic system that seems to have enriched elite minorities into a sort of intellectual complacency, nor do they venture beyond academic paradigms that prevent more holistic and transdisciplinary readings of cultures and civilizations. At this critical juncture in human history we must redirect our attention away from what Bernard Lewis and Samuel Huntington have called the "clash of civilizations" and focus instead on the centrifugal forces that threaten to implode these cultures apart and leave us with culturally denuded landscapes where, as Robert Kaplan argues in a rightly celebrated essay, anarchy spills over into the last bastions of civilized society.[11]

For Kaplan, whose global geography is determined not by the

neatly drawn borders of culture, the world is threatened by an "environmental scarcity" that ultimately leads to social unrest and war. The immediate challenge facing the world is not culture clashes but the West Africanization of modern societies. The breakdown of traditional communities that are forcibly integrated into the global economic system encourages a sort of anarchy and lawlessness that states are increasingly unable to control. The future map of the world, then, far from being static and determined by millennial tribal or cultural quarrels, "will be an ever-mutating representation of chaos."[12] Matthew Connelly and Paul Kennedy reach a somewhat similar conclusion when they state that, instead of the civilizational fault lines that Samuel Huntington had identified in his by-now controversial essay on the "clash of civilizations,"[13] the real global problems facing humanity in the twenty-first century are "demographic-technological" ones, separating "fast-growing, adolescent, resource-poor, undercapitalized, and undereducated populations on one side and technologically inventive, demographically moribund, and increasingly nervous rich societies on the other." And the two writers hasten to add that not only do the rich stymie the poor by forcing alien and unsustainable development strategies on them, but the conflicts and wars that surge out of these amorphous fault lines are mostly armed by "the five permanent members of the Security Council."[14]

The culturalist argument is not only intellectually constrained by the old Orientalist argument that freezes cultures into unchanging essences, it is also dangerously disabling, since it disconnects Muslims from their larger Third World and global contexts.[15] The attempt to define a slippery notion of the West often erases the long and turbulent past that permitted Europe to develop an embryonic and fragile conception of itself and spread its cultures overseas.[16] And while intra-European wars have abated since the end of World War II, the vilification and persecution of minorities, together with nationalistic resistances to an unintelligible pan-European identity and to American cultural hegemony, continue to problematize the mythical homogeneities that culturalists propose.[17]

No work better exemplifies the confluence of Orientalist claims, culturalist assumptions, and traditional social science paradigms in the 1990s than Samuel Huntington's "clash of civilizations" thesis.[18]

Huntington's argument is, in many ways, shrewd, sophisticated, and refreshingly candid (he often states unpleasant truths about the very West he seeks to defend), and he makes no concessions of false gratitude to comprador intellectuals and nations such as Turkey. He is skeptical of what he calls Kemalism, generally defined as the attempt by a country, suddenly shocked by its own economic and technological disadvantage in relation to Europe, to catch up by dismissing its own past and embracing Europeanization in various aspects of social life, ranging from clothing and physical appearance to the modification of old alphabets or even the adoption of entirely new ones. In Russia, Peter the Great attempted to transform a Christian Orthodox tradition; in Turkey, Mustafa Kemal Ataturk tried to do the same to an Islamic one.[19] The latter set out, single-handedly, to redefine "the national, political, religious and cultural identity of the Turkish people,"[20] only to create a "torn" country that has always been treated warily by the very European Community in which it seeks integration. Indeed, although the Islamic resurgence (not to be confused with "fundamentalism," which is only an aspect of this broadly based resurgence) continues to expand in Turkey and elsewhere, the protection of an alien secularism is entrusted to the military. Would the European Community accept a secular but military regime ruling over an increasingly Islamized society? For Huntington, this prospect looks doubtful, which is why he frankly stated that "while the rejectionist response to the West is impossible, the Kemalist response has been unsuccessful. If non-Western societies are to modernize, they must do it their own way, not the Western way and, emulating Japan, build upon and employ their own traditions, institutions, and values." In other words, Turkey's way out of its impasse is to redefine itself once again, "give up its frustrating and humiliating role as a beggar pleading for membership" in the European Community, and regain its core position in the Islamic world (154, 178).[21]

There are several problems with Huntington's advice, including the assumption that Turkey might, once again, regain its Ottoman prestige (the Ottomans were the latest—and not the only ones—in a series of ruling dynasties in the Islamic world) and the general belief that modernization (usually conflated with capitalist development) is the only available option for internationally dependent peoples to improve their condition. The contradiction implied in such a recommendation becomes more pronounced when the author tells us that, unlike what is commonly assumed, modernization paradoxically leads to de-Westernization that only aggravates tensions and makes Islam's already bloody borders bloodier. To be sure, to delay the West's inexorable decline, Huntington suggests, among other things, a form of civilizational dialogue, if only to protect shared values against the onslaughts of multinational corporations and Mafia cartels. Yet Huntington suggests (when he uncritically quotes a former British defense minister) that "liberal capitalism and free trade" are a distinguishing feature of Western civilization. In so doing, he imposes serious limitations on his definition of the West and simply overlooks the impact capitalism—increasingly dominated by the very multinational corporations he suspects—has had on social arrangements and future prospects.

To construct a homogeneous West, Huntington overlooks the permanent tensions between Europe and the United States, or among European nations themselves; he also practically ignores sub-Saharan Africa and, unable to decide to what civilizational bloc Latin America belongs (at one point he seems to agree with Octavio Paz that Mexico is essentially an Indian nation), recommends further "Westernization" (through the sort of trade treaties President Salinas implemented) of the continent's already decimated indigenous peoples (149, 312). He knows that the West triumphed through the application of "organized violence," that universality is always the outcome of hegemony and imperialism, that universal standards are impractical in the field of politics and often lead to double standards, and that "what is universalism to the West is imperialism to the rest" (51, 92, 184); yet by wanting the West to retain its power as long it can, he implicitly accepts—and provides no alternative to—the ways in which sovereignty could be dissociated from Machiavellian calculations and endemic cultural suspicions. Moreover, his hardheaded realism could encourage historical amnesia—the most catastrophic wars in human history, Hobsbawm reminds us, happened primarily among Europeans less than a century ago—and a rather bleak view of the future of cultural relations, his final suggestions for better cultural awareness notwithstanding. If, as Huntington states, Fatima Mernissi, one of the most cosmopolitan Muslim intellectuals in the world today, is unable to appreciate the value of individualism, where, then, is the hope for a meaningful dialogue with Islam?[22]

Huntington's prognosis may have been inspired by the Orientalist argument that the West and Islam are condemned to live in perpetual tension, since Islam, an impressive civilization and once a major world power, deeply resents its present humiliating condition in the world order. This is, in fact, what Bernard Lewis wrote in 1990 (during the height of the Rushdie controversy and on the eve of the Gulf War) in an *Atlantic* magazine issue, provocatively illustrated with medieval-looking Muslims obviously threatened by and enraged at the devilish power of the United States—represented as a tricolored serpent. If the problems with Muslims are never-ending, it is because they transcend the real but contingent pressures of imperialism and neocolonialism; the West is faced with "the perhaps irrational but surely historic reaction of an ancient rival against *our Judeo*-Christian heritage, our secular present, and the worldwide expansion of both" (my emphasis). But if Islam inspires in a few of its adherents hatred against "us," the West must refrain from reciprocating in an equally irrational fashion and strive to appreciate Islamic history and culture better.[23]

Perhaps, as Huntington suggests, one outcome might be to live in a state of "cold war" ("the term *la guerra fria* was coined by thirteenth-century Spaniards to describe their 'uneasy coexistence' with Muslims in the Mediterranean");[24] but then, didn't the Spaniards, as Lewis has demonstrated, also establish the statute of purity of blood (*estatuto de limpieza de sangre*) in 1449 to discriminate against and persecute Moriscos (crypto-Muslims) and Marranos (crypto-Jews)? In fact, Huntington's conception of the West (primarily the realm of Latin Christianity) and with which Bernard Lewis so naturally identifies, was forged out of a long history of persecuting Jews—often seen as mirror images of Muslims. If the Muslim is the impure par excellence, it is not clear that other non-Christians are less so. Once a common European front was established (perhaps for the first time) to wage the first crusade on Muslims following Pope Urban's call at the Council of Clermont in 1095, the first victims were not Muslims but pagans, heretics, and especially Jews:

The first outbreaks of violent anti-semitism seem to have occurred in France shortly after the Council of Clermont. They then spread to Germany and eastern Europe, where they were associated with the first wave of crusaders leaving for the East in the spring of 1096. On 3 May the storm broke over the Jewish community at Speyer, where a South German army under Emich of Leiningen, the most merciless of the persecutors, had gathered. Emich proceeded to Worms, where the massacres began on 18 May, and then to Mainz, where he was joined by more Germans and by a large army of French, English, Flemish, and Lorraine crusaders. Between 25 and 29 May the Jewish community at Mainz, one of the largest in Europe, was decimated. Some crusaders then marched to Cologne, from where the Jews had already been dispersed into neighbouring settlements. For the next month they were hunted out and destroyed. Another band seems to have gone south-west to Trier and Metz, where the massacres continued. Meanwhile another crusading army, probably Peter the Hermit's, forced almost the whole community at Regensburg to undergo baptism and the communities at Wesseli and Prague in Bohemia suffered probably from the attention of yet another crusading army, led by a priest called Folkmar.[25]

The crusaders "found it impossible to distinguish between Muslims and Jews," and "throughout the twelfth century every major call to a crusade gave rise to pogroms against the Jews" (16–17). Whether it is motivated by the zeal of religion, theories of race, or mere economic opportunism, and despite occasional interludes and progressive enfranchisement following the Reformation in Europe, Jews have rarely been, by Lewis's own account, part of the Western tradition as defined by the culturalist thesis—that is, West European Christianity and its extension overseas. The sort of prejudice and racism that emerged from the Reconquista and the slave trade would not only exclude Jews from the community of white Christian Europe (the American immigration law of 1924 was both racist and anti-Semitic) but would lead to the most gruesome holocaust in all of human history (which happened, again, less than a century ago).[26] If the Judeo prefix that precedes the adjective of Christian is an attempt to bury this history under the assumption of a common heritage, why would the Muslim become the Jew's Other, especially if Lewis himself states that "Jewish and Muslim theology are far closer to each other than is either to Christianity" and that the initial formulations of Jewish theology are still "profoundly influenced by Muslim patterns of thought"?[27] If, as Huntington predicts, the cultural element, based on old histories and frozen essences, is going to reassert itself in world politics, then there is no reason to expect Europe's long history of anti-Semitism to vanish without a trace; only if the Jew successfully melts into the mainstream Euro-American cultures could the ominous prospect of exclusion be effectively avoided.

Supposing that the rise of Western civilization was forged through the application of what Huntington called "organized violence" (the use of violence is a universal trait, but the systematic domination of other peoples by a few European countries since the conquest of the American continent seems to be unmatched in human history),[28] how then do we conceive of a millennial epoch in which Islam is redefined as a progressive culture actively participating in the building of a multicultural and more egalitarian world civilization? To merely wish for a universality in the abstract is to sanction imperialism as the only vehicle through which such a tenuous project can be achieved.[29] How does one reinterpret the Islamic tradition in a highly secularized intellectual world that, if it is not already under the sway of Orientalist notions, is nevertheless endemically suspicious of religion?

The problems confronting the world are more complex than the simple "us" versus "them" syndrome: the present capitalist economy is not only undermining the myths that many Western essentialists and Islamists want to defend, it is also creating the conditions for the kind of dystopian social horror that Kaplan manages to evoke in his article. Two recent books on the growing power of transnational corporations provide an insight into the much-heralded process of globalization, and the social impact of the acceleration of capitalist consolidations can be surmised from the careful reading of any periodical or newspaper in the world.[30] Richard J. Barnet and John Cavanagh describe the "postnational order" as a world run and controlled by a few transnational corporations—"world empires of the twenty-first century"—which "control the human energy, capital, technology" and create the global village in which relatively few people with disposable incomes are offered a dizzying variety of consumer products while the bulk of the world's population is reduced to mere window shopping.[31] Indeed, because the middle- and upper-class markets comprise a relatively small percentage of the world population, astronomical sums are poured into an increasingly differentiated advertising ($240 billion in 1989, or what amounts to "$120 per person in the world, almost double what the average person in Mozambique earns in a year") and the construction of shopping malls to lure consumers. In such a ferociously competitive market, children and young teenagers, whose annual combined income is estimated to exceed $25 billion, are attractive targets (163–83). Cigarette companies, embattled in the United States, have turned their main product—the cigarette—into "the most widely distributed global consumer product on earth, the most profitable, and the most deadly" ("nicotine is more addictive than either alcohol or cocaine") (184–85). Indeed, since tobacco exports have been "one of the few bright spots in the [United States's] generally depressing international trade experience in recent years," Philip Morris, the maker of Marlboro, is determined to break down the "psychological barriers" that might slow down their expansion, especially into the lucrative Asian markets.[32]

By importing raw materials—tobacco, coffee, "counterseasonal" fruits and vegetables, etc.—and recycling these resources into corporate food staples, multinational corporations are not only disrupting indigenous patterns of development, they are also impoverishing the global diet and fueling the human migrations (both to sprawling, uninhabitable Third World cities and to richer countries) that Western nations want to keep at bay. Meanwhile, workers are subjected to increasing pressure and degrading working conditions (206–47). A few countries, like Malaysia and Guatemala, orientalize and impose slave-like working conditions on their own female citizens to lure investors. A late-1970s Malaysian investment brochure, for example, praised the "oriental" female's dexterous small hands and asked: "Who . . . could be better qualified by nature and inheritance to contribute to the efficiency of a bench-assembly production line than an oriental girl? . . . Female factory workers," the brochure added, "can be hired for approximately US $1.50 a day."[33]

This exploitative economic system, supported by neocolonial and supranational financial institutions such as the International Monetary Fund, the International Bank for Reconstruction and Development (commonly known as the World Bank), and the World Trade Organization (WTO), not only breaks down sustainable human and ecological structures, it replaces viable human communities with the new corporate family of the "Pepsi generation" or the endless inorganic "communities" sprouting up in advanced capitalist economies.[34] Authoritarian and even tyrannical, these increasingly monopolistic organizations (monopolies are a logical outcome of capitalism, since too much competition is destabilizing) have managed to coerce many intellectuals into accepting their practices as perfect embodiments of Western economic thought, despite Adam Smith's strong suspicion of monopolies as antisocial.[35] Few defenders of the West remember Abraham Lincoln's and Rutherford B. Hayes's fear for the nascent American democratic ideals from the already indomitable corporations that, in 1886, were transformed into natural citizens entitled to Constitutional protections by a corporate-biased Supreme Court.[36] While this free-market fundamentalist ideology remains conveniently unexamined, almost unnamed in the United States (72), world cultures continue to be eroded by the escalating anarchy and oppression resulting from the abdication of authority still precariously monopolized by the nation-state.[37]

Capitalism's danger to human life is now starkly evident everywhere in the world. Slavery and slave-working conditions are returning to the workplace as competitive advantages in low-income countries and communities; underremunerated and part-time occupations are the norm even in the "robust" economy of the United States.[38] While the Peruvian government is cracking down on militant organizations fighting for social justice in Peru, its rich archaeological heritage is being plundered, looted, and sold to international collectors and investors in the United States, Japan, and Western European countries, leading a former head of the National Institute of Culture in Peru to blame "international capital" for consuming Peru's "cultural patrimony." Indeed, all ancient cultures—part of the human cultural patrimony—are targets of a new form of organized crime based on looting. Sales of Mayan antiquities are reported to gross $120 million a year. In boycotted and internationally sanctioned Iraq, "looters and grave robbers working with international smugglers" are pouring "precious artifacts from the world's oldest civilizations" into the same international market.[39]

Kidnapping for ransom is also a thriving business in much of the Third World. One *New York Times* reporter explained that "huge income disparities, inefficient police forces, and near-total impunity for kidnappers are transforming Latin America into the world's top region for ransom kidnapping, and the threat is inhibiting investment in the region and is forcing wealthy Latin Americans to use private guards, high walls and armored cars for protection." (In Mexico, kidnapping has grown into such a sophisticated business with differentiated functions that professional gangs act as "service providers specializing in the successive phases of the crime, including the armed captures, negotiations with the victims' relatives and collecting the ransoms." No wonder the same country has become a lucrative market for the private security industry, whose global revenues are estimated to reach $200 billion by 2010.) In the Philippines, where members of the successful ethnic Chinese community are the prime targets, even police officers belong to kidnapping rings.[40] And to add to the global catalog of fear, piracy is also making a comeback: there are now reports of whole ships with their entire crews hijacked from the seas.[41]

If the rich and world trade can be thus threatened by the chaotic capitalist system, the poor and dispossessed are almost compelled to forfeit their cheap and inconsequential lives. On the second day of the quincentennial of the "discovery" of the American continent, John Noble Wilford reported that indigenous people worldwide are still being "massacred and terrorized," especially in places where "the march of economic exploitation tramples on their once-isolated domains"; for "more widespread and respectable is the economic argument that a few people should not be allowed to hold up development." More important than the natives' rights and environment is the search for gold and riches.[42]

As social fabrics disintegrate under the pressures of "globalization," the rights that have been secured for historically vulnerable social categories are rapidly eroding. At the end of 1999, UNICEF, the

United Nation's Children Fund, studied the condition of women in former Soviet and East European countries and concluded that they were worse off under the new market system than they had been under communist rule. Many of the women of the once proud and resilient—although arguably grim and economically unsustainable—states of Eastern Europe are now being sold into sexual bondage, an industry described by the *New York Times* as "one of the fastest-growing enterprises in the robust global economy." The United Nations estimates that "four million people throughout the world are trafficked each year"; Western Europe alone, according to another organization, absorbs 500,000 women within its borders. The volume of trade in women has grown so rapidly in countries like the Ukraine that the latter "has replaced Thailand and the Philippines as the epicenter of the global business in trafficking women."[43]

The number of children exploited in the global economy is also rising; with 250 million employed in various (mostly hazardous) occupations, children constitute a major segment of the global working class. (Furthermore, around 300,000 children have been drafted into military conflicts and serve as "regular soldiers, guerrilla fighters, spies, porters, cooks and sexual slaves—even suicide commandos.") Many poor children, including infants, are kidnapped and sold for adoption in rich industrialized nations; the same markets also sell their body parts.[44] The prostitution of children in Asia, especially in Thailand, where the number of child prostitutes is estimated to constitute 40 percent of the prostitute labor force, has become so profitable for the Thai economy (which had been growing at an average 7 percent in the thirty years before the Asian crisis of 1997) that it has blossomed into a multinational enterprise. Remittances of Thai overseas prostitutes to their parents were estimated to be $2.5 million a month in the early 1990s. Reporting on this issue, James Petras and Tienchai Wongchaisuwan wrote: "Thailand, a former center of Buddhism, has become the global center of sexploitation. Thailand, with a rich complex cultural past, has become the center of cultural anomie and moral decay. In the new international division of labor of this 'interdependent global economy,' the Thai state functions as a pimp and procurer for the leisure world of advanced capitalism."[45]

Lest one believe the rich industrialized countries to be immune from the scourge of an antisocial, antidemocratic capitalist ethic, one need only look at rising inequalities in most of these countries, starting with the largest economy of all, the United States. Only a few months before the year 2000, at a time when unemployment was significantly reduced, the country was facing a labor shortage, consumerism was booming, and returns on stock market investments had skyrocketed to new heights, it was reported that "the richest 2.7 million Americans, the top 1 percent, will have as many after-tax dollars to spend as the bottom 100 million," that "four out of five households, or about 217 million people, are taking home a thinner slice of the economic pie today than in 1977." Moreover, the "poorest one-fifth of households" had actually seen their income decline by 12 percent.[46] Although statistical reports on these mounting social disparities often avoid making recommendations for change, the effects of these economic polarizations are not difficult to discern. Earlier in the 1990s a "wide-ranging, three-year study of young American children" concluded that because of their parents' poverty and other social hardships, "millions of infants and toddlers are so deprived of medical care, loving supervision and intellectual stimulation that their growth into healthy and responsible adults is threatened."[47] In 1996, researchers at Harvard and the University of California reaffirmed the obvious correlation between poverty and high mortality rates; even the rates of sexual and physical abuse of children are significantly higher among poorer sectors of the American population.[48] And while the lives and health of American children are endangered by poverty and lack of resources, it was reported that the U.S. government had spent at least $5.48 trillion on nuclear weapons since 1940, and American adults gambled $638.6 billion legally in 1997 alone—and lost about $51 billion in the process![49]

In Japan, meanwhile, not only are overworked and overcrowded people beginning to question the very system that has allowed that country to prosper, but middle-aged family men, unable to cope with the ruthless pace of the economy or with sudden unemployment, are resorting to suicide in ever larger numbers, leaving behind equally vulnerable spouses and children. As income distribution gaps widen and the country plunges further into the perilous capitalist culture, taboos are being gradually unveiled. The homeless now litter the social landscape; even child abuse, once considered unthinkable in the traditionally strong Japanese family, has become a public issue, caused partly by the same economic pressures driving parents into suicide. Similarly, the road to capitalism in the former Communist states of Eastern Europe is littered with the corpses of human casualties and expanding misery. Lower life expectancy and higher suicide rates are gradually stripping these countries of their male populations. In Russia, a formidable military superpower until the late 1980s, declining living and health standards, together with a fatalistic indifference to both, have become a national security issue. Confronted with the stark apocalyptic landscape in many Eastern European countries, the United Nations concluded in 1999 that "the transition to a market economy has . . . been accompanied by a demographic collapse and a rise in self-destructive behavior, especially among men." These former Communist countries are surely, in the words of the same report, paying "a high social and human cost" for pursuing the promises of capitalist prosperity.[50]

The rise of complex international criminal organizations trafficking in anything from narcotics to human beings and human parts, the lucrative arms industry, the frenzy of a speculative capitalism dissociating profit making from real productivity, the reduction of democratic politics to a mere spectacle orchestrated by public relations and marketing firms, and the mindless association of the American Dream with consumer freedom (especially as entertainment has become a crucial export item for the United States) are a few of the practices that are uprooting the traditional social structures that the defenders of a besieged West want to preserve.[51] If, say, protecting U.S. national security means ensuring that country's control over the world and its resources, then the country will have to transform itself into a permanent military fortress. Since the United States, with 4 percent of the world's population, consumes one-fourth of the total world annual production of oil, and a baby born in the United States accounts for 35 times the environmental damage of an Indian baby, and 280 times that of a Chadian or Haitian one,[52] how will the West prevent smuggling and immigration without a radical review of the very economic system that has empowered it to both control access to the world's resources and concentrate vast amounts of wealth in fewer and fewer hands? We know that the world population could be better fed and substantially healthier if poverty and inequality were to be reduced;[53] yet such measures remain out of reach at a time when the capitalist mode of production is increasingly prescribed as the long-delayed therapy for "emerging" countries.

This brief list of social failures and demographic instabilities (some would call them mobilities) not only provides a sense of the relationship between the global economic system and the crises afflicting human communities and cultures but also highlights why and how the structural limitations of the Orientalist and culturalist theses (Eurocentrist and Islamist alike) have been unable to either grasp the interconnectedness of issues or situate cultures in a larger global context in which boundaries themselves have become separate cultural and economic zones.[54] Although the antidemocratic simultaneous processes of cold "globalization" and intense "retribalization"—Jihad vs. McWorld, in Benjamin Barber's terms—do not spare any region of the world (rich or poor),[55] it is their total erasure from the works dealing with Islam that, in my view, renders these works ideologically and theoretically problematic. The persistence of long-discredited Orientalist and social science paradigms into the twenty-first century have perpetuated cultural impasses that must be superseded if scholarship is to reclaim its explanatory powers and its long-term view of human histories.

That postcolonial theory has been particularly inattentive to the question of Islam in the global economy exposes its failure to incorporate different regimes of truth into a genuinely multicultural global vision. An almost universal consensus exists that any criticism of freedom of speech and human rights as universal goods must be regarded as hypocritical and indefensible gestures whose goal is to perpetuate Third World authoritarianism. That such concepts could be complex, fluid, derive from particular histories, or can be equally manipulated by all governments is rarely raised—only archaic, authoritarian societies must be pressured into universal norms of civility. Yet it was none other than the reliably iconoclastic Foucault who cautioned against the adoption of such facile beliefs. For Foucault, liberty is primarily a "practice" and cannot simply be engineered by the institution of laws (progressive as they might be). "The liberty of men is never assured by the institutions and laws that are intended to guarantee them." Foucault's assertion not only complicates the European liberal orthodoxies used to discredit non-Western institutions, it also resituates oppression in a complex network of relations that cannot be addressed by mere legislation. In another context, Foucault explained that

> In defining the effects of power as repression, one adopts a purely juridical conception of such power, one identifies power with a law which says no, power is taken above all as carrying the force of a prohibition. Now I believe that this is a wholly negative, narrow, skeletal conception of power, one which has been curiously widespread. If power were never anything but repressive, if it never did anything but to say no, do you really think one would be brought to obey it? What makes power hold good, what makes it accepted, is simply the fact that it doesn't only weigh on us as a force that says no, but that it traverses and produces things, it induces pleasure, forms knowledge, produces discourse. It needs to be considered as a productive network which runs through the whole social body, much more than as a negative instance whose function is repression.[56]

The rise of nationalism and a whole new vocabulary rearranging history and redefining identities is also insufficiently debated in postcolonial studies. Arab nationalism, for instance, has invented a new global identity whose effect was to sever the Arabic-speaking peoples from a larger ecumene (community with common cultural traits) that included black Africa. As a secular, European concept, nationalism was introduced to the lands of Islam during its phase of political decay and was part of a deliberate strategy to weaken Muslims and other colonized peoples. Through powerful propaganda mechanisms during the twentieth century, nationalism became an inextricable part of the identity of Arabic-speaking peoples. Black Muslims and the Turks thus became the Arabs' Other in what has been termed the "postcolonial" world, as if the scourges of forced dependency and Orientalism have been magically removed with political independence. "Post-al" theories—the theme of my next chapter—do suggest that, somehow, everything is behind us, that we are now in some sort of no-man's-land, a twilight zone between history and the future in which even reality has ceased to be real.

My examination of postcolonial theory and the Arab identity deployed by nationalists to counter imperialism might open the door to a better examination of the African literary canon and help explain why a progressively defined Islam—one that is democratically available to all—may be a desirable option for Muslim peoples. The increasing reliance of Muslim feminists on the canons of their own traditions may break the theoretical impasse that seems to block the emergence of viable non-Western, indigenous alternatives. One of the best ways to protect the endangered human patrimony from the ravages inflicted on it by a uniform mode of thinking and the deculturing effects of capitalism (nowadays cheerily proclaimed as globalization) is to allow the world's cultural traditions to speak for themselves, through their retrieved memories, revitalized vocabularies, and historically imagined futures. Though I contend that Islamic cultures—like many of the world's cultural traditions—could help "provincialize" the West and offer other ways to be in the world,[57] I have no interest whatsoever in theological disputes that seek to prove the truth of one religion over another. Because my primary interest in Islam is almost exclusively cultural (a historical consciousness combined with literary critical methodologies is bound to complicate the most sacred of foundational narratives), I expect my discussion to be applicable to other nonsecular religious traditions. In all cases, the passion of faith needs to be sweetened by the prospect of a viable multiconfessional world in which different religions are allowed to flourish side by side. By stating that Allah has deliberately divided humanity into many nations and tribes, then challenged us to know one another, the Qur'an clearly revealed that God's design is for a world of diversities competing in pious deeds. There is no reason to believe that such a divine intent is less inspiring than the one that champions a brave new world of interest-seeking individuals whose collective endeavors, we are told, automatically add up to the coveted blessings of happiness and social harmony. Whatever their inspiration, dialogic relations are maintained by actual practice, not by written laws or ideological purities.

1

Can the Postcolonial Critic Speak?

Orientalism and the Rushdie Affair

Postcoloniality is the condition of what we might ungenerously call a comprador intelligentsia: of a relatively small, Western-style, Western-trained, group of writers and thinkers who mediate the trade in cultural commodities of world capitalism at the periphery. In the West they are known through the Africa they offer; their compatriots know them both through the West they present to Africa and through an Africa they have invented for the world, for each other, and for Africa.—Kwame Anthony Appiah, *In My Father's House*

A form of freedom, I'd like to think, even if I am far from convinced that it is.—Edward W. Said, *Out of Place*

The ascendancy of postcolonial theory in the American academy has had an ambiguous effect at best, for though it has opened a debate on the concerns of hitherto marginalized peoples, it has also obfuscated some of the enduring legacies of colonialism, including the pauperization of the Third World. For Muslims who are trying to question the dominant logic of late capitalism, this has meant challenging a rearticulated discourse of Orientalism that continues to portray Islam as an undifferentiated monolith, condemned to clash with the most cherished values of the West. In this context, new theories have emerged to redefine military strategies and redraw the map of the world along cultural lines. Since the Gulf War, Samuel Huntington states, "NATO planning is increasingly directed to potential threats and instability along its 'southern tier.' "[1] Just when postmodern theories were thought to have taken us to a new dimension of thinking about ourselves in the world, essentialist views of civilization are being resurrected to account for continuing tensions, without criticizing the structures of capitalism and the lasting effects of colonialism on the shape of the world today.

The heroic efforts of postcolonial critics such as Edward Said to highlight the nefarious consequences of an Orientalist scholarship that once was the intellectual handmaiden for the project of colonialism has most certainly given a new meaning to cultural criticism in the West; however, as Arif Dirlik argues, "postcolonialism has been silent about its own status as a possible ideological effect of a new world order situation after colonialism." Not only is "postcoloniality . . . the condition of the intelligentsia of global capitalism" and the discursive power of "newfound power" by Third World intellectuals in First World academe, but it has also been "designed to *avoid* making sense of the present crisis and, in the process, to cover up the origins of postcolonial intellectuals in a global capitalism in which they are not so much victims as beneficiaries."[2] I would, however, qualify these dubious benefits; for despite the high visibility of a select group of intellectuals (mostly of Indian origin),[3] their sense of alienation and loss can barely be disguised and so they must continue to be seen as victims of a larger enterprise whose origins go back to the earliest colonialist phase. For the seemingly liberating discursive "post-al" theories notwithstanding, one must decide whether the struggle for liberation from neocolonial policies that support the global transactions of capitalism is, as Frantz Fanon once put it, "a cultural phenomenon or not." Fanon's question is obviously rhetorical, since his answer is unequivocal: "We believe that the conscious and organized undertaking by a colonized people to re-establish the sovereignty of that nation constitutes the most complete and obvious cultural manifestation that exists."[4] But since, according to Dirlik, Third World intellectuals such as Homi Bhabha have been "com-

pletely reworked by the language of First World cultural criticism"
and have largely managed to obfuscate realities without a mapping of
which no viable struggle can be mounted,[5] it is doubtful whether
their insight on cultural practices can be useful to the liberation of
Third World peoples. For, to invoke Fanon once again, "the business
of obscuring language is a mask behind which stands out the much
greater business of plunder."[6]

Because the postcolonial state is more colonial, inasmuch as its
culture is more thoroughly infiltrated by the ideologies and cultural
practices of former metropolitan centers, the restoration of an indigenous vocabulary is not the nostalgic and sentimental gesture that
many of its critics make it out to be, but is the very act of cultural
affirmation and political expression needed to reconnect individuals
with their traditions. Many of the categories used by secular(ized)
intellectuals to dismiss alternatives rooted in religion can be convincingly critiqued; yet the latter continue to cast a cold eye on the
significance of Islam, especially in the wake of the controversy over
Rushdie's *The Satanic Verses*. While extremism can take on both
secular and religious aspects, it is the progressive Islamic contestation
of both that has been conspicuously absent from the debate. The
reason, one suspects, is the cyclical dominance of a few theories,
associated with a few academic names, and either the dismissal of
religiously inspired discourses as serious alternatives to capitalist relations or the widespread but confining methodologies used in the
fields of Orientalism and area studies generally.

Gayatri Spivak, Akeel Bilgrami, and Edward Said were, for example, among the postcolonial critics who rightly protested Khomeini's
fatwa on Rushdie, exonerated Islam from such "bigoted violence,"
and reaffirmed their "belief in the universal principles of rational
discussion and freedom of expression" in a letter to the editor of the
New York Times.[7] Spivak's signature on the letter may have been
politically strategic; but when, later that year, *Harper's* published a
forum on the canon, she failed to defend Islam against Orientalist
(mis)characterizations of the Qur'an. At one point during the debate
over the canon, Roger Shattuck asked both ends of the political spectrum whether they had read the Qur'an:

"Have you read the Koran [*sic*]?" he asked Hirsch.

"No," answered the well-known defender of cultural literacy in the United States. Then, after announcing that he had read the Qur'an "three times in two different languages," Shattuck turned to Spivak:

Shattuck: . . . Gayatri, have you read it?

Spivak: No.

Shattuck: Okay. Look at what you find in the Bible and in the Koran. As classics, these books are not moral equivalents or literary equivalents or equivalents in greatness. [Shattuck goes on to explain how the Bible is superior.][8]

Spivak and Hirsch, however, did not accept this proposition: Spivak, because she doesn't believe in hierarchical structures or value binarisms; Hirsch, because to say so (and he agrees with Shattuck on the issue of quality) is not "politically feasible." Although it is not clear whether Shattuck read the Qur'an in the original (since the *experience* of reading the Qur'an in Arabic is ultimately untranslatable), he succeeded, by this simple gesture, to legitimize the virtues of the classical liberal education challenged by new pedagogical and curricular theories and to question the reliability of postcolonial intellectuals in the West as adequate speakers for Muslim subjectivities. Spivak, who had defended Islam against intolerance, had not read the most central and defining text of Islamic cultures.

My goal here is not to critique Spivak or other leading Third World writers and intellectuals in the West—on the contrary, my project would most certainly have been difficult, if not impossible, without their groundbreaking work—but rather to question the representation of Islam and Islamic identity in postcolonial studies and to suggest that progressive Islamic alternatives are necessary for the emergence of a new multicultural order based on dialogue, not hegemony. At a time when issues of subjectivity are rigorously debated, many Muslims—whether familiar with Western theory or not—continue to be denied access to this debate. Thus Edward Said's diagnosis of a self-perpetuating Orientalist tradition of distortion and prejudice is being applied to the Western culture at large, since Muslims' inability to represent themselves—partly because of their passive participation in their own Orientalizing—is not only related to repressive regimes and inadequate facilities in the Islamic world,[9] it is also actually hindered by the pervasive proliferation of a few theories (e.g., Orientalism as a discursive gesture or deconstruction as a self-negating technique) that have now become the standards against which all postcolonial theories are tested.

Dirlik's suspicion that postcolonial theories encourage the exploitative tendencies of global capitalism will need to be persuasively answered if the postcolonial project is to have legitimacy for billions of people worldwide; despite Spivak's and Said's tireless efforts to steer the course of Western cultural criticism away from its historically parochial confines, both scholars' excessive familiarity with the most arcane and inaccessible philosophical and literary traditions of the West makes them appear unsettlingly unreliable to many non-Westernized Muslims. Spivak has had to struggle with the issue of her own reliability: regarding theory as a form of Orientalism, she concedes, after a lengthy examination of two French intellectuals' coming to terms with the irreducible problematic of representing Others, that the "subaltern" (the leftovers, *le déchet* of social strata, the Other of the Other, the nameless muted Hindu woman, etc.) "cannot speak." The impossibility of representation properly acknowledged, she nevertheless refuses to "disown" her female intellectual's "circumscribed task" with "a flourish."[10] The pull of the American cultural apparatus (along with the inescapable urge to speak itself) cannot be easily resisted; this apparatus, after all, describes Spivak as "one of *our* best known cultural and literary theorists."[11]

Although the nameless speaking Subject of this generous evaluation reproblematizes the position of the self-consciously acculturated Third World intellectual and pushes us to inquire further into the questionable program of postmodernism as a "final solution" to the crisis of identity, and although Spivak may be more comfortable in the United States than she would in India, and rootlessness may be a virtue, she still resists total assimilation—at least symbolically—by refusing to apply for U.S. citizenship or to vote. She defines her role as that of a scholar who brings metanarratives to a "crisis," a strategy that is useful in "contact politics" (questions of subjectivity), for "the only thing one really deconstructs are things into which one is intimately mired." The Subject of Spivak's evaluation thus transforms a depoliticized (in the traditional, grand narrative sense) scholar, permanently alienated from her homeland since the age of nineteen, a woman who yearns to be Bengali and Indian again,[12] into the mediator of an unequal cultural exchange, a dialogue conducted almost invariably in one of the modern European languages. For while the Western academic conscience is readily assuaged by the symbolic representations of the Other, it refuses to ask the equally significant if not troubling question: At what price postcoloniality? Dirlik doesn't address this important aspect of postcoloniality—if Third World intellectuals in the West are empowered by the insight of their displacement, their pain is nonetheless real. To forget this is to encourage a disturbing lack of sentience and perpetuate the myopic limitations of reified scholarship. If the goal of postcolonial theory is to abolish certainties at the superstructural level, the liberatory project it presumably espouses cannot be completed, as E. M. Forster concluded on friendship between political unequals in *A Passage to India,* without genuine political sovereignty. Only at that moment does displacement lose the coercive power of necessity and becomes the purely intellectual force it otherwise can and should be.

Edward Said, the prototypical "specular border intellectual" familiar with two cultures but "unable or unwilling" to be in either, not only embodies the harrowing predicament of the Third World critic in the West, but his very presence in the Western academy and the "tense productivity" of his scholarship are expressions of the Palestinian predicament, the people who (at the time of this writing) have been condemned to be at home in their homelessness (to use one of JanMohamed's metaphors). In fact, to question Orientalism itself can been seen as an act of protest that aims to unmask the cultural face of domination without necessarily being interested in offering "an alternate positivity."[13] This is why postcolonial theory transforms itself into a discursive gesture that is simultaneously informed and co-opted by the very assumptions of Western humanism it questions in the beginning. For if Said once had to defend himself against the surprising charge of Eurocentrism when a black woman historian found his allusion to "white European males" excessive, it is because he seems to have been severely constrained by a struggle that demands that he first legitimize himself to that nameless Subject that claims and disclaims, the panoptical powers of Western institutions whose capricious selectivity finally drains the energies of Third World resources—both human and natural.[14] Said's "*worldliness,*" therefore, though ideal under conditions of global economic socialism, not only risks displacing the struggle of Others as one of the most effective ways to be heard and ushering in the very conditions of equality and reciprocity that Said advocates, but it may also evoke images of a utopian cosmopolitanism unachievable in the present capitalist system. Said is surely aware of all this; what is unconvincing, however, is the status he confers on the migrant or the exile as the best-situated intellectual and contrapuntal reader of culture in the age of global capitalism. It is, he writes, "no exaggeration to say that liberation as an intellectual mission, born in the resistance and opposition to the confinements and ravages of imperialism, has now shifted from the settled, established, and domesticated dynamics of culture to its unhoused, decentered, and exilic energies, energies whose incarnation today is the migrant, and whose consciousness is that of the intellectual and artist in exile, the political figure between domains, between forms, and between languages."[15]

If the "specular border intellectual" is equipped to examine the synchronicity of culture in the (post)modern era, exile remains, as in Said's case, the condition of disempowerment whose "salutary" effects are to be decided against "the normal sense of belonging."[16] A Christian who is culturally a Muslim, Said's critique of "the forces of resistance to Islam" does not address the "major epistemological problems" of "modernity," "heritage," and "authority" that Arab and Muslim scholars are now examining.[17] Yet these Islamic perspectives have been occluded, and explaining "the return of Islam" has been entrusted to scholars whose impressive credentials in Western culture are not enough to disqualify others whose project is precisely to theorize Islamic alternatives to Western hegemony.

Take the case of Akeel Bilgrami's reading of the Islamic identity in a special issue of *Critical Inquiry* about identities, guest edited by Kwame Anthony Appiah and Henry Louis Gates Jr. (summer 1992). Here moderate Muslims appear to be besieged by the mounting crescendo of an antihistorical absolutist dogma, a belief that has outlived its functional context (since it is decidedly antisecularist) and therefore becomes excessive, much like neurosis. This is the "surplus phenomenology of identity." Bilgrami recognizes that the absolutist surplus renders opposition from Muslim reformers and moderates difficult, since this surplus is "the product of a certain history of subjugation and condescension, which continues today in revised but nevertheless recognizable forms." He rightly wants the reformers and moderates to reclaim their own active voices by questioning the authoritarian pressures of the absolutists, whose discourse has been unable to move beyond the typical complexes of colonial victimization. But Bilgrami ignores the fact that the ambivalence and silence of the moderates and reformers stem from the legitimacy conferred upon the absolutists by their better knowledge of—or merely their reliance on—Islamic texts (however badly interpreted) and their deployment of recognizable Islamic signifiers. For the reformers to be successful and engaged, they need to (re)educate themselves in their own cultures and histories, a venue that has been denied to them by neocolonial models of education and social organization. In other words, successful Islamic reform requires a better knowledge of Islam and Islamic history, subjects that have been made insignificant in the postcolonial era or simply relegated to small, often secondary and less rigorous sectors of public education. Merely reducing Islam to a "deist core" in a secular modern social arrangement cannot empower the anticolonialist reformers and moderates; it will simply prolong the hegemony of the absolutists who draw their legitimacy from their better knowledge of Islam.[18]

Edward Said's critical project of Orientalism is, as he emphasizes in *Culture and Imperialism*, to show how cultural practices precede, support, and justify hegemonic practices (in this case, imperialism);[19] yet his monumental influence notwithstanding, the Orientalist discourse continues unabated. As long as the secular premises of Western scholarship are not interrogated, it is unlikely that the discursive interventions of a few highly talented Third World critics can effectively contribute to the emancipation of all Third World peoples. No matter how insightful and liberating Western self-critique can be, it still partakes from the secular assumptions of the liberal tradition and cannot persuasively intervene in any discourse without accepting the limitations of this condition. Moreover, when radical critiques of the West are articulated in one of the European languages, they end up, as John Tomlinson has argued, reproducing the very hegemonic structures they want to eradicate.[20] This irresolvable paradox, borne out of existing power relations, can only be overcome with the liberation of the entire humanity from the clutches of an anticultural capitalism.

But even within this seemingly inescapable structure, the term *postcolonialism* is strategically disabling, as its prefix not only seems to relegate colonialism to a past that no longer is but also suggests a "dubious spatiality" that erases the concreteness of inequality.[21] (Besides the problematic claim that countries such as the United States and Australia are postcolonial, Said's contrapuntal reading also suggests, rather ironically, that the whole world is *postcolonial*, a suggestion that may be totally incomprehensible to billions of people.)[22] The project of Eurocentric Third World discourses in the West might be more relevant if exiled Third World critics continued to see themselves—if only strategically—as colonized, despite their commitment to equality and reciprocity, and despite the privileges that have accrued to many of them in their displacement. Collapsing irreducible differences into an uncritical universalism or advocating the adherence to regnant Western paradigms would only obfuscate the basic structures of the present global system and complicate the struggle needed for the emancipation of the wretched.[23]

The cultural rights of Others must be presented even if they are radically at odds with secular premises. Such a thing is not always easy to do, for the line between capitalist ethics and cultural ones has become so blurred as to render any criticism of capitalism into an attack on Western values; by the same token, non-Muslim critics of Islam could appear motivated by the same Orientalist prejudices that have vilified Muslims in the West and would therefore lead Muslims to reject the suspect outsider's attempt to analyze their condition or culture. The dilemma is somewhat reminiscent of the two positions Stanley Fish called "boutique multiculturalism" and "strong multiculturalism," both of which assume an initial dialogic relationship with the Other (the first based on respect, the second on tolerance), but which eventually collapse when absolute differences cannot be accommodated without substantially altering one's very identity. In the end, both approaches are forms of what Dirlik called "cultural relativism," since, in the final analysis, they confirm the distance implied in the hegemonic culturalist thesis. "Sympathy neither precludes condescension, not, at least, as a sense of the irrelevance of the Other, no matter how admired."[24] Fish argues that if cultural incompatibilities are seen as two equally valid forms of rationality, and if the Other's enmity is seen as a (negative) reflection of one's own relative moral code, not a fixed, transcendent essence, then it is best to adopt temporary strategies, or "adhoccery," in order to avoid liberal platitudes.[25] This strategy, however, cannot be applied at a global level, since the positions are assumed within a certain form of culturalist outlook and do not take into account the corrosive forces generated by the global capitalist economy. To suspend judgment is a first good step, but the world needs some standard against which people can negotiate cultural identities that would prevent violence against both vulnerable segments of local cultures and outsiders whose values are uncompromisingly different. Here, as in the rest of this book, I identify that universal standard as a form of (self)-critique that resists the logic of capitalism and articulates a progressive cohabitation with global diversities. It is more important to understand how the world's cultures are shaped by capitalism, whose synchronic powers makes them clash and retreat into fanatical isolation simultaneously.

The concern over the Islamic resurgence has reinvigorated the Orientalist discourse precisely because Western(ized) academics, including those on the Left, cannot accept and are not willing to learn why certain basic universalist tenets of Western civilization are, in fact, historically and culturally specific. François Burgat explains that while it is ready to accept the Other,

> the Left has retrenched to its finicky attachment to secular symbols, and today seems to be a prisoner of its own inability to admit that the universalism of republican thought can be called into question, or that anyone might dare to write history in a vocabulary other than the one that it has forged itself.

But it is precisely the rupture in language and syntax—the discarding of Western political terminology—which is the core of the

Islamist recipe. Henceforth, the potential for misunderstandings becomes vast.[26]

Since the secular reading of faith as religion "has its origins in the post-Enlightenment West," Western academics, John L. Esposito believes, "have been a major obstacle to understanding Islamic politics and so have contributed to a tendency to reduce Islam to fundamentalism and fundamentalism to extremism." Relying on the unshakable tenets of "secular liberalism and relativism," they act as "conservative clerics" when they fail to see Islam as a dynamic "faith-in-history." And this is how a new form of Orientalism is disseminated.[27] So the question that Said asked in *Covering Islam*, "What is it about 'Islam' that provokes so quick and unrestrained a response [in the West]?" is as valid now as it has always been, for Islam continues to be seen as a "threat to Western civilization." Said suggested that the answer may lie in the insularity and "guild orthodoxy" of Orientalism, especially since meaning depends at least as much on "affiliative" ("related to what other interpreters have said") configurations as it does on reading alien cultures.[28]

However, Akbar Ahmed's contention that, under the tutelage of its dominant Greek heritage, Western culture has erected its foundations on elitism, sexism, impatience with human frailty, and arrogance—a legacy of ruthless humanism that stands in sharp contrast with the Semitic (including Christian) insistence on humility and obedience—broadens the argument further and helps shed light on those irreducible cultural differences discursive universalisms cannot mend. While the Semitic tradition is predicated on the "fall from [divine] grace" and salvation, the Greek legacy, the most recent expression of which in the academy are current theories of postmodernism, is predicated on a human-bound notion of "progress":

> Consider three of the most important founding fathers of the modern Western mind, Marx, Nietzsche and Freud. Marx's doctoral dissertation (1841) was on the materialist and antimetaphysical philosophers Democritus and Epicurus; Nietzsche became a professor of classics in 1869 before he was 30; and Freud was fascinated by many aspects of Greek culture—for example, Platonic love and catharsis—long before he coined the term "Oedipus complex" in 1900.[29]

Westernized African and Asian intellectuals enter this history with varying degrees of assimilation and resistance (their attitude partly reflecting their class origins, determined, in recent history, by colonialism), but Muslims (especially those who have had a fair exposure to Islamic education, such as remembering the Qur'an and praying during childhood) seem to experience the dichotomous pull of the two historical currents much more intensely. Indeed, their very location in the West is itself a monumental challenge to their being, for as Fredric Jameson suggested in another context, the practice of faith needs a relevant context; otherwise, the monadic experience of the subject in late capitalism commodifies belief and renders its meaning superfluous.[30]

This may also help explain why the idea of monotheism troubles postmodern writers, for without the anchor of faith, without the ability to transcend the circulation of images, the inevitable instabilities that Jean-François Lyotard celebrates and the instant perishability of meaning in the era of the *petit récit* (call it the regime of untruths, if you will),[31] it is the most apt representation of the increasingly irrational human and social life under the destabilizing flexibility of transnational capitalism. In such a milieu, progressive definitions of Islam and other Western narratives of emancipation, such as Marxism, become archaically suspect—the first because it no longer fits into the main ideology of bourgeois liberal democracy; the second because, paradoxically, it harks back to the now discredited assumptions of the philosophies of the Enlightenment. Thus any intellectual attempt to question the capitalist system is a nostalgic gesture that doesn't account for the system's built-in mechanism for its own undoing, as Otherness simply melts into a potpourri of cultures, colors, ethnicities, etc.

Needless to say, such Benetton-like claims have been rigorously critiqued by Western intellectuals who are less interested in whether postmodernism signals a break with modernism or the continuation of a modernist tradition, but who read the whole movement as simply the cultural expression of the latest and most intensified phase of capitalist exploitation and decay (ruinous overconsumption in the midst of spreading social precariousness). The dissolution of the subject and the social, the devaluation of the past in a structure of "eternal presentness" (the time frame of the instant gratification economy based on extending credit for the consumption of goods generated by an ever more efficient production system), the indeterminacy of meaning (truth), the "elevation of space" ("relations of nearness and distance in space, rather than in time, become the measure of significance"), and the rise of fluid, discontinuous, and invented narratives of the Self are characteristic features of this movement. As Krishan Kumar described it, the postmodern world is "a world of eternal presentness, without origin or destination, past or future; a world in which it is impossible to find a centre, or any point or perspective from which it is possible to view it steadily and to view it whole; a world in which all that presents itself are the temporary shifting and local forms of knowledge and experience. Here are no deep structures, no secret or final causes; all is (or is not) what it appears on the surface. . . ."[32] This apocalyptic theory of disillusionment and retreat, initially promoted by failed 1960, French radicals who later found themselves both middle aged and part of the new middle class, is characterized by a return to the aesthetic.

> In various aspects of life one could detect a similar association of certain kinds of consumption with forming oneself into a particular kind of person; among the most important was a narcissistic obsession with the body, both male and female, less as an object of desire than—when disciplined by diet and exercise into a certain shape—as an index of youth, health, energy, mobility. This stylization of existence (to borrow Foucault's phrase) is surely best understood against the background, not of New Times, but of good times for the new middle class, a class which found itself in the 1980s with more money in its pocket and easier access to credit, without the pressure to save to which the old petty bourgeoisie was subject.[33]

So if Islam implies "submission" to divine revelation, postmodernism is also a form of "submission," surrender to a mirage, to the condition of double alienation (since the possibility of alienation is ruled out in a world in which general truths have vanished and the only positive mood left is the one tirelessly promoted by marketing specialists: consumer satisfaction), and no Muslim or genuinely religious intellectual can convincingly accommodate alienation by uncritically espousing such theories. Even Spivak admitted that we all have irreducible essences, and that essentializing, although preferably minimal and perpetually self-critical, is inevitable.[34] Collapsing differences into a capitalist-dictated universalism obliterates the promise of non-Western systems to struggle for cultural plurality, without which encounters are condemned to remain one-dimensional and hegemonic. But how does one equalize cultural encounters under the logic of transnational capital and the "corporate takeover of public expression"?[35] How are the estimated 3,500 spoken languages that exist in the world today given an equal status in the family of human languages when more than two-thirds of global communications are produced in 5 European languages?[36] This insurmountable hurdle legitimizes the right of alternative emancipatory models to be taken seriously, even supported, as Sartre knew, unconditionally; for only the total liberation of all peoples and the end of imperialism can give birth to a new human consciousness emanating from an egalitarian and enriching multicultural world.

The search for universality has led theory to transform the catastrophe of homelessness, rootlessness, and just plain displacement into a virtue. Hybridity (the cause of so much trauma in the Third World) and syncretism are proposed as the best available models to dismantle the unproductive polarizations inherent in the totalizing narratives of difference (and which are necessary for a gradual emancipation). However, both conditions are effects of unequal global relations; their unthinking propagation risks becoming complicitous with the systemic violence inflicted on billions of people worldwide. Although the salutary effects of contrapuntal or deconstructionist readings cannot be denied, the darker aspects of theory need to be highlighted in order to construct a more organic relationship between theory and real-life conditions. Modernism ushered in "the most extreme forms of the self-critical and anarchic models of twentieth-century culture which . . . can be seen to depend on the existence of a post-colonial Other which provides its condition of formation."[37]

Euro-American cultures, Edward Said and Walter Rodney have shown, are both built on and affected by the colonization of non-Western peoples.[38] Furthermore, the containment of Third World peoples through a Westernized elite has always been a deliberate design of colonialism,[39] a policy that was most succinctly articulated in 1835 by Lord Thomas Babington Macaulay in what is known as his "Minute on Education": "We must at present do our best to form a class who may be interpreters between us and the millions whom we govern; a class of persons, Indian in blood and colour, but English in taste, in opinions, in morals, and in intellect."[40] Thus European colonialists embarked on a campaign of cultural annihilation, imposing new languages on their captives to disrupt the necessary continuity between language and memory, causing a massive identity crisis, including among the "interpreters" themselves (Soyinka's novel by the same title is an ironic illustration of this confusion).[41] Seen in this light, hybridity and syncretism become no more than a state of mind, the theory of most diasporic Third World intellectuals,[42] *penseurs* of the highest caliber suffering stoically, reaching out for a world that is no longer theirs, unable to feel at home in a world that has become theirs by default. Thus homelessness-as-home or home-as-homelessness is celebrated as a cultural achievement by an academic apparatus eager to congratulate itself on the unmitigated pain of both homeless intellectuals and indigenous peoples, an apparatus devoid of sentience and unable to break away from the imperatives of a narrow professionalism that insists on productivity *avant tout,* and rarely on genuine cultural emancipation.

Western(ized) intellectuals who have turned Rushdie's predicament into a cause célèbre, transforming a native-born Indian from a Muslim family who had to immigrate to England into a convenient hero, rarely paused to remember the consequences of the other *fatwas* articulated not by Iranian Ayatollahs but by British Lords: Macaulay and Lytton in India, and Lugard in Nigeria. Instead of using the Rushdie affair for soul-searching and healing, the cultural apparatus rallied to reiterate that Western values are indeed universal, and that Islam and Islamists are yet to be civilized. On the thousandth day of the *fatwa,* the *Times Literary Supplement* (8 November 1994) published the commentaries of prominent Western writers who used this occasion to depict Islam—as the following excerpts show—in the dark colors of the worst Orientalism.

Then came the holy war against *The Satanic Verses* in which the enemy was a single fiction, a single writer, and the whole might and money of the Islamic world was deployed in the *fatwa:* death to Salman Rushdie. (Nadine Gordimer)

The lethal pitch of Islam is all the more understandable since Islam is among the youngest of the existing creeds; intolerance is the mark of its age as well as its means of transportation. (Joseph Brodsky)

Clearly, fundamentalists are nowhere near accepting the vital Western principles of the rule of law, religious tolerance, and freedom of speech and enquiry—the underpinning of what V.S. Naipul now identifies as "our universal civilization" . . .

[Pressure must be increased] to secure the lifting of the *fatwa* . . . to persuade Islamic fundamentalism that it will remain outcast until it comes to terms with Western standards of civility. (Ferdinand Mount)

Gordimer suggests that such a publishing event is an innocent, harmless act (although she must have been aware of the death toll that resulted from it) and transforms one leader's *fatwa* and a few million dollars into "the whole might and money of the Islamic world." She implies that writing in a global village dominated by former imperial languages and powerful disseminating systems is a harmless activity, perhaps just irritating; she thus fails to see, as does Ali Mazrui, how writing itself can be a "lethal weapon."[43] In her view, the whole Islamic world participates in the conspiracy to execute Rushdie; she never wonders whether the Islamic world, in its state of dependency, has any "might" at all. The oil-producing Islamic countries drained their money reserves to cover most of the expenses incurred during the Gulf War ("one of the rare wars out of which a major power [the United States] actually made a profit"),[44] an event that only demonstrated how postcoloniality is an empty expression in the Arab and Islamic worlds.[45]

Brodsky chose to attribute the "lethal pitch of Islam" and its "intolerance" to the religion's youth (a rather intriguing argument, since Islam has been more tolerant than the Christian West, in which the oldest of monotheistic religions, Judaism, suffered relentless persecutions that culminated in the Holocaust); he is, however, curiously silent about the newness of the "New World" itself, in which indigenous civilizations were gruesomely decapitated—to use Marx's expression—and replaced by political and economic orders that still exclude and punish non-Western peoples. Still, Muslims are condemned to remain uncivilized and barbaric, as Ferdinand Mount clearly suggests, until they accept "the vital Western principles of the rule of law, religious tolerance, and freedom of speech and enquiry."

Thus a whole page in one of the most prestigious book reviews in the West uncritically propagates the supremacy of Western civility, carrying on the mission of Orientalism, recently decried by a no less prestigious scholar, without evoking the slightest sense of incongruity. The imperative of Eurocentric secular scholarship prevents a more textured reading of the political tensions in question and simply reasserts the supremacy of Western values as a solution to ancient cultural impasses. It was perhaps for this reason that Salman Rushdie "has been perceived by many Muslims as being guilty of cultural treason."[46]

Theoretically, Rushdie is a postcolonial writer who has been inserted in the postmodern moment by the Western cultural apparatus.[47] Mark Edmundson, for instance, sanctified Rushdie as a "prophet" because *The Satanic Verses* "is infused with innovative power, with a capacity to prophesy, and maybe even to provoke change"; the novel, with its unprecedented creativity, is a "harbinger" for a "*positive* postmodernism." Not only is Rushdie's style "*post*-contemporary," but Rushdie himself is posthistorical, wanting "to be ahead of time, doing some of history's work for it." What is this exceptional talent that allows Rushdie to anticipate history? Rushdie's "rewriting of Muhammad ... means speeding up the work of secularization by vaporizing—in good, negative postmodern fashion—the prophet's holy aura."[48]

Partly for this reason, Muslim (or other Afro-Asian) intellectuals have uncritically adopted these views. Claiming that Rushdie's novel speaks for the constituency of apostates in the Islamic world, Qadri Ismail sees Western liberalism (or neocolonialism) and Islamic fundamentalism as allies in the defense of purity, since both ideologies fear hybridity; *The Satanic Verses* becomes in this case a double-edged, simultaneous critique of both systems.[49] Meanwhile, Aamir Mufti's more serious argument reiterates the same statements Edmundson makes: "By questioning the infallibility of the Revelation, by refusing to accept the required code of strict reverence in speaking of the Prophet and his close circle of relatives and companions, and, more generally, in secularizing (and hence profaning) the sacred 'tropology' of Islam by insisting upon its appropriation for the purposes of fiction, [*The Satanic Verses*] throws into doubt the discursive edifice within which 'Islam' has been produced in recent years."[50] Edmundson makes it clear that the desacralization of the Prophet Mohamed sacralizes Rushdie as an artist. Rushdie himself, being "a member of that generation of Indians who were sold the secular idea," ascribes powerful possibilities to art. For him, "redescribing the world is the first necessary step towards changing it," and good books should expand the horizons of possibility, even "when they endanger the artist by reason of what he has, or has not, *artistically* dared."[51] The powers of art are unlimited: in its "secular definition of transcendence," it can replace religious dogma, whereas religious faith "must surely remain a private matter"; indeed, with the collapse of communism, literature is left alone to battle the sweeping march of capital by bringing certainties to a crisis.[52]

That cultural practice could acquire revolutionary meaning seems to be a shared belief among certain postmodernists. Spivak, in a debate about postmodernity, argues that deglamorizing *grands récits* works against a capitalism that needs all the ammunition of unexamined certainties to carry on its mission of pillage.[53] Perhaps it is this belief that has created an aura of radicalism around some cultural journals, where the main concern seems to be the dismantling of traditional convictions and the releasing of people into a liberating hybridity—the rapture of rupture, as Lyotard would have it. The revolutionary project having failed in France, the authoritarianism of grand narratives must now be denounced, and with it any visionary agenda of social reconstruction and a better world for humanity. However, replacing utopian social projects with theoretical playfulness, struggle with disenchantment, may just ominously signal the inability of oppositional intellectual forces in advanced capitalist societies to mount a credible resistance to the overwhelming power of transnational capital, partly because to the extent that they "have been absorbed into structures of domination that represent alienated social power,"[54] their alternatives are more likely to be reduced to variations on the single theme of secular democracy. This may explain why, even before Khomeini's *fatwa* was issued, Rushdie had been depicted as a besieged champion of freedom of speech in the West, from whose shores he dared the prime minister of an important Third World country to lift the ban on his book: "This is now," Rushdie wrote, addressing the late Rajiv Gandhi in the *New York Times*, "a matter between you and me."

While it is understandable that major newspapers would support a writer's right to free speech, the most disconcerting aspect of Rushdie's daring challenge to Gandhi is to equate the literary aspirations of a writer—one who, as Ali Mazrui would say, "elevates the pleasures of art above the pain of society"[55]—with the responsibilities of the head of a strife-ridden and religiously explosive state, a prime minister who would be assassinated precisely because he could not contain ethnic tension in his country. Ironies of history: it was Khomeini who replied a few months later, thus provoking massive indignation in the West. A furious debate erupted after the *fatwa* and reached every corner of the globe. *The Rushdie File* records its initial phases,[56] which revolved around issues of censorship, responsibilities of writers, sources and markers of identity, and tolerance; but what really emerges from reading these various positions is that the project of the Enlightenment, with its premise of freedom of expression, is not—and has never been—as "universal" as the postcolonial writers so unequivocally state in their letter to the *New York Times* editor.

To problematize the universality of human rights is not to accept the unliberating legacy of clerical, orthodox Islam; in fact, many scholars are beginning to question the premises of Islamic law itself in an attempt to take the Islamic nation (*umma*) to a new plane of consciousness that is neither uncritically traditional nor blindly Western. In *The Second Message of Islam*, the late scholar Mahmoud Mohamed Taha (brutally executed by the Numeiri regime for his enlightened and reformist views), defines freedom as the overcoming of fear, since fear is the greatest obstacle to love and to a harmonious, balanced, and spiritual existence. Only Islam, which connects the individual with the community, is able to liberate people in this fashion; for Westernization (not Christianity), premised on a thoroughly materialistic view of life, has failed to create the conditions for a better world. Since Islam is a total way of life, freedom to develop means freedom from the various obstacles that hamper such development, including the freedom from political oppression and economic exploitation. For Taha, then, a "superior state," or the "good society" is one that provides the means for total emancipation, not just freedom of expression:

> The good society is one that is based on three equalities: economic equality, today known as socialism, or the sharing of wealth; political equality or democracy, or sharing in political decisions which affect daily life; and social equality which, to some extent, results from socialism and democracy, and is characterized by a lack of social classes and discrimination based on color, faith, race, or sex. In the good society, people are judged according to their intellectual and moral character, as reflected in their public and private lives and demonstrated in the spirit of public service at all times and through every means. Social equality aims at removing social classes and differences between urban and rural life by providing equal opportunity for cultural refinement.

Such a society, furthermore, "enjoys tolerant public opinion, permitting different life-styles and manners, *as long as these are beneficial to society.*"[57] This latter qualification needs to be highlighted, for the crisis of contemporary capitalism stems from its failure to produce a social imaginary that would give social existence a meaning that goes beyond the pursuit of productivity and consumption for their own sakes. It is precisely because capitalist modernity is experienced as a "loss,"[58] an anticultural process that fetishizes culture into marketable commodities, that Islam, drawing its inspiration from divine revelation, appears as a profoundly disturbing effect to the reigning global complacency. The Islamic social narrative is antimodern only to the extent that it refuses to treat free (bourgeois) expression as the final-ity of the social project; societies need to strike a balance between individual and communal needs, and a progressive interpretation of Islam provides just one answer to secular modernity.

Because secularism is originally a Western idea born out of specific historical circumstances,[59] its rejection in the Islamic world is part of Muslims' struggle for self-definition. Most Arab intellectuals interviewed on the subject of human rights seem to agree that defining one's identity is an indispensable foundation for any discussion of human rights, which is one reason why the Western notion of liberty in the Arab world has been controversial. "The liberation of our spirits from the hegemony of Western thought," according to one Islamist, "is an indispensable condition without which we will not free the land nor the economy and without which we will not manage to reunify our ranks," for to be alienated is to be underdeveloped, hence "the first step [in the process of liberation] is to destroy in ourselves the idol of the West."[60] Unsurprisingly, Kevin Dwyer discovered that the Western notion of human rights is seriously questioned, if not rejected out of hand, across the political spectrum, even in the most Westernized Arab countries, such as Morocco, Tunisia, and Egypt. To explain this, Dwyer concluded that the Islamic resurgence is "a response to urgent contemporary problems," including "the desire to construct societies free from the ills of 'modern' Western society: its materialism, lack of social cohesion, lack of common purpose, absence of a sense of community."[61]

The preservation of community weighs more on the scale of justice than do the defying articulations of individuals. Even the secular Article 19 of the International Covenant on Civil and Political Rights that protects freedom of opinion imposes restrictions for the "respect of the rights and reputations of others" and for "the protection of national security or of public order (*ordre public*), or of public health or morals."[62] In Islam, as in precapitalist societies, the idea of atomized individuals exercising their "rights" through participation in an electoral "democratic" process has no historical roots in the people's collective memory. When the West resorts to the moral argument of human rights, it precludes peoples' right to self-determination and denies the right to equal economic opportunity, since capitalism is inherently a system of uneven development. Although the notions of freedom and rights cannot be disputed on moral grounds, these concepts have been so diluted by ideological agendas that a careful sorting out of fact from fiction has become indispensable (see chapter 4). In the Third World, introducing democracy simply means democratizing poverty and containing threatening alternatives; otherwise, one would have to address freedom in capitalist democracies, including the United States, where the triumph of capitalism has managed to confine thought and privatize censorship: "Every day of the week something is being censored in the US media. Programs are denied funding for fear of offending advertisers, subscribers. . . . Otherwise reputable publishers turn down manuscripts, edit out ideas, or surgically remove chapters likely to offend powerful groups in the nation."[63]

While freedom of speech remains a contentious and unfinished project in the West—its meaning and extent defined by prevailing power relations—this right has been used to portray the widely diffused picture of an intolerant Islam, despite repeated reservations by people who are more familiar with Islamic history. Though some leaders may have been perplexed by and strongly objected to Khomeini's unilateral leadership in the Rushdie affair, many Muslims read the freedom of speech principle as the latest tactic in the West's crusade against Islam,[64] a crusade that has managed to put Muslims on both sides of the divide—Rushdie (and other intellectuals) versus common believers—in an extremely precarious situation that does nothing but exacerbate the pain of the colonized and perpetuate long-simmering tensions.[65] For although Rushdie wants to celebrate "hybridity, impurity, intermingling, the transformation that comes of new and unexpected combinations of human beings, cultures, ideas, politics, movies, songs" and "our mongrel selves"; although he wants the "freedom to offend," "to satirize all orthodoxies, including religious orthodoxies," *The Satanic Verses* is ultimately "the story of two painfully divided selves [Saladin Chamcha and Gibreel Farishta] and "their quest for wholeness."[66]

To the extent that the novel struggles with questions of identity at home and in a race-conscious imperial society, it is part of a larger Afro-Asian literary and cultural tradition, one in which alienation bedevils ambitious and talented young people caught in the simultaneously promising and deadly web of Westernization (see chapter 3). And if, as Mufti states, pastiche "becomes a means of appropriating and rewriting the colonial text,"[67] this stylistic strategy is, as Jameson argued, the hollowed artistic gesture of late capitalism.[68] So even the revolutionary potential ascribed to style does not possess the redeeming qualities ascribed to it, for as with most cultural productions, it remains symptomatic of the larger and more concrete historical event of late or global capitalism. This is why the term *colonized* is preferable to *postcolonial*: In what language does the Western academy—and the American one in particular—address Rushdie? If the dialogue is monolingual and conducted in Western terms, then only dazzling feats of self-deception, through the recourse to equally labyrinthine cultural theories, would manage to obfuscate the painful subjugation of the South to Western models of living. Cultural hegemony is real, and the presence of the Third World intellectual in the West—despite the proverbial exceptions and other conscious complicities—is a stark manifestation of this reality.

No leftist or radical Western scholar seems to measure accurately the degree of Third World intellectuals' alienation, to read the exotic presence of Others in the Academy as a reminder of their vulnerabilities and organic uprootedness; even if Third World migrants prefer to be here—and they mostly do—they do it out of the paradoxical necessity to overcome structural hardships at home and to benefit from the very system that has marginalized their economies and transformed their nations into neocolonial, even undemocratic, states.[69] It is yet to be proven that Britain is a more beautiful country than India, or that Euro-American people are better than others; but what seems to be indisputably clear is the systematic uprooting of non-Western cultures in the last five hundred years or so, has led to a painful and maddening identity crisis whose symptoms have been unscrupulously interpreted to be the sign of a liberating order.

That the quest for (a lost) identity is the dominant theme in Rushdie's novel should make us look beyond the colorful posturing of theory and into the real meaning of pain and suffering that loss engenders. Whether Gibreel Farishta, the fallen movie star and satanic archangel, and Saladin Chamcha, the multivocal impersonator, are intertwined or not, their fall from the hijacked plane *Bostan* (garden of Eden?) is really a time of reckoning: at this stage, they have both, through different trajectories, reached an irreversible point of crisis. Their identities need to be urgently recovered if they want to avoid death ("To be born again, first you have to die"). Gibreel Farishta would eventually succumb, defeated by his ego, inflated on stages, and broken by Allie. But Saladin seems to have embarked on a journey of healing and self-restoration (he recovers his real name, Salahuddin) in the end, finally coming to terms with a most traumatic past. Even the unbelieving skeptical Mizra Saeed Akhtar, who suffers from the postmodern affliction of emotional "detachment," of not being able "to connect" himself to "things, events, feelings," and is therefore unable to follow Ayesha's perilous crossing of the Arabian Sea, seems to yield to the mysteries of faith.[70]

Let us also remember that it is Gibreel, troubled by doubt (92) and afflicted with schizophrenia (429), who dreams up (and distorts) the power of faith: Mahound, the intolerant prophet, with his "terrifying singularity" (102) within the religious multiplicity of Jahiliya; Ayesha, in her carnivalesque, postmodernist journey amid great social commotion in India (488); and the exiled Imam (whose resemblance to Khomeini is too striking to be a matter of coincidence), who condemns History as "the intoxicant, the creation and possession of the Devil, of the great Shaitan, the greatest of lies—progress, science, rights" because "the sum of knowledge was complete on the day Allah finished his revelation to Mahound" (210). Leaving aside all speculation about the author's intentions, it is significant that both Mahound and the Imam, with their firm (but satirized Islamic?) convictions and alternative visions, are the only successful revolutionaries in the novel. And although Khadija offers Mahound "the reassuring certainty" he needs, Gibreel is further weakened by the hybridized Allie, "the bringer of tribulation, creatrix of strife, of soreness of the heart" (321). Gibreel doesn't even have a Zeeny, the fatalist intellectual of the homeland who interpellates Saladin back. He finds no redemption, no inspiring source of hope; he is "destroyed," as Rushdie puts it, "by the loss of faith." Gibreel's blasphemous imaginings are "punishments and retributions," and "the dream figures who torment him with their assaults on religion are representatives of the process of ruination, and *not* representative of the point of view of the author."[71]

The author is, on the contrary, another product/victim of Macaulay's scheme and its limitations. Like Salahuddin, he has been "Englished," as his alienation from his people and culture increased.[72] He is the son of Muslim elites who could not resist the temptations of India's former colonizers. As with most promising children of the early nationalist bourgeoisie, he was sent to school in England, where he ultimately lost his faith:

> God, Satan, Paradise and Hell all vanished one day in my fifteenth year, when I quite abruptly lost my faith. I recall it vividly. I was at school in England by then. The moment of awakening happened, in fact, during a Latin lesson, and afterwards, to prove my new-found atheism, I bought myself a rather tasteless ham sandwich, and so partook for the first time of the forbidden flesh of the swine. No thunderbolt arrived to strike me down. I remember feeling that my survival confirmed the correctness of my new position.[73]

There is no doubt that Rushdie's naive defiance of Islam is merely the heartbreaking scream of another casualty of colonialism and the confused elite it created in its aftermath. One simply cannot accept the rebellious gesture of an estranged fifteen year old as the legitimate and unchanging foundation of a new prophecy, a new theory; but one can recognize how such a boy, already a displaced resource, is transformed, through the maneuvers of Eurocentric ideologies, into the body/stage on which an old conflict is reinscribed. Only a cold scholarship with its myopic insistence on fact can fail to see the tragedy in Rushdie's statement, the disorientation of a child exiled to England for no other reason than because that country had once occupied his.

The same is, in different degrees, true of major Third World intellectuals such as Spivak and Said who left their homelands in search of better educations in capitalist centers.[74] To be sure, because of these scholars' gigantic intellectual efforts, and the unavoidable presence of Third World people in all spheres of capitalist production—from underpaid backbreaking jobs in agriculture to high-tech innovation in the corporate world—Eurocentrism has been somewhat attenuated; but such demographic shifts do not change the fundamental structures of the world economy, or even bestow independence on poor countries. Indeed, the occasional anxiety over the decline of the West, often based on the same postcolonial assumptions, is premature: wealth and power are still mostly concentrated in the hands of the same colonial powers that dominated the world at the end of the nineteenth century.[75]

The voice of the West's Other, spoken in unpressured indigenous idioms, needs to be reasserted in order to challenge complacent intellectuals who define themselves as progressive into a *multilingual* dialogue. If the monotheistic religion of Islam, premised on the notion of the sacred and cultural authenticity,[76] represents a significant portion of the Third World, the answer is not in conjuring up a world of civilization clashes, in which a Sino-Islamic alliance will finally push back Western democracies into an isolationist stance, but in seriously contemplating new economic and political structures that may enlarge the scope of freedom without undermining both cultural diversity and humane cultural encounters. (Fault lines can be reimagined as innovative border zones where syncretic arrangements and cultural borrowings flourish outside states' regulatory policies.)[77]

A positive analysis, as the *Economist* had done even before the publication of Huntington's first "clash" essay, needs to apply an equally critical look at the West's own legacies. Though its dystopian article anticipated much of the nostalgia that permeates Huntington's "clash" thesis, the *Economist* also subjected the whole project of the Enlightenment to critical scrutiny. Written from the vantage point of the year 2992 about the "disastrous 21st century," the article imagines the West to have collapsed under trade wars as hypernationalisms rise to meet the stifled needs for identity. With Western democracy on the defensive, the United States, under the Buchanan Doctrine of 2003, retreats to a sort of gentler pan-American nationalism. Two new giants arise: China and the New Caliphate of Islam. A coup in Saudi Arabia in 2011 lures other Muslims to join in a new empire, while an exhausted West watches helplessly. The last section of the article, "The end of a cycle," describes the rise of individualism and

Reason to counter the excesses of the Age of Faith, and then explains why such correctives have turned into their opposites:

> By the 18th century it was being argued that man had now reached an Age of Reason, in which human beings could understand and master every aspect of their lives. This proved false. It led, among other things, to the French revolution of 1789 and the Russian revolution of 1917, both of which claimed to speak for human rights but in fact crushed them, and both of which did irrational things in the name of reason. The fascist upheaval of the 1920s and 1930s was in part a reaction to this, a violent return to the idea that blood and feeling were the true guides to human action. Nationalism, and its son hypernationalism, were milder versions of the same reaction.
>
> It was time for a new readjustment. A new balance was needed between the analytic part of the human mind and the instinctive part, between rationality and feeling; only then could man address the world more steadily. And a new balance had to be struck between the claims of individual freedom and the claims of individual morality; only then could law and liberty swing evenly on the scales. Because they did not tackle these problems in time, the democracies marched straight from the climax of the 20th-century victory into anti-climax. They did not know what to do next.[78]

Obviously, the *Economist* is warning the "democracies" that by dispatching expeditionary forces and boycotting small countries they will not reverse their decline and mend the fissures growing within their ranks;[79] only a new way of seeing (*une autre manière de voir*— the theme launched in the last decade or so by *Le Monde diplomatique*) and a new reassessment of the very Western tradition being defended could renew the fraying and embattled progressive spirit of Euro-American cultures.

There is hope: the clash thesis has not totally obliterated other self-critical views, and contemporary theory has not convincingly erased the glaring fact that Afro-Asian peoples (intellectuals or not) continue to be alienated by a capitalist regime that encircles the globe and rewards only those who—dazzled by the ephemeral promise of winning in such a system—have unscrupulously abandoned the memory and wisdom of their ancestral traditions. The truth is that the hard lives of global outcasts cannot be easily theorized away. Only when Third World societies can reclaim their resources, their Rushdies and others like him, only when these societies become self-sufficient and are motivated by different ideals will they stem the flood of people and resources to the North and end the pain of displacement that many postmodernists have eagerly celebrated. Yet these ideals must be carefully articulated in nonexclusionary languages. While critically assessing the representation of their traditions, Muslims are also challenged to question their own intellectual and cultural legacies, expand the scope of their inclusionary visions, and determine the extent to which they, too, have lived under the iron grip of false ideologies. In the following chapter, I examine how a progressive notion of Islam has been stifled by the rise of nationalism (both in its secular and religious manifestations) in the Arabic-speaking parts of the Muslim world.

2

Millennium without Arabs?

But only now, putting together the Christian and missionary
inspired origins of Arab nationalism in Syria and the use the British
made of the idea to mobilize the "Arabs" against the Ottomans, did I
realize the extent to which Arab nationalism had emerged as a way
of opposing the Islamic Empire. And only now did I realize the
extent to which Egypt had not only *not* been Arab but actually had
been mostly on the opposite side of the Arabs.
—Leila Ahmed, *From Cairo to America—A Woman's Journey*

The obdurate insistence of Arabs on their own particularities,[1] even
at this advanced stage of capitalism and highly integrated financial
world, may have prompted *Time* magazine, in a 1992 special issue on
the new millennium, to conclude that the only solution left is to
remove these unreformed people from history. The proddings of the
media, the latest inheritor of the whole repertoire of negative Orientalism, have been unable to instigate other outcomes. Erasure from
global memory is now the final solution.

In an article titled "How the World Will Look in 50 Years," the
Arabs are relegated to the dustbin of history, since by now, the West,
having outgrown its dependence on Third World resources (including oil), finds the increasingly unstable Arab states of the Middle East
of "declining interest." Not surprisingly, a corollary consequence of
the drying up of Arab oil is the isolation of the Islamic world, deemed
"powerfully resistant to modernization."[2] In this lavishly illustrated
issue, which anticipates the persistence of class struggle and eco-

nomic wars, and in which some room is made for a warning against the pitfalls of "progress" by the fiery puritan of American intellectual life, the late Christopher Lasch,[3] a very telling illustration accompanies the Arab/Muslim terminal illness: the caricature of a stereotypical Gulf Arab stretching his arms in the double and paradoxical gesture of supplication and defeat toward an ankle-high shrunken oil well from which only three long green leaves surprisingly sprout. The word "decline" (the last four letters crumbling precipitously) is inscribed on the illustration, and the whole caption is boldly titled: "A Region about to Fade." The Arab, regarded as mere oil producer in the world economy,[4] is left to make preparations, write historical wills, and sit in anxious envy of the West's infallible judgment and brave new world of capitalism.

Time magazine's essay is of course the projection of various interrelated but illogical desires of an elitist agenda: maintaining supremacy in a dangerously wasteful economy, reducing the risk of dependency on poorer nations, and banishing the troublesome Other from consciousness.[5] There is obviously no alternative to Western capitalism and the various ideologies—such as nationalism, secularism, civil society, progress—that have become the ideological pillars of late capitalist society. Religion as a different cosmology entailing its own distinct sets of belief systems and practices is a troubling excess. It is especially excessive when it appears as a disruption of dominant ideologies that secure political consensus and ensure the uninterrupted march of capitalism; it is repulsively atavistic when it refuses to relinquish tradition and identity. Islam, in other words, can no longer insist on its autonomy without fundamentalizing itself; hence it is reduced—by both critics and adherents—to banal descriptions and crude oversimplifications that perpetuate imaginary rivalries. The terminology deployed in these crusades and anticrusades is contingent and unstable, relying on indeterminate designations such as the "Arabs," the "Middle East," and the "West"—words that exist only discursively, not in the sense that capitalism exists as a real system of social relations, or Islam as a cultural economy with its specific proposals for arranging reality. They are mere slogans paraded to a world (of scholars) fiercely attached to unexamined certainties whose primary ideological function is to obscure the destructive processes of the global economic system. While processes with real effects on human societies and destinies remain conveniently unnamed, a whole set of misnomers proliferate with an amazing frequency to invent pseudorealities on which a whole apparatus of scholarship is erected.

Would it then be an excessive postulation or exaggeration if one agrees that the Arabs are, discursively speaking, fading away, and that they may very well exit the global stage as swiftly and dramatically as when they burst onto it in the two major moments of history: the early expansion of Islam and the rise of Arab nationalism at the turn of the twentieth century? The veteran Moroccan historiographer, Abdellah Laroui, after all, insists on a procedural, positivist historicism that is chronically suspicious of memory and traditional parochialisms and open toward a multicultural universalism as the only way out from the impasse of Arab intellectual thought.[6] Yet even Laroui himself postulates on the historically problematic premise that there is a transhistorical "Arab" essence and implicitly accepts the construction of a new identity, forged in modern Levantine history, engineered by British diplomats in Egypt and the Arabian peninsula, and exported to Arabic-speaking peoples as the secular substitute for a mutilated "imagined community" of Islam onto history.

Mohamed 'Abid al-Jabri, the Moroccan philosopher, did, in fact, undertake the daunting task of locating the structure of the "Arab mind" in the early Abbasid period when the Arabs who oversaw the expansion of Islam outside its Arabian confines were suddenly confronted with the sobering realization that the universal message of Islam was eroding their ethnic privileges and political supremacy. Although the pre-Islamic Arabian past had been erased in the initial phases of Islam, the emergence of the phenomenon of the *shu'ubiya* with the conversion of non-Arabs forced the Arabian ruling class to rewrite Arabian, pre-Islamic cultures and record them as cultural foundations for the expanding corpus of Islamic studies and law. The Age of Recording (*'asru tadween*) was an attempt to recuperate the once deliberately annulled and superseded traditions of the Jahiliya (the pre-Islamic period; literally, the time of ignorance). The collection of the language of *al-a'arab* in the authoritative dictionary *Lisan al-'arab* was, in fact, the invention and establishment of a new vocabulary reflecting the parochial cultural environment of pre-Islamic

Arabia, not the cosmopolitan thought expressed in the Qur'an. In this way, the vulgar Bedouin, the "al-a'arabi" of the Jahiliya, was transformed into the cultural legislator of a long tradition; he became the ultimate *'alim,* the "scholars' master" (*ustadh al 'ulama*).[7] His grammar and rhetoric stamped the laws of *fiqh* with their indelible structures and were decreed as immutable references for the rest of history.

The work of Al-Jabri, critically acclaimed as the "most serious attempt in the Arab world to go beyond ideology to epistemology in order to analyze the working of the Arab mind,"[8] inadvertently posits Arabness as a fictional ethnicity invented as a political ploy to contain dangerous foreigners attracted by the egalitarian and liberating promise of Islam. That attempt ultimately failed in the late Abbasid period, and the word *Arab* was subsequently confined to its original meaning, "becoming in effect a social rather than an ethnic term."[9] Still, a small group of besieged autocratic rulers had managed to keep the "Arab ethno-national ideology" (the whole set of cultural traditions invented during the Age of Recording) "in a state of latency" and infuse it into the universalist and complex Islamic civilization.[10] For the Arab nationalist ideology to reemerge, it needed "(1) worldwide ascendancy of ethno-national ideologies with linguistic demarcation; (2) a tendency to secularization; and (3) last but not least, the rise of a multiconfessional Arabic speaking bourgeoisie with common interests, engaged in a more or less unified struggle."[11]

Up to this period, there is general consensus that Islam is what defined identities and unified people in the far-flung and politically fragmented realms of Islam. The Muslim, despite endemic rivalries, was a citizen of Dar al-Islam (Realm of Islam), and was protected by a universal and autonomous Islamic legal code (*Shari'a*) whose primary purpose and genius was to secure the separation of temporal and religious powers, and put a check on the caliph's arbitrary rule.[12] Today, when fundamentalized Islam inevitably appears as "surplus," it is easy to forget that it was the *'ulama* who championed the *mawali* (non-Arab converts) in their revolt against the despotic Arab Ummayads and worked out additional strategies to balance individual rights against the rights of the community.[13] When the institutions that preserved the *Shari'a* were incorporated into the state structure during the Ottoman period,[14] it became too conservative. As a result, no access was allowed to the knowledge and sciences of the emerging "technicalistic" Europe.[15]

Eventually, the sacral culture of Islam founded primarily on a sacred script (the symbolic marker of identity) was pressured by the force of European imperialism into reconfiguring its relationship to language and to copying European nationalist principles.[16] The latter were closely tied to a "lexicographic revolution" that had displaced Christendom's sacred Latin and ushered in vernaculars often arbitrarily imposed on delineated geographical entities.[17] This revolution became the ideological cornerstone of imperial policies and the cultural program for maintaining Europe's hegemony over its (former) colonies.[18] Thus the idea of nationalism began to enter Islamic lands through vernacular revolutions: not only was the first vernacular press in Istanbul published by a man (Ibrahim Sinasi) who had spent five years in France, but Arab Maronites and Copts, trained in Levantine Christian academic institutions, were to become "major contributors to the revival of classical Arabic and the spread of Arab nationalism."[19] As in previous European history, Arab and Turkish elites were (re)inventing traditions to place themselves in a mutual form of Otherness that only strengthened European imperial policies.[20] Once again, political strategies were giving shape to a new cultural tradition.

If the Otherness engendered by nationalist sentiments took the shape of anti-imperial struggle in the Third World, it was not because nationalist leaders were motivated by real political alternatives but because they realized their ultimate exclusion from the hierarchical mobility initially promised by colonial education;[21] otherwise, indigenous bilingual intellectuals, with access to Western culture, were indispensable mediators and reliable agents for the long-term goals of colonialism. The viceroy of India, Lord Lytton (1876–80), expressed this goal succinctly when he outlined his vision before his legislative council on March 14, 1878:

> It must be . . . remembered that the problem undertaken by the British rulers of India . . . is the application of the most refined principles of European society, to a vast Oriental population, in

whose history, habits, and traditions they have had no previous existence. Such phrases as "Religious toleration," "Liberty of the press," "Personal freedom of the subject," which in England have long been the mere catchwords of ideas common to the whole race, and deeply impressed upon its character by all the events of its history, and all the more cherished recollections of its earlier life, are here in India to the vast mass of our native subjects, the mysterious formulas of a foreign, and more or less uncongenial, system of administration, which is scarcely, if at all, intelligible to the greater number of those whose benefit it is maintained.

Then he added that "it is a fact which there is no disguising . . . and also one which cannot be too constantly or too anxiously recognized that . . . we have placed, and must permanently maintain ourselves at the head of *a gradual but gigantic revolution—the greatest and most momentous social, moral, and religious, as well as political revolution which, perhaps, the world has ever witnessed.*"[22] Such a project required the invention of a new social class of cultural mediators caught in an often paralyzing bifurcated identity and operating in highly nationalized universes with their own set of pilgrimage patterns (to major colonial towns and, later, to the metropoles themselves).[23] As anticolonial nationalists, they were promoted by colonial powers to maintain Eurocentric views and economic interests. It is in this sense that secular Arab nationalists turned out to be surrogate colonialists.[24]

Mostly relying on the existence of a shared interregional language, Rodinson once stated that "there is such an entity as an Arab nation."[25] If that were the case, one might have called medieval Europe a Latin nation; but Latin was for Christendom what Arabic was for Islam: a sacred language that was not in and of itself the source of identity. Even the history that Rodinson claims to have united the Arabs was not as "common" as he suggests. One can easily show how the secular histories of various geographical regions in the so-called Arab world were very varied, that the history of, say, Morocco is substantially different from that of the recently invented states in the Middle East, or even of the Ottoman provinces. Rodinson's claim is difficult to sustain historically; the author himself states elsewhere

that the idea of Arab nationalism was first developed among Levantine Arabs as a response to Ottoman "maladministration" and imperialist pressure, and eventually led to the dream of Arab unity "first
formulated around 1930 by the tiny communist parties of Arab countries, which formed a bloc with the Third International."[26] Outside
these historical circumstances, the Arabs' only irrefutable ideology is
an Islam "based on a definite corpus of ideas and practices."[27] Rodinson is on surer terrain, however, when he identifies the Arab nation
as a "tendency" (instead of a nation),[28] since this would accord with
Al-Jabri's account of the ideological circumstances in which crucial
aspects of the Islamic corpus were forged.

The desacralization of Arabic in the Levant meant that language
would be restricted to the utilitarian function of copying European
secular ideologies and for the invention of new nations with names
mostly retrieved from antiquity.[29] The "territorial units for which so-
called national movements sought to win independence, were overwhelmingly the actual creations of imperial conquest," the paradoxical products of Orientalist fantasies, "since the very colonialists who
encouraged Arabs to revolt against the Ottomans never truly believed
in the actual existence of an Arab race or even considered the possibility (despite several promises and declarations) of Arabs govern-
ing themselves." As in the hastily invented Third World, these new
nations represented "religio-cultural zones rather than anything that
might have been called 'nations' in Europe."[30] Moreover, the colonialists who played a crucial role in inventing Arab nationalism didn't
see the Arabs as one people; "that idea was new (and controversial) in
the Middle East at the time and had not been heard in Europe."
Europeans versed in the Bible and the classics "knew more about the
region as it had been two thousand years before than it was in their
own time." To them, the Middle East seemed like "a patchwork of
races, some with pleasantly Biblical names. It certainly appeared very
different from the sort of society conjured up by the modern expression 'the Arab world.'"[31] Even the famous Arab Revolt against the
Turks led by Sherif Husayn of Mecca (June 10, 1916) was "an ironic
beginning," since Arab nationalist sentiment had been almost non-
existent among the Hijazis; the latter, at least up until 1908, seemed
to have been "reasonably happy with the Ottoman-amirate govern-

ment." Despite the appearance of nationalist literature envisaging the Hijaz as the new center of the Arab caliphate, the Hijazis themselves remained indifferent to these sentiments. They were, as far as they knew, only Muslims; beyond "localistic patriotism," their loyalty was to the Islamic community, the *umma*.[32]

Epistemologically, one can in fact read the emergence of Arab nationalism as a secular quest for the fragmented *umma* and an attempt to salvage the Islamic tradition (*turath*) after the abolition of the Ottoman Caliphate in 1924.[33] For just as the sacralized Arabic language contained the imagined ontologies of the pre-Islamic Bedouin, the *a'rabi,* invented and recorded in the early Abbasid period to secure the privilege of an Arab minority, a secular version of the same language cannot erase the sacrality proffered on Arabic by Islam. Ghassan Salamé has argued that the overlapping and tense existence of Arab ethnic and Islamic universalistic epistemologies in the Arabic language render categorical delineations between the discourses of Arab nationalism and Islamic resurgence difficult. If Arab Islamism doesn't signal the passing away of pan-Arabism but simply its metamorphosis, a "profound mutation," the nationalist concept of the *umma* is, by the same token, a "true usurpation of the referent, an illicit secularization ("laïcisation illicite") of the term. One paradox of Arab nationalism is its attempt to dehistoricize Arab identity by removing it from the religion that made it possible in the first place:

> La romantisation de la nation arabe butera en permanence contre cet obstacle hérité de l'histoire, à savoir que l'islam a non seulement unifié les Arabes, mais leur a donné la grande possibilité de conquête. C'est par l'islam qu'ils ont fondé leur moment impérial, c'est en le donnant au monde qu'ils furent acceptés comme conquérants et gouvernants d'autres nations, et c'est en référence à cette "mission" qu'ils revendiqueront une place priviligiée dans le monde. Les nationalistes arabes se mettaient ainsi dans un dilemme auquel ils n'arriveront jamais à donner une réponse convaincante, celui de vouloir s'approprier un passé islamique tout en le dépassant dans une modernité à propension sécularisante.

> [The romanticization of the Arab nation will stumble permanently against this obstacle inherited from the past, namely that Islam not

only unified the Arabs but it also gave them the great possibility of conquest. It is through Islam that they founded their imperial moment, and it was in giving it to the world that they were accepted as conquerors and rulers of other nations. Because it is in reference to this "mission" that they claimed a privileged place in the world, Arab nationalists were putting themselves in a dilemma for which they would never have an answer. They wanted to appropriate an Islamic past while overcoming it in a secular modernity.][34]

Even under Nasserism, Arab nationalism was confined to the realm of "high politics" while Islam remained deeply rooted among the masses, in the domain of "low politics."[35] The inability to remove long entrenched epistemologies from the Arabic vocabulary, together with a series of setbacks for Arab nationalists, brought the two camps together in a nationalist-religious debate, sponsored by the Lebanon-based Research Center for Arab Unity—historically the guardian of the Arab nationalist doctrine—in 1989.[36] A new compromise trend emerged from these encounters, best represented by the work of Maghrebian scholars such as Al-Jabri, whose goal is to reexamine the foundations and structures of the Arab mind and to propose syntheses that combine tradition and reason, the same intellectual traditions once adopted by Al-Jabri's Maghrebian and Andalusian predecessors, Ibn Hazm, Ibn Rushd (Averroës), and Ibn Khaldun, and later defeated by the conservative pressures embedded in the "Arab mind." If the Maghreb, whose population is overwhelmingly Muslim, reappears now as a strategic location from which to theorize the relation between nationalism and Islam,[37] it may be because the accelerated "demographic dechristianization" of the Levant has diluted the imaginary separation between Arabic and Islam. And so if Arab nationalism began as "a sort of de-islamized religion,"[38] it is now reappearing as an Islamized nationalism or simply Islamism:

L'arabisme semble connaître, avec l'effrondrement (et dans certains cas l'effrondrement pur et simple) des appareils d'État, le modèle israélien et les effets pervers de la mal-distribution pétrolière, une mutation où, sous le langage religieux, on retrouve le même refus fondamental de l'Etat d'Israël, la même soif d'identité culturelle différente de l'Occident et la même exigence d'une meilleure place dans le monde. Les islamistes n'enterrent l'arabisme que pour en être pleinements les héritiers.

[With the crumbling of state structures (and, in certain cases, just pure crumbling), the Israeli model and the perverse effects of the maldistribution of oil, Arabism seems to have experienced a mutation whereby the same fundamental rejection of the Israeli state, the same hunger for a different cultural identity, and the same insistent demand for a better place in the world are expressed in a religious language. The Islamists have buried Arabism only to be fully its inheritors.][39]

A language-based nationalism is hard to sustain. It is not only vulnerable to the pressures of bilingualism or even multilingualism, but the phenomenal rise of transnational corporations, international nongovernmental organizations, and the growing insignificance of "national" economies that relegated the stubborn Arab to the outer limits of history can no longer, Hobsbawm predicts, be contained "within 'nations' and 'nation-states' as these used to be defined, either politically, economically, culturally, or even linguistically." The "supranational restructuring of the globe" will, with one or two exceptions, undermine the precarious sovereignty of hastily invented states in the Arabic-speaking regions.[40] One might say that this is yet another opportunity for pan-Arab nationalism to renew itself; but if the borrowed ideology of nationalism couldn't be sustained even during its high epoch (because of the irresolvable epistemological and ontological contradictions inherent in modern Arabic), why should it be expected to do better now that the whole ideology of nationalism is being displaced by transnational capitalism? Since the nationalist movement that reinvented the Arab at the turn of the century is on the wane, it is only logical to expect the Arab to follow on its footsteps, as *Time* magazine predicts. The Arab appeared on the stage of history during strong nationalist waves that mobilized the entire cultural apparatus of the state for the purpose of legitimation; the commitment for such an undertaking may not always be available, as Islamic countries are adopting more pragmatic outlooks (including contingent alliances) in a frenzy to cope with the massive and turbulent shifts engineered by global capitalism.[41] So if Arabs, browbeaten by superior forces, are quietly exiting the fictitious stage of the Middle East, who will take their place? Arabized Muslims?[42] This conceptual challenge has yet to be adequately addressed by the various constituencies working on Arab cultures and Islam; even the theses of major scholars such Al-Jabri and Laroui are trapped in the very epistemologies they seek to overcome. The Arab intellectual crisis simply indicates that Arabs have not been able to theorize their own identity within the bifurcations and polarities engendered by the colonial experience. Is the rewriting of a traditional Islamic authenticity the answer?

To examine this issue we must first shed the now already outdated definition of the Islamic resurgence as a fundamentalist movement and the equally sensational idea that the technologically insignificant, poorly armed, and economically dependent Islamic nations are a "threat" to the West.[43] Fundamentalism, or even the more accurate French word *intégrisme*, need to be discarded as valid descriptions of a phenomenon whose meaning is determined by global power relations and the struggle for symbolic hegemony in the era of transnational capitalism. In the first place, "Islam has never ceased to be intégriste," and the appeal to the egalitarian message of the Qur'an has always roused the masses against perceived injustices and continues to do so to this day. One could even argue that today's Islamists are far more moderate and open when compared to precolonial Muslims; for the latter, merely encountering or traveling in Christian lands was considered a serious threat to one's faith.[44] Today's Islamist who speaks European languages and wears European clothes would have been branded a heretic in many precolonial Islamic societies.

The Islamist movement makes sense only within the context of the world capitalist system, especially since Islamism is still largely informed by the nineteenth-century modernist agenda of "catching up" with the West.[45] The integration of Islamic societies in the global capitalist economy makes the cultural aspect of the Islamist agenda an undesirable surplus, perhaps the expression of frustration at a long but so far futile effort at overcoming the Arabs'/Muslims' structural weaknesses in the world economy. This cultural agenda is, in turn, countered by more notions of social organization borrowed directly from Euro-American vocabularies, most notably the ideas of secularism and civil society espoused by traditional Arab nationalists and now promoted by global capitalist regimes. Both camps (Arab nationalists and Islamists), however, agree on the urgent need to catch up with the West; they only disagree about appropriate methods or ideologies to use in that process.

Although catching up with the West as a historic necessity is not an issue for the two competing ideologies, the Islamists' only difference from secular nationalists is that they want to both catch up with Western modernity and still somehow preserve cultural authenticity. It is here that the crisis in Islamist/Arab nationalist thought is most evident: for not only is the West defined primarily in cultural terms, but Muslim/Arab intellectuals have not been able to envisage a postcapitalist, post-Eurocentric world, one that is not modeled on the social, economic, and political structures of capitalism. If they did, they would realize that mainstream Arab and Muslim definitions of the West do not obtain in the contemporary period and that, furthermore, catching up with Western modernity is a nonprogressive, unrealistic option at this historical juncture. Not only is there no concrete geographical "West" to "catch up" with, but the continuing quest for integration in the global economy will certainly prolong the Muslims' dependency. Because the proposed culturalist solutions do not take the real destructive powers of capitalism into account, they block out the articulation of new paradigms whose main goal is the collective destiny of human societies, not the perpetuation of old, unsustainable cultural rivalries.

While the polarized agendas of what Laroui called "Westernization" (modernization, development, etc.) and "medievalization" (Islamism, golden age, etc.) have been alienating responses to the hegemonic agenda of capitalist expansion.[46] One also needs to remember that capitalism has produced terrifying excesses everywhere, including in Europe itself.[47] The West, which has long been detached from its geographical and historical matrix, is now, like nationalism, reproducible,[48] and continues to uproot indigenous alternatives and peoples and increase dependency on the financial centers located in the old metropoles. Moralizing efficiency and ranking nations according to their degree of technicalization have forced Muslims and all the world's indigenous peoples to deny their own ethnocide by claiming that they are only importing skills and technologies, not values and ideologies.[49] But as Jalal Amin, an Egyptian economist, has suggested, the recuperation of a liberating economic model is ultimately inseparable from the rediscovery of self-confidence and energy in tradition. In Boullata's assessment, "this latent energy can burst forth only through religion which, in the case of Arabs, is Islam."[50]

The upsetting of the former relative parities within the "agrarian-ate" economies (whose center was, for centuries, Dar al-Islam) by the advent of technicalistic Europe meant that the gulf between early technicalistic societies and Islam would prove to be permanent.[51] (After all, the goal of Westernization was precisely to secure the gulf if not widen it further.) The rush to acquire Europe's secret meant a scramble for modernization and the occasional banning of traditional attire (e.g., the fez in Turkey, the veil in Iran) and the rewriting of local idioms in the Latin script;[52] but these measures now appear, in retrospect, only psychological attempts to believe oneself capable of repudiating a dysfunctional and embarrassing past. Wearing European clothes has so far failed to advance "Arab" and Islamic societies; the stubborn pursuit of development within the context of nation-states has simply increased dependency and aggravated tensions. Hodgson knew that "catching up" with the West is a "heart-breaking problem," since as a Third World region, Islamic societies are condemned to remain increasingly poorer suppliers of raw materials to the hypertechnologized advanced capitalist countries:

> Moreover, even independence remained precarious so long as a way was not found for a sudden and drastic reshaping of the local social and economic order. The ever-accelerating pace of technical change which technicalism has meant poses the heart-breaking problem of "catching up": for whatever advance a low-investment land may make, necessarily the lands of high investment have been able to make a greater one meanwhile, and the actual economic gap in productivity can get steadily greater. One particular facet of this situation has become still more pressing after independence than

under imperial rule: the "terms of trade" as between a country producing raw material and one producing finished manufacture may become steadily worse for the former; that is, it gets steadily less for what it produces and hence has less for other investment. Though this may not be theoretically necessary, yet *the dynamic of the development gap does impose this sort of outcome time and again. In general, "underdevelopment" and "imperialism" remain two sides of the same coin; without special measures, it seems impossible for an "underdeveloped" land to avoid "imperialistic" domination.*[53]

Although it is not clear what "special measures" are needed to catch up in a system in which catching up is systemically impossible (peripheralization being an inevitable feature of capitalism), the Islamic resurgence, like Westernization, appears as a phenomenon that cannot be understood without reference to the "hegemonic Western modernity under the context of expansionist colonialism."[54] Inasmuch as Islamic revivalist movements are informed by a modernist agenda, they are only proposing the folkloric shell of authenticity; but if delinking the Islamic social imaginary from a capitalist-driven process of Westernization could help maintain, expand, or even reclaim noncapitalist spaces of social relations, then Islam could be (re)imagined in more utopian terms and become a founding bloc in a multicultural world governed by a strong ethic of reciprocity. Many traditional *'ulama* are opposed to catching up with the West, not because they are committed to the nationalist discourse of "cultural authenticity" but because of the fundamental duty to maintain an adequate space for the proper practice of the faith.[55] For them, Islam, as a religious practice, simply cannot survive within the anticultural, mechanistic world of advanced capitalism; the coexistence of Islam with modernization is, as Latouche thinks, merely an empty expression.[56]

Yet many secular intellectuals exclude the Islamic option out of the conviction that Islam abridges freedoms and encroaches on what is termed civil rights. Under the diffusionist pressure of "international" organizations, the "Arabs" are advocating yet another Eurocentric solution to the specific and unique condition of Muslim people and, in the process, legitimize the very economic system that has pe-

ripheralized their societies. One effect of universalizing secular notions of freedom is to affirm the despotic nature of precolonial Muslim societies. The nation-state is assumed to be an eternal structure of
social organization, and, by the same token, indigenous articulations
of the meaning of freedom are delegitimized. Yet as Laroui indicated,
when looking for liberty in pre-nineteenth-century Islamic societies,
one doesn't have to be strictly confined within the parameters of
modern secular vocabularies; for if one were to look merely for the
Arabic word "hurriya" (freedom), then one is not likely to find it. But
a historian needs to look instead at the world of signs, not words
(*mots*) to decipher the meaning of the concept. The Bedouin, the
clan, the practice of piety (*taqwa*), and Sufism are four examples of
how liberty was understood and practiced in different measures and
different contexts.[57] These practices were the guarantors of what we
now call civil liberties, since the state's power was limited to sporadic
outbursts or displays of force. Not only that, but there were more
freedoms under traditional social arrangements.[58]

> Disons pour conclure que l'expérience historique de la liberté dans le
> monde arabo-islamique est infiniment plus large que ne le suggère
> l'organisation étatique traditionnelle. Le Bédouin appartient à la so-
> ciété, mais il échappe à l'Etat; soumis à des lois géographiques immu-
> ables, il maintient vivante l'idée d'une liberté naturelle. A l'intérieur
> de l'Etat, l'individu barricadé derrière la tribu, la famille, la corpora-
> tion, etc., ignore l'ordre sultanien. Ce qui reste d'autorité particulière
> fondée sur la piété; il peut même la nier totalement en "se détachant
> de tous et de tout." Dans l'Etat sultanien, la liberté, pour être conçue,
> exige la négation de cet Etat; exclue du champ politique, elle s'ex-
> prime négativement sous forme d'utopie. Mais l'utopie en tant que
> telle, influence à son tour le comportement de chacun et en fin de
> compte les relations entre gouvernants et gouvernés. N'oublions pas
> cependant que le champ étatique est restraint; et plus il l'est, plus le
> domaine du non-étatique est large.

> [Let us say, by way of conclusion, that the historical experience of
> freedom in the Arab-Islamic world is infinitely larger than what is
> suggested by the traditional state structure. The Bedouin belongs to
> society but he eludes the State; subjected to immutable geographical

conditions, he maintains alive the idea of natural freedom. Barricaded behind the tribe, the family, the corporation, etc., the individual ignores the Sultanian order within the State. He can even totally deny the particular authority founded on piety by "detaching himself from everyone and everything." For freedom to be conceived in the Sultanian State, the State must be negated; excluded from the political realm, the State expresses itself negatively under the guise of utopia. But utopia as such in turn influences the behavior of everyone and, in the final analysis, relations between governor and governed. However, let us not forget that the realm of the State is limited; and the more limited it is, the larger the non-State domain.][59]

With European colonialism, the state's reach expanded at the expense of traditional institutions, giving rise to new demands for freedom coined in a new terminology. Paradoxically, at the very time when freedom was being proclaimed as a social right, the state's power over its subjects became greater than ever.[60] While the extent to which individuals are truly free in bourgeois systems has yet to be determined, the Islamic definition of freedom as being in total harmony with the environment has proven so far difficult to achieve under the political institutions of capitalism.[61] The Islamic faith that had consolidated trust across the far-flung and politically divided realm of Islam since the late Ummayad period, and which managed to make an international economic system possible, has not been surpassed in a modern "Arab" world locked in colonial geopolitical models. Contractual agreements inspired by capitalist ethics have not been able to replicate the degree of trust and establish the bonds that prevailed during the medieval Islamic period; they have not done so in the West, and there is no reason to expect them to succeed in Islamic countries. Even the *Shari'a,* antiquated in several aspects, is not entirely to blame for the stagnation of Islamic peoples. In Fawzy Mansour's secular account of the Arab world, it was the corruption of public and private life that "froze the development of the law," and not "the law which froze the development of society." The cause of stagnation, as Amin wrote in a preface to Mansour's book, is to be found in capitalism.[62] It is capitalism that explains the persistence of nativist sentiments and intellectual culturalism, including the traditionalization of Islamic thought, whether in the shape of nationalism or Islamism.[63]

One of the mirror images of Islamism and Arab nationalism in West European societies are Orientalist assumptions. As one expression of Eurocentric culturalism, Orientalist thought refuses to examine the material conditions of the Europe or West whose superiority it often assumes; it rarely examines how a culture's production of knowledge about the Other is better examined against the existing "structures of power" and how these structures differ "according to historically changing systems of discipline."[64] Scholars who want to understand their local histories "must also inquire into Europe's past," especially the culture of the Enlightenment, which created many of the social science categories that define several academic disciplines.[65]

Consider the case of philology, which stamped the study of Others with indelible prejudices, arbitrary essentializations, and false determinisms.[66] Not only did prominent philologists like Ernst Renan belittle the "Semitic" languages of Jews and Muslims when compared to Indo-European and even other "Semitic Oriental languages" (145), but in his hands these linguistic generalizations could be expanded to "anatomy, history, anthropology and even geology." The "Semitic" became a "transtemporal, transindividual category, purporting to predict every discrete act of 'Semitic' behavior on the basis on some pre-existing 'Semitic' essence." By the nineteenth century "it was assumed that if languages were as distinct from each other as the linguists said they were, then too the language users—their minds, cultures, potentials, and even their bodies—were different in similar ways. And these distinctions had the force of ontological, empirical truth behind them, together with the convincing demonstration of such truth in studies of origins, development, character, and destiny" (145, 149, 231, 233).

The integration of these subjectively delineated language families into Biblical mythology was, of course, to have deadly consequences for the "Semitic" peoples in modern history. The genocidal campaign against Jews was the culmination of an old pattern of demonizing the Other, one whose modern shape probably appeared in the Iberian peninsula with the expulsion of the Moors from Spain in the late fifteenth century. Many Jews who had been persecuted at least since the Crusades would be emancipated during the Enlightenment; but their increasingly successful assimilation inevitably fueled resentment, so the science of philology provided a new reason for their persecution.[67] Modern anti-Semitism is thus a logical outcome of a major trend in Orientalist scholarship. Sustained by dangerous myths, it was introduced to Islamic societies through the agency of Francophone Christian Arabs who disseminated these views to the rest of Arabized Muslims.[68] And if anti-Semitism was "Islamized" during the Palestinian struggle, as Bernard Lewis demonstrates with ample evidence from the Arab press (196, 204), so, too, has anti-Muslimism—expressed in hateful and demonizing rhetoric—in contemporary Israeli politics.[69] Hence the nationalist ideologies embraced by both Jews and Muslims have turned out to be deculturing processes, canceling out the very ideals that supposedly are being upheld.

No one can deny the pioneering effect of early Orientalists in introducing new cultures to the West, but their ideas "have become mimetic, a storehouse of oriental stereotypes and exotica."[70] According to Abdellah Laroui, Orientalist scholarship is mostly "valueless," since, as a "system" that owes much to the German-born field of cultural anthropology, it makes reality conform (through omissions, exclusions, etc.) to one idea or nation and fails to grasp "factual history" from which "all progress ultimately comes." Although all social sciences lend themselves to political use, Orientalists' inability to see change in Islam says more about the theoretical backwardness of the field than about Arabs and Muslims.[71] Al-Azmeh has argued that because Orientalism's "overriding need [is] to speak ill [of Islam]," it has managed to inoculate itself against the corrective impact of observation. From being simply evil in the medieval period, Islam is now characterized by a series of deficiencies reflecting Europe's dominant values.[72] Orientalism as a form of intelligibility is thus a reading of Others, especially Islam, as a list of "absences"—capitalism, cities, civil society, democracy, etc.—and the transfer of the West's anxieties to the Orient.[73] Viciously solipsistic in its textualistic approach, it is remarkably immune to global changes and remains "captive to a metahistorical schemata" in which the "homo islamicus" is frozen into an unchanging past.[74]

Fred Halliday's more recent argument that the discourses of Lewis and Said, and those of Islamists, are equally responsible for perpetrating false myths fails to consider the balance in global relations in which the dissemination of information and the deployment of power are very much a one-sided affair; if it is true that scholars such as Said and Lewis focus primarily on discourse, they are separated by the respective subject positions of the nations or cultural entities they presumably represent.[75] Not only Said's, but all Muslim scholarship, secular or not, is one of protest, an attempt to escape the maddening crisis of marginalization and dependency. Laroui and Al-Azmeh opt for a thorough positivism and uncompromising secular modernization (if only for the sake of expediency); others resurrect a primitive version of the *Shari'a* to counter cultural imperialism. In the final analysis, both tendencies fail to move away from "Westernization" and "medievalization." Laroui's call for a sort of multicultural universalism—accomplished through the rigor of positivist historicism—as the best solution to centuries of mutual differentiation is unrealistic, since the liberal bourgeois revolution he prescribes as an initial step toward an eventual transition to socialism fails to account for the contradictions, class divisions, and strengthening of the capitalist structures in the interim.[76] That every inch of the world must first come under the iron grip of capitalism before people make the transition to socialism is a theory that has not only been problematized by scholars such as Samir Amin, but it is also impractical, given the threats the earth faces from the depletion and pollution of natural, life-sustaining resources and the growing instabilities engendered by economic inequity and excessive and wasteful consumption.

Fazlur Rahman is on somewhat firmer ground when he calls for a wholesale critique and historicizing of all Islamic sciences (including the *hadith*—sayings attributed to the Prophet—and the Qur'an itself) while warning against the futile attempt of trying to dismiss Islamic traditions, since "no community can annul its past and try to create a better future for itself—as that community."[77] While the *Shari'a* needs to be continually interpreted, it must ultimately flow from the normative values of the (historicized) Qur'an. Like Laroui and Al-Jabri, Rahman privileges both history and philosophy as the most important branches of knowledge in the project of liberating Islam from its hybernation, but he also warns against a restless modernity that is more symptomatic of the West's malaise (147–48, 156, 157–58, 161). And though he sees the Islamic resurgence as a futile and negative reaction to the West, he also believes that a mental "disengagement" from the West (through a reformed educational system) can lead to a more positive relation with the latter (130–40).

The futility of getting rid of the Islamic past is also a premise shared by Leonard Binder, who realizes that the monolithic and universalizing assumptions of liberal development theory and the fundamentally essentialist views of Islam have prevented scholars (even prominent ones such as Said and Gellner) from taking local and cultural specificities into account.[78] Binder argues that, by invoking structural anthropology and humanist Marxism as possible points of reference, and by presenting Islam "as emptiness, a form without content, or more precisely as authenticity whose only purpose is to be different" (124), Said is, effectively, "in constructive agreement with the positions of Gellner and Lewis as well as Geertz" (120). Because "no other cultural region is so deeply anxious about the threat of cultural penetration and Westernization," Islam, Binder urges, must be appropriated by the "bourgeois ideology before it is appropriated by some rival force" (17). Only a "vigorous Islamic liberalism" (19) is capable of rehabilitating Muslims and saving them from the superfluousness that seems to be their inevitable lot. Hence Laroui and Binder agree that bourgeois capitalism (whether in the short or long term) are inevitable options for Arabs and Muslims.

Polarized in debates over the future of the Arab and Muslim worlds, Muslim and Western culturalists have failed to realize that the very model of development to which the entire Third World aspires is now bankrupt at every level, and that "progress" has turned out to be a cruel myth that has thrown the world in the throes of an impending catastrophe. Capitalism and its consumer culture have done more damage to our living environment than previous systems of social organization: it has engendered more poverty, created more health problems, endangered the planet, idled tens of millions of people worldwide, and reduced work to a numbing and meaningless monotony.[79] Richard Douthwaite's carefully documented study of the ideology of economic growth leaves no doubt that "we are all victims of an economic totalitarianism and have little freedom to determine what we think and do in the economic sphere." Declaring that the "widespread feeling that things were better in the past is not false," he sees only one option left to Third World peoples, that is, roughly what Samir Amin calls "delinking" from the world system.[80] Since infinite growth is unsustainable and trying to replicate the American economic experience is materially impossible, the very idea of catching up that sparked Arab nationalism and Islamist movements has become utterly impractical and as dangerous as the Western hegemony it seeks to resist and overcome.

By the same token, Orientalists who have misread the laws of capitalist change as the essential characteristic of an ever evolving and progressive West not only conspire to hide the dangerous effects of capitalist development but also overlook crucial elements of the very "Western tradition" they champion. Both in ancient Greece and in the Judeo-Christian tradition, the notion of infinite change was considered unnatural and symptomatic of disease; in a world locked in a finite materiality, only the hereafter was believed to be infinite. But when infinity was domesticated into the secular canons of the early capitalist phase, the process of maturity was impelled to abandon its traditional "fixed reference point." As Cornelius Castoriadis, the distinguished Greek-French philosopher, put it,

> We must consider the emergence of the bourgeoisie, its expansion and final victory in parallel with the emergence, propagation, and final victory of a new "idea," the idea that the unlimited growth of production and of the productive forces is *in fact* the central objective of human existence. This "idea" is what I call a *social imaginary signification.* To it correspond new attitudes, values, and norms, a new social definition of reality and of being, of what *counts* and what does *not* count. In a nutshell, henceforth what counts is whatever can be counted. On the other hand, the philosophers and scientists apply a new and specific twist to thought and knowledge; there are no

limits to the powers and possibilities of Reason, and Reason *par excellence* is mathematics, at least insofar as the *res extensa* is concerned: *Cum Deus calculat, fit mundus* (As God calculates, the world is being made—Leibniz).[81]

As a political slogan deployed against others, the West has become the cultural expression of an expansionist and deculturing capitalism that, among other things, produces a false consciousness that precludes the practice of the essential Greek attribute of "autonomy" (akin to what Marx called the ruthless criticism of everything existing, including the essentialized notions of the West).[82] Since that is the case, resistance to the prevailing intellectual complacency in the face of impending global perils must come from new vocabularies expressing radically different ontologies. The relevance of a progressively defined Islam may be precisely its ability to introduce a new vocabulary that shatters postcolonial somnolence by presenting a much needed "ideological and symbolic autonomy" to Arabs. As Burgat explained,

> The recourse to a political vocabulary nourished by categories (less religious than cultural) produced by the local societies, or perceived as such, restores to the references of the parent culture the universal qualities which had been lost to the political language of the North. Consequently, this restoration permits a double reconciliation: It reintroduces in political expression references that colonial expropriation had progressively relegated to "private" culture, and it permits the Arab political individual to renew his relationship with his or her own living and intuitive culture. In reconciling the individual with his or her ancestral culture, in which a symbolic affiliation becomes once again possible, the historical continuity that the imposition of Western categories had interrupted is restored in the collective imagination. In doing this (and it is here that the secret of its formidable capacity for mobilization resides), the colonial parenthesis is closed at the symbolic level, at precisely the point where the more or less brutal recourse to representations fabricated by other social systems were able to have their most traumatic effect.[83]

Even the *Economist* acknowledged that the cultural significance of the Islamic resurgence could provide some inspiration to atomized

Western societies. Islam's insistence on human freedom and social welfare may inspire Western societies to revitalize their own human-itarian traditions. Just as "contact with Muslims helped to bring about the West's great leap forward out of the Middle Ages," Islam may yet again remind the West "of the common underpinning of what they both stand for." Although the *Economist* still assumes the West to be a distinct place, and wants the "long quarrel between cousins" to end,[84] it still cannot conceive of the necessity to preserve and possibly expand alternative noncapitalist zones in the global economy. Arab nationalism (whose vision is still largely locked in the cultural origins of the emerging capitalist Europe) and militant Is-lamism (having re-Islamized secular nationalist ideologies and fur-ther alienated itself through a regressive reading of the Islamic past) have been unable to articulate a different position that takes the collective fate of humanity into account. A more courageous form of resistance to the destructive tendencies of the global economic sys-tem would simply be a rebuilding of human-scale economies and a creative form of delinking from the expanding and intensified pro-cess of capitalist exploitation. A postnationalist, Islamically progres-sive identity can contribute not only to Muslims' autonomy but also to the forging of new cultural solidarities in a polycentric world.

3

The North as Apocalypse

The Thin Line is clear at present. Everything got misty in front
of my eyes so that it would be clear. It said to me: you are black.
You are a black from generations back, crossed with white. You are
about *to cross the line.* To lose your last drop of authentic black
blood. Your facial angle opened up, and you are no longer wooly-
haired or thick lipped. You were the issue of the Orient, and
through your painful past, your imaginings, your education, you
are going to triumph over the Orient. You have never believed in
Allah. You know how to dissect the legends, you think in French,
you are a reader of Voltaire and an admirer of Kant. Only the
Occidental world for which you are destined seems to you to be
sewn with stupidities and ugliness you are fleeing from. Moreover,
you feel that it is a hostile world. It is not going to accept you right
away, and, at the point of exchanging the box seat you now occupy
for a jumpseat, you have setbacks. That is why I appear to you.
Since the very first day I appeared to you, you are nothing
but an open wound.—Driss Chraibi, *The Simple Past*

In what is probably one of the most powerful literary passages in
modern Moroccan literature,[1] a young man, Driss Ferdi, son of a
Berber petit bourgeois merchant during the French Protectorate in
Morocco (1912–56) and a student in a French missionary school, gets
an unsettling—if not terrifying—vision of himself as de-Africanized

and unable to believe in Allah just when he is in the midst of prayer on the most sacred night of the Islamic calendar. The event takes place in Fez, the oldest Islamic city in Morocco and one of the most important Islamic cultural centers in the world. Driss's identity crisis is the culmination of his exposure to the French colonial educational system in Casablanca (a modern financial center) and his rebellion against the oppressive and hypocritical male patriarchy of his Islamic society. He later passes his high school exam after writing a paper stating his commitment to French culture, a feat that earns him the dubious title of the "Moroccan Martin Luther" from school officials. But before he leaves for France to pursue his higher education, he realizes the violence in his and his nation's ambition and remains cautiously hopeful.

While Driss Chraibi's novel might be included in the Moroccan, Maghrebian, or even Arab literary canon, but it is doubtful whether it gets adequate attention as African (including Berber) literature. Although Driss Chraibi (the autobiographical element in *The Simple Past* is, as in many African novels, barely disguised) describes the vanishing of black African features into a suspect whiteness, the author would undoubtedly be qualified as "white" by U.S. racial categories, or as North African and Arab by other geographical or nationalistic definitions. Such geographical markers not only have hindered a fuller appreciation of the African colonial and postcolonial experiences in their wider and varied cultural contexts, but they also have perpetuated dangerous racist myths uncritically adopted as valid academic and intellectual paradigms. The reason Driss Chraibi's novel is emblematic of a more general trend in (post)colonial African literature is not merely the Africanness he asserts as his primary identity but because he knows—despite his refusal to believe—that he is culturally a Muslim. It is as an African Muslim that the young rebellious protagonist tries to navigate the uncharted terrain of the European colonial experience; and it is in this sense that a few classics written by African writers from Senegal and Sudan are best read. For authors such as Cheikh Hamidou Kane, Tayeb Salih, and, more recently, Ken Bugul (pseudonym for Mariétou M'Baye), identity is primarily rooted in Islamic consciousness, not in blackness, or some other colonial category. The Islamic continuum in Africa bridges temporal, spatial, and gender gaps remarkably well, and thus points to new cultural, economic, and political configurations that might serve as alternatives to the failed nation-state model that has brought the continent to the brink of ruin. Muslim African writers who underestimate this Islamic component and privilege either color or nation as better defining components of their identity tend to reiterate colonial prejudices, despite their best intentions and revolutionary rhetoric.

Another renowned Moroccan writer in French, Tahar ben Jelloun, member of the Haut Conseil de la Francophonie and, recently, a candidate for the Nobel Prize, doesn't identify himself as African because "in Morocco one tends to feel more Arab than African. We're really in the northernmost part of Africa and we have a very different history." While insisting that his statement is not meant to be "pejorative" or "mean," he confidently explains that he doesn't "feel at all African" because he has "no ties to Africa."[2] Ben Jelloun's privileging of the Arab cultural space over Morocco's geographic location has permitted him to redefine Moroccan identity along the lines of Arab nationalism and, by the same token, erase the role of Islam (and therefore Africa) in Moroccan (precolonial) history. Islam, to Ben Jelloun, is simply an orthodoxy that must be challenged, whereas French (his "mistress,"[3] he calls it) is rather acceptable for allowing him and other writers from the Maghreb the possibility of self-expression in an otherwise censorious Arabo-Islamic environment. His remarkable self-assurance ignores the concern over the language issue—a crucial component in the debate over identity—that has bedeviled many an African writer and presents the Francophonie as a benign enterprise, not part of the colonial war the French have been waging on Africans since the nineteenth century. His views are at odds with those of Mahdi El Mandjra, another internationally renowned Moroccan intellectual who has called attention to France's hegemonic policies through the cultural agenda of the francophonie and urged Maghrebian states to abandon that organization. Not surprisingly, El Mandjra also vigorously objects to the Arab/African split, and in fact emphasizes the still unappreciated fact that (at least) 75 percent of Arabs are also African, and that all ethnic groups, including Berbers, are part of the Islamic civilization.[4] Still, for Ben

Jelloun Africa is primarily the domain of the wild hinterland, the land of the black, a view that, partly owing to the large influence of "négritude" and the late Cheikh Anta Diop, has even been largely sanctified by academic departments in the diaspora.

Ben Jelloun's position also legitimizes a certain discourse about Africa that equates Islam's legacies with those of the imperialist West and presents Islam as the enemy of "African culture and unity."[5] The fact that even larger parts of the continent would have been integrated into the wider Islamic ecumene had not the Europeans scrambled to check that spread is conveniently obscured by these (neo)nationalist discourses. Roland Oliver, a seasoned historian of the continent, stated that

> At the start of the colonial period [in Africa, Islam] was, of course, by far the most widely spread and deeply rooted of the world religions. It had been predominant in Egypt and North Africa since the eighth century, in the Sahara since the eleventh century, in the Sudanic belt since about the fourteenth century. The jihadic movements of the eighteenth and nineteenth centuries had carried it almost to the southern Atlantic coast of West Africa. Throughout the northern third of the continent, to be connected with either the ruling or the trading elite, or even to be a plain city-dweller, was almost inevitably to be a Muslim. North of about the tenth degree of northern latitude, virtually every substantial settlement had its mosque and its Koranic school presided over by a literate holy man who lived on the gifts and services of his people.[6]

Assessing how European colonialism underdeveloped Africa, Walter Rodney argues that literacy rates in late-nineteenth-century Africa (connected with the Islamic religion, except in Christian Ethiopia) were comparable to those in Europe and Asia, and that it was colonial education, whose purpose was to assimilate small numbers of indigenous peoples into the metropolitan cultures in order to assure the permanence of domination into the future, that disrupted local patterns of learning. (Significantly, the Alliance Française, the cultural arm of French imperialism, was designed to accomplish this colonial mission through the strategic institutionalizing of the French language.)[7]

Africa's actual impasse, Basil Davidson has concluded, reflects the failure of African nationalists to restore Africans to their own past, and—just as the colonizers had so ingenuously planned—the nationalists' success in initiating "a new period of indirect subjection to the history of Europe."[8] More than forty years of scholarship on Africa has prompted Davidson to urge us to look back, unromantically, at the period "*before* dispossession" for viable alternative models.[9] In *The Search for Africa,* Davidson finds that "Africa's two largest internal systems of economic and political development between roughly the sixth and sixteenth centuries" were mostly influenced by Islam. And if the domain of African Islam extended as far north as Spain (Al Andalus being "essentially an African kingdom in Europe") thanks to an international economic system fortified by the most powerful currency of the day, the Almoravid *dinar,* minted from West African gold, East African cultures were enjoying an equally prosperous period of international trade and political strength. Much of the international trade in medieval times "was dominated by the circuits of North Africa and Muslim Spain, exploiting their markets from Morocco to China and their control of a unique gold standard based on West African supplies of the metal."[10] The three largest urban centers in the Western Sudan—Gao, Timbuktu, Djenne—whose populations ranged from fifteen thousand to eighty thousand in the fifteenth and sixteenth centuries, were all integrated in the trans-Saharan, long-distance trade. In this complex enterprise, it was Islam that provided the moral code for commercial negotiations. According to the economic historian A. G. Hopkins, Islam "helped maintain the identity of members of a network or firm who were scattered over a wide area, and often in foreign countries; it enabled traders to recognise, and hence to deal readily with, each other; and it provided moral and ritual sanctions to enforce a code of conduct which made trust and credit possible. It was through Islam that Dioula and Hausa merchants established the commercial networks, or diasporas, which made them so prominent and successful in long distance trade."[11]

Because integration in the larger Islamic ecumene required communication, Arabic literacy spread; by one account, more than thirty languages were written for the first time in the Arabic script. Not only is Arabic Africa's largest and most global language, but both Swahili and Hausa languages contain strong Arabic elements.[12] Literacy and the use of the Arabic script allowed "major vernacular Islamic literatures—Swahili, Zenaga, Fulfulde and Hausa—[to] share certain characteristics of content and format," and thus create a common trans-African consciousness. The historian Hiskett further adds that the "strong similarity in content and format that exists across the written vernacular Islamic literatures of Africa testifies to the depth to which Islam has penetrated into the life-style of the people, who still cherish these literatures to the present day; and the remarkable evenness with which Islamic mainstream culture has imposed itself upon what were originally diverse indigenous societies ranging from cattle nomads to primitive agriculturalists and hunter-gatherers."[13]

If the Latinization of the Hausa and Swahili languages in the 1930s (a process legitimized at a more global level under the aegis of UNESCO in the 1960s) is part of the colonial disrupting process that, among other things, dictates its own geographies and identities—North versus sub-Saharan Africa, blackness as the quintessence of Africanness, colonial language communities, or just mere state nationalism—then the retrieval of the precolonial Islamic cultural continuum provides yet another layer of meaning to postcolonial literatures of the African continent.[14] Although these literatures are indelibly marked by European colonialism and its legacies, one needs to examine how such responses are informed by their particular histories and cultural outlooks. To merely lump novels from the African continent together under an assumed homogeneous Africanness is, in effect, to erase Africa's various and complex histories and reduce a large continent to the monolith of race.

Though Islam is experienced differently in Africa, a dominant motif of canonical postcolonial works by Africans of Muslim descent is the young educated protagonist's wrenching deracination from his or her indigenous culture, followed by catastrophic, even suicidal, journeys to the Northern metropoles. In fact, the remarkable consistency of thematic concerns attests to a shared prior cultural experience and certainly reconnects the peoples of the African Islamic ecumene both in their common defeat and in their creative negotiations with (post)coloniality. Colonialism may have rearranged African spaces and separated the Maghreb from West Africa by transforming the Sahara into the southern and northern hinterlands of both regions,[15] but it also paradoxically stimulated the literary genre of the dangerously alienated Western-educated Muslim. Samba Diallo (in Cheikh Hamidou Kane's *Ambiguous Adventure*), Mustafa Sa'eed (in Tayeb Salih's *Season of Migration to the North*) and Ken Bugul (in *The Abandoned Baobab*), echoing the predicament of Driss Ferdi in this chapter's epigraph, are all inserted in colonial educational systems that delink them from their traditional milieux and interpellate them into a modernity experienced as a series of multiple alienations.[16]

One aspect of this alienation was to marginalize the Arabic language, which, colonial administrators quickly found out, promoted a strong anticolonialist Islamic consciousness. Thus, as Ngũgĩ Wa Thiong'o wrote about a more general context, "Learning, for a colonial child, became a cerebral activity and not an emotionally felt experience." Because "culture is almost indistinguishable from the language that makes possible its genesis, growth, banking, articulation and indeed its transmission from one generation to the next," the educated native is coerced into a negative bilinguality that dissociates her learning experiences from her "natural and social environment."[17] The net result of a bifurcated worldview is a general spread of ignorance (colonial literacy limited to a small comprador class, the masses deprived of education altogether) whose effect is to perpetuate dependency on the colonial centers. Ngũgĩ cautions us not to generalize the petit bourgeoisie's predicament to the rest of the people who have no access to colonial literacies; yet the novels listed above do not depict the colonially educated elite as opportunistic buffoons preying on their own people (as is the case in other African novels),[18] but as talented men severely wounded by their (post)colonial privileges.

To be sure, the rise of new terminologies and the remapping of Africa has led to a form of what Edward Said has called "self-Orientalizing," leading distinguished Moroccan authors such as Tahar ben Jelloun to disown their Africanness and to minimize the unifying role of "Islam within Africa by setting the Sahara as a significant cultural *boundary,* and this despite the fact that Islam extends well south of the desert and that the desert has never been an absolute barrier."[19] Yet, if Ben Jelloun rewrites history along colonial lines, most of his fiction remains fraught with the trauma of alienation, both within an oppressively patriarchal Islamic society and a racist European community.[20] Such postcolonial complicities must therefore be read as an *effect* of (post)colonialism, unless one is willing to endow individual authors with an agency that eclipses the material conditions in which such educations are acquired in the first place. Indeed, at an early stage of resistance, Westernization (which is the inevitable outcome of "modernizing" local institutions, despite the persistent attempt to separate one from the other) is seen as the only viable way out of the degrading conditions of colonialism and the best vantage point from which to repudiate regressive local customs. Westernization is then drafted in the struggle against the West, to strengthen local polities and economies, and ultimately catch up with the colonial powers and protect one's culture from aggression. That is why Driss Ferdi in Chraibi's *Simple Past* is sent to France and Samba Diallo is registered in the colonial educational system, despite the fact that the Sufi Teacher already has chosen him for the awesome task of preserving his people's Spirit.

Ambiguous Adventure opens with this very struggle over how to incorporate Westernization into the local Afro-Islamic culture of the Diallobé. The whole country—emblematic of Africa—is going through an identity crisis and is in the process of deciding how best to resist "the assault of strangers [who have] come from beyond the sea" (23). Predictably, the values of the Sufi Teacher lose out to the ambiguous vision of the charismatic Most Royal Lady. She is driven solely by the pragmatic need for the short-term protection of her people. She detests the foreign school and knows, as does the Knight, Samba's father, that it is the newest form of war on her people (37); yet she sees no alternative to it, as if Africa's only option is to abdicate its own traditions and adopt European cultural models. The "arrival of foreigners" (47) has left her people no choice but to let this dilemma be played out in the lives of the younger generation. By killing her culture in elite, promising children such as Samba (37), she hopes to save future generations from her people's predicament (46–47). The Most Royal Lady's "clear gaze" has seen beyond military occupation and seems to be resigned to an even more insidious phase of cultural imperialism:

> The new school shares at the same time the characteristics of cannon and of magnet. From the cannon it draws its efficacy as an arm of combat. Better than the cannon, it makes the conquest permanent. The cannon compels the body, the school bewitches the soul. Where the cannon has made a pit of ashes and of death, in the sticky mold of which men would not have rebounded from the ruins, the new school establishes peace. The morning of rebirth will be a morning of benediction through the appeasing virtue of the new school.
>
> From the magnet, the school takes its radiating force. It is bound up with a new order, as a magnetic stone is bound up with a field. The upheaval of the life of man within this new order is similar to the overturn of certain physical laws in a magnetic field. Men are seen to be composing themselves, conquered, along the lines of invisible forces. Disorder is organized, rebellion is appeased, the mornings of resentment resound with songs of universal thanksgiving. (50)

This "strange dawn," this "morning of the Occident" (48) casts a mood of profound sadness on Samba Diallo and his father, foreshadowing Samba's tragic realization in France that the French language has transformed his alienating hybridity into a permanent condition. When Adèle, the granddaughter of Pierre-Louis, a retired black magistrate,[21] asks Samba Diallo how he was "conquered," Samba thoughtfully comes face to face with his own entrapment and attributes his condition to the French schooling system. " 'Perhaps it was with their alphabet. With it, they struck the first hard blow at the country of the Diallobé. I remained for a long time under the spell of those signs and those sounds which constitute the structure and the music of their language. When I learned to fit them together to form words, to fit the words together to give birth to speech, my happiness knew no further limit' " (159). He explains how he was excited by his ability to write and how his initiation into the Teacher's universe was interrupted by this new imperative. "That is how it is, Adèle. But they—they interposed themselves, and undertook to transform me in their image. Progressively, they brought me out from the heart of things, and accustomed me to live at a distance from the world"

(160). Soon afterward, he expresses the standard anxiety that afflicts Third World writers and intellectuals in exile, that he has probably lost the privilege of experiencing life from one single perspective (160).[22]

Ken Bugul, the first woman in her family to go to French school, also remembers colonial education as a dramatic turning point:

> At the beginning I took [school] as another one of the thousands of games with which the bush, which protected my village, provided me. But all my expectations shattered with the sound of the French letter the teacher pronounced and wrote on the blackboard: *i.*
>
> That brief and also very abrupt sound cracked my cheeks when I pronounced it, almost screaming. I felt the blood circulate through my body and go to my head. The sound of the *i* scared the birds who used to sing all day long among the leaves. The termites chose to build their hills elsewhere.
>
> The entire class repeated it after the teacher, that first letter of the French school in the region of Ndoucoumane, the French school that was to upset a thousand worlds and a thousand beliefs hidden behind the baobab trees, paralyzed into taking human forms. (98)

The French alphabet here appears as a violent eruption into the local culture, creating new sounds echoing other people's histories and alienating indigenous cultural expressions. (When I was in primary school in Tangier, Morocco, I remember a Berber student's humiliating moments in class when he repeatedly failed to pronounce French vowels—especially "u"—properly. Whether French hindered his progress or not, he later dropped out of school and joined his parents in a successful business.) The violence also manifests itself in the very lives of Westernized children who will, as Frantz Fanon, the psychologist of the wretched put it, suffer "serious psycho-affective injuries" and become "individuals without an anchor, without a horizon, colorless, stateless, rootless—a race of angels."[23]

The estrangement that begins with the French colonial schooling system produces hybrids whose double acculturation—European and African Muslim—propels them into disabling exilic conditions whose effects are the radical opposites of Islamically sanctioned journeys, such as the *hijra* (flight or migration, as in the title of Salih's novel) and the pilgrimage to Mecca. Just as Islamic history begins with the Prophet Mohamed's flight from persecution, and the Islamic realm was consolidated during that period, the pilgrimage (obligatory on those who can afford to do it) encourages renewal through travel, the forging of spiritual, nonexploitative relations, and the further consolidation of the *umma* (Islamic community).

> The pilgrimage allowed West African Muslims to broaden their horizons, re-establish contact with West African communities who had settled in the Near East (often to escape some of the realities of European conquest and colonial rule), and to contemplate the possibilities for obtaining Islamic higher education abroad. These educational opportunities were not seized upon nearly so much as they are today, in the era of the petrodollar and the scholarship, but they were exploited by a small number of West Africans who might then return home and try to sustain the older standards of learning.[24]

The migrations of Samba Diallo, Mustafa Sa'eed, and Ken Bugul to European metropoles would not have been undertaken if European colonialism had not violently remapped the world and traced out new routes whose purpose is to keep all Africans in a state of dependency. This is important, because without an adequate assessment of the context in which the literary work is conceived and produced,[25] the critic risks adopting a theory of the aesthetic that precludes the historicity of imperialism and blocks out of consciousness the instabilities engendered by capitalism. The strategic "contrapuntal" readings that Edward Said recommends for reading modern literature, and his privileging of the exile as the best-situated critic to make sense of the entire experience of (post)modernity, inadvertently affirm the permanence of colonial rearrangements, and risk emptying non-Western, noncapitalist cultures from their radical alternatives.[26] As the following close reading of the three novels mentioned before will try to show, the experience of exile produces an identity crisis that no amount of aesthetic judgment and critical ability can alleviate. If the Third World critic's hybridity enables her to read cultural production in the age of capitalism better than less cosmopolitan folk (i.e., the struggling poor who have not been graced by colonialism's benefits), such an academic privilege is at best totally irrelevant and, at worst, the expression of a false consciousness that endows bourgeois cultural production with revolutionary content. For Afro-Muslim societies, only the repudiation of capitalism and its colonialist legacies, accompanied by a progressive cultural agenda that draws its sustenance from indigenous traditions, can point to configurations away from the current impasse so movingly described in fiction.

In Saree Makdisi's reading of *Season of Migration to the North*, the unstable, "multilayered" text, with "different registers of textuality, narrative, form, chronology, and history" prevents closure and points toward the direction of synthesis, of a hybridity that resists both Arab traditionalism and European modernity. As an expression of an Arab modernism that rewrites imperialism, the novel "necessarily looks away not only from the premodern but beyond imperialism and toward some alternative future that is in the process of inventing." Tayeb Salih is not only "struggling for the creation of a postimperial Arab society" but is, in fact, "struggling for the creation of a genuinely postimperial world." Mustafa Sa'eed's life story, Makdisi tells us, is dedicated to a reader who could not possibly exist, while "*Season of Migration to the North* is dedicated to readers who do not yet exist: those who can simultaneously see with two eyes, talk with two tongues, and see things both as black *and* as white."[27] Although such a reading captures the complexities of Salih's narrative, it also tends to de-Africanize the novel (inserting the novel in the Arabic literary canon downplays the crucial significance of Mustafa Sa'eed's color in Europe and disconnects Arabness from its African context) and upgrades a cosmopolitan hybridity that privileges the aesthetic over the material.

To be sure, the novel can be read at a variety of levels (transition to modernity, process of individuation, an African version of Conrad's *Heart of Darkness*, etc.),[28] but it is British colonialism and its aftermath that finally determine the lives of both Mustafa Sa'eed and the Narrator of his story. The significance of Mustafa Sa'eed is that he is a pioneering exile, a "prodigy" who, abandoned by his father early in childhood, makes most of his decisions on his own, including the irreversible one of enrolling in the much suspected school (20). That decision would be a "turning-point" in his life, an opportunity that he exploits to the fullest. Cold to the world and indifferent to his own success, he soon obtains a scholarship for Cairo, "a city at the height of English rule" and thus a sort of "antechamber to London,"[29] where Mrs. Robinson awakens in him a "vague sexual yearning" (126). Thus English women (and sexual promiscuity) would henceforth be associated with the Western(ized) metropolis and, in England, as in the case of Jean Morris, they become metaphors for the North itself.

Not only does Mustafa Sa'eed prey on women and invariably drive them to their death, but he is "the first Sudanese to marry an English-woman," or any European, for that matter (55). Mustafa Sa'eed is on a penile conquest of England, cynically describing himself as "a colonizer" and "an intruder," for he knows full well that his is only a mad fantasy, a desperate act of revenge on the English who introduced schools to his country in order to teach submission to Europe's cultural imperatives, to infect the natives with "the germ of the greatest European violence, as seen on the Somme and at Verdun, the like of which the world has never previously known, the germ of a deadly disease that struck them more than a thousand years ago" (95). Mustafa Sa'eed is "a drop of the poison which [the West has] injected into the veins of history" (95), and his reconquest becomes a mad crusade of lies and deception. He makes full use of England's entrenched myths about Africans as simultaneously gods and slaves (109) and turns his London house into an Oriental and African museum of seduction and death.[30] His deliberate self-exoticizing is deployed as a weapon against the English themselves, turning them into victims of their own malignant myths. This is why his house is

the den of lethal lies that I had deliberately built up, lie upon lie: the sandalwood and incense; the ostrich feathers and ivory and ebony figurines; the paintings and drawings of forests of palm trees along the shores of the Nile, boats with sails like doves' wings, suns setting over the mountains of the Red Sea, camel caravans wending their way along sand dunes on the borders of the Yemen, baobab trees in Kordofan, naked girls from the tribes of Zandi, the Nuer and the Shuluk, fields of banana and coffee on the Equator, old temples in the district of Nubia; Arabic books with decorated covers written in ornate Kufic script; Persian carpets, pink curtains, large mirrors on the walls, and coloured lights in the corners. (146)

Despite the appearance of defiance, Sa'eed's self-orientalizing is also a form of resignation to the English (especially the liberals') insistence that he conform to their own image of the African. Furthermore, his anger may stem from his torturous awareness that he has internalized much of the West, despite his continuous resistance. He falls in love with Jean Morris against his own will because he sees his own image in her: not only is she "exceedingly intelligent" and "exceedingly charming" and is like "some mendicant Scheherazade" who probably has no family; but, like him, she also lies "about the most ordinary things and would return home with amazing and incredible stories about incidents that had happened to her and people she'd met" (155). He knows that she is "brazen in word and deed," that she abstains from nothing, including "stealing, lying and cheating" (156).

But Jean Morris is, by the same token, the image of the cold, foreboding, and hostile North. The "ordered world" of England he goes to (27) is also "the world of Jean Morris" (29). She is the personification of the West "in the shape of a woman": "She was my destiny and in her lay my destruction, yet for me the whole world was not worth a mustard seed in comparison. I was the invader who had come from the South, and this was the icy battlefield from which I would not make a safe return. I was the private sailor and Jean Morris the shore of destruction" (160).[31] Through his fatal love affair with Jean, Mustafa Sa'eed tries to come to terms with his own alienation, his exile in the West. By killing her in a highly eroticized love scene, he tries to exorcize the West from his consciousness; or, at least, he wants to accomplish a symbolic triumph over the North. When she lays down, after tormenting him for months, ready to be conquered, he once more declares that his ships are sailing "towards the shores of destruction" (164). His refusal to commit suicide after he presses his dagger between Jean's eager breasts (164–65) indicates that he still hopes to retrieve his mutilated identity. His passionate murder of Jean Morris is an attempt to exorcize the irresistibly seductive attraction of the West from his infected being.

Only when he is back in his adopted Sudanese village does he finally realize that the Northern germ is ineradicable, that once a Muslim African is Westernized cultural alienation becomes a permanent condition, that his precociousness and sexual bravados cannot restore the equilibrium in the global balance of power. Furthermore, as Westernization is being deterritorialized and Western-style education universalized, cultural differences are emptied of their radical content and reduced to folkloric shells. While his two sons, Mahmoud and Sa'eed, ride a donkey to go to school six miles away from the village where he has settled (88), he implores the Narrator, whom he appoints as guardian over his family, to spare them the "wanderlust" that has ruined his life (65–66). It is obviously a futile wish, for although displacement may not be physical, the school to which he sends his sons will almost invariably create in them new hopes and desires that might not be accommodated by village life.

If Mustafa Sa'eed himself, painfully aware as he might be of the dangers of Westernization, continues to succumb to the West's irresistible pull, even in this remote village, it is wishful thinking to expect better outcomes from people who, like succeeding generations of Africans, define their own emancipation, whether personal or collective, in Western vocabularies. The tragic itinerary of Mustafa Sa'eed is symptomatic of the "black African Muslim in a world dominated by the White European."[32] The secret room that he allows the Narrator to open is a testimonial to his thorough Westernization: if in his London house Sa'eed craftily exploits Orientalist myths to seduce and wage a war on women as embodiments of the West that he both loathes and loves, his room in the village grimly indicates Sa'eed's inability to reconnect himself with his traditions. Not only does his secret room contain an incongruous fireplace, but his extensive library doesn't contain one single book in Arabic. Even the Qur'an is in translation. The room is a "graveyard. A mausoleum. An insane idea. A prison. A huge joke. A treasure chamber" (146), exclaims Sa'eed's horrified trustee. We now understand why Sa'eed drowns in the Nile, which flows irrevocably northward and "pays heed to nothing," surmounting every hurdle on its way until it reaches its appointed destination (69). The magnetic powers of the West are comparable to the forces of nature, the steady flow of the river northward,[33] as if human destiny simply cannot avoid the lure of Westernization. (The Narrator himself will—upon leaving Sa'eed's secret room and finding himself confronted with his own and, until then, carefully repressed identity crisis—throw himself, naked, into the Nile. But even when he makes the conscious decision to resist its pull, to no longer remain adrift, forget and "live by force and cunning" [169], this reader remains unconvinced that he will be saved as he struggles in the water. Thus the novel doesn't offer alternative visions; it simply tries to articulate the crisis of colonially educated African Muslim elites.)

Like Mustafa Sa'eed, Ken Bugul also grows up as a rather abandoned child, with an old patriarchal father who becomes blind when Ken is only five years old, and who furthermore is more concerned with the hereafter in his old age than with his own health or the well-being of his daughter. He is like the Teacher in Kane's *Ambiguous Adventure*, or perhaps more like the Knight, for he refuses to seek modern treatment for his blindness, insisting that he has seen it all (26). (The new Westernized world is not appealing.) Yet years later, in cold Belgium where Ken receives news of his death, she cries for the double alienation that would haunt her throughout her life: that she cannot even be alienated in the traditional sense; for, with her mother always gone when Ken was still a schoolchild, she only experiences a fragile rootedness—symbolized throughout the account by the sturdy yet not invulnerable baobab tree. In fact, Ken seems to be the victim of the clash of traditions: parents who care but cannot accommodate the new demands of modernity, and a colonial modernity that cannot tolerate the older ways represented by the father.

Obviously, Ken experiences her predicament as a woman, which initially adds another layer of oppression to the unfolding tragedy of her displacement. The myth of the civilized West is quickly dissipated upon arrival to the European continent, as her disillusionment with the lack of "real structure" (71) in her family is now compounded by her shock at realizing that what she had come to know as her "ancestors" in the French school, the Gauls, are, in fact, rapacious colonialists who separated Africans and frustrated their search for unity.[34] To be a woman, "a child without any notion of parents, to be Black, and to be colonized" (93) in the "Century of the West" (94) turns out to be the worst of possible fates. Triply alienated (as a black colonized woman), despite her remarkably resilient and ingenious ways of coping, insanity begins to haunt her, especially as she is unable even to theorize or launch a viable program of emancipation from both the (Islamic) patriarchy and the hegemony of Western imperialism.

Her own set of problems weaves a complexity around Ken's account that goes beyond the novels discussed above. For instance, although she grows to realize that all women—regardless of race or national origin—are persecuted by a more universal, violent patriarchy, and believes that women should spend more time together (52), she ultimately rejects the assumed universality of all women's conditions and concludes that relationships among Western women are "in decay" (89). As a woman, she may be sexually exploited in both cultures—her first sexual relationship is with her social science teacher in secondary school (43, 48); but that doesn't make all cultures (despite their predominantly patriarchal structures) undifferentiated. That is why, after a heartbreaking disappointment in the human relations within the capitalist metropolis, she concludes that only friendships among women in her village are real and genuine (84). Indeed, it is after a futile attempt to rebel against the village traditions and to partake in the libertinism of the West that she realizes that "sexuality is culture and atmosphere" (52), and that the loss of her virginity to her high school teacher has, in fact, severed her connection to the mores and traditions of her society (48). (The fact that Ken is initiated into nontraditional sexuality with a teacher highlights the role of [colonial] education in disrupting traditions.)

Ken is inserted in a postindustrial West whose postmodern culture is based on simulacra and nostalgia. She finds a cold and dehumanized society where the exotic South is sometimes experienced as a poster or postcards (35–36, 82). She had been warned by her mother about "the country of the white people" (27), but it is only during her sojourn that her excitement and anticipation begin to wane, now that she is immediately ensnared by the logic of consumerism: "The stores attracted me like lovers. I began by buying myself almost anything at all. All these seductive store windows were egging me on to buy paper, soap, candy, scarves, sweaters, dresses, jewelry, pajamas, even if I didn't wear them. I felt quite at home as I was shopping. I felt like neither a foreigner nor a newcomer; I was just a consumer like anyone else. I'd pay, and I'd get change handed to me indifferently" (36). Only as a consumer, then, can Ken achieve some sense of equality with white people; otherwise, she feels black, ugly, and foreign in the white city (37–38). She struggles to comprehend why no one greets her (35, 39) and thus, eager to be accepted, allows herself to be loved by Louis (a Belgian student who lived in Africa), becomes pregnant, and finds an executioner-like, racist doctor to perform an abortion on her.

At this point, Ken's universal feminist consciousness begins to develop, only to be eroded by what she later realizes as irreconcilable cultural differences. She meets Jean Werner, an artist, recently divorced with three children, a man of "homosexual tendencies" (58), but soon finds herself sharing Jean's amorous attention with François, Jean's male lover. She is now introduced to the world of avant-gardism and drugs. Surprised by this surreal environment—for Ken had grown up believing in the West's superior values (60)—she begins to long for the home she never had. Her search for a "home" and acceptance continue to lead her into a world of deceptions and destructive emotional traumas. Gradually, she resorts to self-fetishism and self-exoticizing, increasingly living the lie that Mustafa Sa'eed adopts partly as a survival mechanism. She adorns the walls of the room she shares with an American GI (and later, Souleymane, a displaced compatriot) with photographs of her nude body. Discovering that the body can be alienated from "feeling and thought" (70), she works in a sauna, giving massages to men, partly because she is unconsciously and "irresistibly attracted to that whole side of the West that nobody had ever talked about in the school texts" (72).

Ken moves further into the world of LSD, alcohol, free love, etc., in the company of "marginals" and "intellectuals of a decadent society" (81–82). Always on the verge of insanity, she loses her scholarship and submits to her role as a black token (84), a "Negress," "that supplementary being, useless, displaced, incoherent" (85). Even the middle-class family of the Denoëls that she befriends want her because they, too, want their part of exoticism, "their part of exoneration" (87). The Westerners, she suspects, envy blacks for the "emotional wealth" (88), which may be why—as the priest does with the unsuspecting Souleymane—they prey on their sexuality (91). Trapped, Ken nevertheless drifts down the precipitous path of destruction, doing odd jobs such as modeling for artists and photographers, dancing in nightclubs, until she prostitutes herself for the sake of "a moment of attention" (106). Allowing herself to be consumed by white men, however, doesn't provide her with the affirmation she needs, for she remains "full of rage and despair" (158) and suicidal. She now decides to return to Senegal, only to find the baobab tree that has served as a reference and focal point in her alienation—the only element of stability and permanence in an otherwise shifting world—dead (158–59). As if for herself, she then pronounces a eulogy.

Throughout her autobiography, Ken struggles with the cultural dislocations that have resulted from colonialism and unsuccessfully tries to articulate or chart a viable alternative for change. Her frustration reflects the failure of the various attempts to find a lasting solution for Africa in the postcolonial era. Colonialism has prevented development and inflicted an inferiority complex that Ken refuses to accept (71). She knows that the West cannot solve Africans' problems and is dismayed by the sort of Africanism (as in Orientalism) heedlessly displayed by Westerners (86). As she begins to realize that the West's promised freedoms have turned out to be mere illusions perpetuated by the educational system implanted back home, she begins to resist the sort of tokenism Mustafa Sa'eed deliberately uses to extract vengeance from the West and rips down the nude photographs of herself (93). Africans, she now realizes, have celebrated their independence prematurely, for what they still need is exorcism and anger (130); but Africans are not united, and an appropriate formula for genuine liberation remains elusive (74). If the Westernized neocolonial elites who rule most of the continent are scared and confused (125, 136), and the people are not united (90–91), how is one to overcome this tragic loss of self and the ghettoization of a whole continent? If the baobab tree, which is now an "empty shell," is a metaphor for the entire African society,[35] then are surrender and defeat, whether in a vacuous mimicry of modernity or collective self-exoticizing, the only options left?

Bugul's autobiography is striking in that it uncannily echoes the same predicament explored by Cheikh Hamidou Kane two decades earlier in *Ambiguous Adventure.* Although the disorientation of Mustafa Sa'eed and Ken Bugul must be read as consequences of violent uprootings from Islamic societies whose (precolonial) structures are not always elaborated on in the novels, *Ambiguous Adventure* deliberately articulates the unbridgeable gaps between African Islam and an imperial secular modernity. The Knight knows colonialism has accomplished its mission when the Chief and the Most Royal Lady announce that they expect Samba, his son, to enroll in the new school. He contemplates the seduction of the West, as the world gives itself "over to an incomprehensible and fantastic mimicry of worship" (70). The Knight, like the Teacher, is the keeper of wisdom that can no longer be sustained, for he also would rather be in the humility of obscurity and prayer, and shun the West's restlessness that passes for civilization (69). He questions the validity of modern science that has transformed Westerners into "masters of the external" (78). He wishes for Paul Lacroix, the school principal, and the West to develop a sense of the tragic, to believe in death in order to save itself, and, indeed, a whole world that, under the compulsion of Westernization, has grown inextricably connected. As a devout Muslim, he laments that God's creatures are now being condemned "to live in the solid shell of appearance" and suffer the "exile" associated with it (83). While Samba reads Pascal's reflections on the alienation of God in the rising culture of productivity and the work ethic, the Knight tells his son that work is justified only when it is done for the sake of God (99–100). For him, work under an atheistic industrial capitalism in which "life and work are no longer commensurable" (101), in which production is increasingly severed from work by valuing profit more than the well-being and happiness of humans, eventually leads people not only to proclaim the death of God but to proclaim their own death as well.

> At the same time that work gets along without human life, at the same time it ceases to make life its final aim; it ceases to value man. Man has never been so unhappy as at this moment when he is accumulating so much. Nowhere is he thought so little of as in the places where this accumulation is going on. That is why the history of the West seems to me to reveal the insufficiency of the guarantee that man offers to man. For man's welfare and happiness we must have the presence and the guarantee of God. (101–2)

Reassured by the words of his father, Samba now knows that "there are those who believe and those who do not believe; the division is clear. It leaves no one outside its neatly drawn line" (102). The West's relativism, then, is the outcome of the same alienation eloquently described by Marx, especially in his early writings; rather than being an advanced stage of development, it signals a disturbing disorientation in the West's psyche, engendered by the triumph of industrial capitalism.[36] Its casualties, however, as the dramatic initiation of Samba into the West so poignantly illustrates, are not only Westerners but also the whole world, the former colonies, the periphery with its bewitched, covetous masses. The "fool," for instance, is a reminder of what's awaiting Samba in Europe. His very presence in the village is an eloquent testimonial on the ravages wrought by Europeans; his strange features and the "inconstancy of his ever-roving glance" suggest that he might know a secret that is "baleful to the world" (87). He has come back to report on and warn about the "obscene chaos in the world" (93), seeking "indulgent listeners" (87); but for his descriptions of the dehumanized and violent West, he is nicknamed "the fool" and his stories dismissed as extravagant (87–92).

In the West, Samba studies philosophy. Concluding that Cartesian thought signals a shift in Western history (114), he finds it offensive that he and his country are coerced to decide between faith and science (116–17). Yet although Samba maintains his values and rejects communism—he only fights for God, not liberty (141)—he gradually changes and unwittingly internalizes the values of both cultures, an outcome even more distressing to him (150–51). Philosophically, he looks at his own alienation, his exile, as a reminder that there still is an alternative to the West, even though that option is not available to Africans born in the diaspora (157). His hybridity, however, paralyzes him. When the Knight, sensing his son's "disquietude" and fearing for his perdition, calls him back, it is too late. The return (*le retour*) doesn't attenuate Samba's alienation, it only accentuates it. Samba confesses on the grave of the dead Teacher that he has lost the ability to believe. He even refuses, under the fool's urging, to pray for his old master. The fool, greatly alarmed, proceeds to kill Samba, most likely because he wants to save his soul. For it is within the darkness of death, from whose fascination he had been dissuaded by the Most Royal

Lady, that Samba Diallo's mutilated identity is made whole again. Death banishes "all that is opposed and aggressive," turns him into "the infinite," not the "nothing" he had become in his disquieting exile. Death is, in fact, the found kingdom of "no ambiguity" (176–77).

Cheikh Hamidou Kane's interest in *Ambiguous Adventure* "is not so much reconstructing the penetration of all external forces, both Arab-Islamic and Euro-Christian, into Senegal (as is the case with Ousmane Sembene's *Ceddo*) as exploring the disintegration of *an already established Islamic society*" (my emphasis). For Kane, "Islam is Diallobé and Diallobé is Islam. Hence the portrayal of the West and its materialist credo as the antithesis of Diallobé spiritualism and communalism."[37] Islam, then, appears as an identity that doesn't need explaining; the author doesn't feel compelled to differentiate his Islamic faith from his Africanness. The Islamic resistance to European colonialism is assumed to be part of the general African struggle.[38] Inspired by "conventional Muslim views," the novel brings into sharp relief, and perhaps prophetically anticipates, the growing impasse between the cultures of Islam and Western secularism in the contemporary period. Indeed, because it insists on privileging indigenous traditions, *Ambiguous Adventure* may still be—although it was originally published in the early 1960s—the most "committed" African novel to propose a "radical alternative."[39]

Westernization and cultural mimicry, in Kane's account, are not solutions to the predicament of underdevelopment. The "fool" returns from the West a paralyzed, incoherent, and profoundly traumatized man; Samba Diallo and Mustafa Sa'eed, having lost faith, can only find salvation in death. The West, whether comprehended through its law (as Pierre-Louis, the retired black magistrate in France advises in *Ambiguous Adventure*) or assimilated (as the Most Royal Lady recommends) is, in the final recourse, irresistible, although it still doesn't proclaim, as Kane himself stated, a death sentence for Muslim societies.

> In my view this is not a hopeless ending. The death of Samba Diallo is only proof that there is a real conflict. You understand, if there had not been the initial civilization in which Samba was rooted, there would have been no problem when he was introduced to Western

civilization; he would have thrived in it. On the contrary, he dies because of it. Why? His death leads to reflection. It means: 1) That we do have permanent values, as I previously stated, and we therefore must nurture them or search for them if they are in risk of disappearing. 2) By not recognizing that, we reach the point of negating ourselves and our specific values; this will destroy us. In other words, Western values inculcated indiscriminately can lead to the destruction of the African who is unable to assimilate them.[40]

The sense of utter despair generated by several Afro-Muslim novels, reflecting the elusive solutions to Africa's debilitating dependency in the postcolonial era, has brought back the precolonial Islamic model as a possibility to overcome the structural challenges facing African nation-states. Spencer Trimingham had long predicted that if Islam were believed to restore harmony to Afro-Muslims, "it is likely to be adopted."[41] Davidson and Ngũgĩ have expressed visions of post-nationalist Africa that re-create patterns of Islamic civilization in the continent. Davidson alludes to the Islamically influenced multi-ethnic, "sprawling political formations" known as *regna* as possible alternatives to the failed nation-state model. Though coercive, these *regna* exercised "a civilizing function on behalf of their subject peoples as well as their ruling peoples."[42] In the mid-1980s, while visiting Dar es Salaam in Tanzania, Ngũgĩ, inspired by the celebrated medieval East African *regnum*, concluded that modern East Africa has no option but to revive the unity that had given East African peoples, unified through Kiswahili, a respectable place in the world:

> With the inheritance of a common geography, a common tradition of resistance, a common language, and with political unity bringing about the economic integration of our 60 million people under one strong federal state, what a wonderful base this would be from which we could face the twenty-first century. This substantial home market would enable us to sustain big modern industries, raise our agricultural production to new heights, open up internal tourism, develop complementary economic activities instead of the current duplication, and exploit all the possibilities of internal commerce long before we need explore foreign markets. . . . A midnight dream of an

amateur fisherman on the high seas? The dream was not mine alone:
It has been with us on the land and on the sea.[43]

To resurrect East African history might mean decentering secular
colonial education and renegotiating the relations between Islam and
Africa. A new pan-African consciousness, such as the one expressed
in a conference on teaching African literature in Kenyan schools held
in Nairobi in 1974, already rejects colonial remappings of the continent. Recognizing the nefarious effects of colonial education, a committee charged with writing recommendations for change stated that
"the centuries old Arab civilization has exerted tremendous influence
on the literature of modern North Africa and also many parts of the
continent. To date their influence has been denied by our educators
and the literature of North Africa and the Arab world has largely
been ignored."[44] Other conferences have also examined the Islamic
past in Africa. In April 1983, sixty scholars from fourteen Arab and
African nations attended a conference in Amman, Jordan, to explore
Arab-African relations.[45] The publication of *Africa and Arabo-Islamic
Culture* in 1987 by the Islamic Educational Scientific and Cultural
Organization (isesco), founded in 1982 and based in Rabat, affirmed
that the "Arabo-Islamic culture as a fundamental unifying factor in
African culture in general and, second, that the recent resurgence of
Arabo-Islamic culture has been a major force in confronting and
liberating Western Africa from Western imperial domination." In
1989 Nigerian Muslims organized an "Islam in Africa Conference,"
restated their commitment to Islam, and condemned, among other
things, "the imperial forces of domination and secularization."[46]

Such attempts to articulate a historically derived alternative to
colonial structures have triggered the typical warning in the Western
media that Africa is being invaded by Muslim extremists. The same
photograph of white-robed Islamic militant women on the march
was the cover of *L'Evénement du Jeudi* in late 1993 and of *Jeune Afrique
économie* one year later. Although the representation of Africa as
militant and resolutely anti-Western dispels the notion that Africans have passively accepted their deplorable postcolonial condition,
Western intervention is still considered indispensable to prevent the
further deterioration of social and political structures.[47] The alarmist

overtones of the media over the renaissance taking place in Islamic Africa is historically myopic and profoundly discriminatory,[48] since it obliterates the very traditions that gave strength and identity to Islamic Africa and, indeed, made it a significant player in the global cultural and economic exchange. The re-Arabization of educational systems in Muslim Nigeria and other parts of Islamic Africa is not a fanatical gesture but is indissolubly linked to the recuperation of a mutilated identity.[49]

If European colonialism purposely engineered the formation of a Westernized elite whose concerns do not resonate among the masses, then the recuperation of indigenous traditions consolidates the struggle for decolonization and may even stimulate multicultural resistances to capitalism on a global scale. When Samba Diallo states that if "those of us who come from the outlying regions" (153) do not awake the "West to the difference which separates us from the object, we shall be worth no more than it is and we shall never master it. And our defeat will be the end of the last human being on earth" (154), he implies that the solution to a perilous Eurocentricity must be sought in non-Western cultures. A contemporary intellectual of his, Frantz Fanon, articulated a similar view in *The Wretched of the Earth:*

> So, comrades, let us not pay tribute to Europe by creating states, institutions, and societies which draw their inspiration from her.
>
> Humanity is waiting for something from us other than such an imitation, which would be almost an obscene caricature.
>
> If we want to turn Africa into a new Europe, and America into a new Europe, then let us leave the destiny of our countries to Europeans. They will know how to do it better than the most gifted among us.
>
> But if we want humanity to advance a step further, if we want to bring it up to a different level than that which Europe has shown it, then we must invent and we must make discoveries.
>
> If we wish to live up to our people's expectations, we must seek the response elsewhere than in Europe.[50]

The promise of the South as a healing and liberating place, a location that cleanses the excesses of European materialism has, in fact, been brilliantly expressed in Camara Laye's account of a lonely white man's mystical journey in *The Radiance of the King*.[51] After failing to impress the African natives with his skin color (the only asset left him in his state of total bankruptcy), Clarence loses all direction and realizes, in the words of one scholar, that "Cartesian categories of thought do not always apply, that the flux of life cannot be comprehended through reason." Clarence's itinerary in Africa turns out to be the reverse of the black man's alienation in Europe. Ironically, it is the white man Clarence who experiences the Sufi experience of *fana* (the ecstasy resulting from the annihilation of the ego and the unity with God) without dying physically.[52] The Sufi rejection of Westernization is not merely an antisocial intoxicating experience, but a fundamental component of the Islamic message proposed by progressive scholars such as Mahmoud Mohamed Taha.

A serious examination of Islam in Africa shatters the dangerously reductive rubric of "Africa" that is the premise of most academic studies today and throws serious doubt on the nationalistic concepts borrowed from Europe's history that not only have divided the African peoples along false lines but also have severed the Arabs and Berbers from their unmistakably African origins. If a progressively interpreted Islam could redefine Arabic-speaking people's conception of themselves and liberate them from historically and ideologically questionable myths, it could also redefine, revitalize, and, best of all, liberate African cultures from the iron cage of race and irrelevant national designations that have come to define their identities and literatures.

4

Women's Freedom in Muslim Spaces

The gender question should be reexamined, as the gender
revolution was intended in Islam but never took off. It was aborted
arguably for two reasons: a) mainstream Islam turned royalist from
the Ummayids [first ruling Islamic dynasty] onwards, and the
harem developed and became more secluded as a more aristocratic
version of Islam developed, and b) the doors of ijtihad [intellectual
effort] closed and the gender revolution was thereby aborted.
—Ali Mazrui, "Islam and the End of History"

We strongly affirm that feminism strives for the broadest
and deepest development of society and human beings free of *all*
systems of domination.—Gita Sen and Caren Grown,
Development, Crises, and Alternative Visions

The current interest in the discourses of feminism, human rights, and
democracy have encouraged many Muslim intellectuals to explore
indigenous models of emancipation for the masses in general, and
women in particular. Although the widely held assumption that
women have been historically persecuted by all patriarchal cultures is,
to a large extent, incontestably true, the discourses of Western feminism, largely shaped by gender relations in Christian capitalist cultures and by the exhausted paradigms of Western social thought, have
hindered a more subtle appreciation of women's issues under Islam.
François Burgat has argued that "the relationship between Islamism
and 'women's rights' is often presented in an unusually heated en-

vironment," a situation that leads to "short cuts in analysis." Describing the Islamic resurgence as a strategic component in the South's (Third World) attempt to contest Western hegemony in the domains of culture and ideology, Burgat is rather suspicious of "the ideological repositioning of the South [and its confinement] into the analytical ghetto of 'misogyny,' or with even less nuance, an 'apartheid' which is erected as a central and absolute principle 'explaining' the [Islamist] phenomenon." Although Burgat is referring more to the political phenomenon of Islamism, his reading is equally applicable to Islam in general, since the discourses of Western feminism and human rights have far-reaching consequences for all Muslim peoples, especially as "the social status of women constitutes one of the terrains on which the invasion of Western references has disturbed the dynamic of the internal normative evolution of the universe of Islam."[1] Although one must expose Islamist ideologies to rigorous criticism and categorically reject all coercive and intolerant practices espoused in the name of religion, the recovery of a long obfuscated egalitarian conception of Islam, together with an effort to reconceptualize a progressive Islam for the future, are necessary undertakings if one is to go beyond a negative critique of homogenized Islamic cultures and rethink a possible indigenous path to women's emancipation.

To conduct dialogues and expand the spaces of freedom in the Islamic world today, it is necessary to critically redefine and thoroughly reassess Islamic traditions, including entrenched but Islamically questionable assumptions about women. Islamic societies are products of history; they bear the imprints of time and change. To rely uncritically on old canonical documents as the foundation of a new Islamic revival would run counter to the best tendencies in Islamic intellectual history. In fact, even certain aspects of the Prophet's life have not always been translated into general practice among Muslims. After carefully studying the Prophet's relationships with women, and implying that his marriage to the six-year-old 'Aisha (consummated when the bride was nine) has not set a legal precedent in Islamic countries, Leila Ahmed wonders "whether the religion is to be allowed to remain permanently locked into replicating the outer forms of the specific society into which it was revealed, or whether the true pursuit and fulfillment of the Islamic message entails, on the contrary, the gradual abandonment of laws necessary in its first age."[2] Although the answer to such a proposition should be fairly simple (at least to progressive elements within the Islamic tradition), a practical solution has remained elusive, especially as Islam evolved from an initial phase of tolerance to the gradual subjugation of women and their enclosure in the dark world of a theologically illegitimate patriarchy. This debilitating climate of oppression needs to be shattered through a revolutionary understanding of Islam and the restoration of "early Sufi and Qarmati thought," long eclipsed by a conservative, male-dominated clerical Islam. Only through the retrieval of this emancipatory tradition, Ahmed convincingly argues, would Muslim women "not be compelled to make the intolerable choice between religious belief and their own autonomy and self-affirmation" (691, 679).

Yet clerical Islam is no more problematic than the ideologically suspect discourses of unexamined Western social science theories. Marnia Lazreg has clearly demonstrated the bankruptcy of these exhausted paradigms for interpreting the Middle Eastern and North African worlds and has criticized both U.S. and "Eastern" feminists for failing to represent the heterogeneity and complexity of Arab societies.[3] Not only do U.S. feminists often assume that in order for Arab women to become real feminists they must dissociate themselves from Arab men and their own culture, but their attitude is often informed by an unmistakable bias against Islam. Indeed, many Arab women become complicitous allies in propagating this reductionist interpretation of their societies; passing for social criticism, their "personal confessions" are often given a conspicuous forum in the West, even as these Arab women themselves are transformed into representatives for the millions of women on whose behalf they were never allowed to speak. The fetishization of Islam, Lazreg explains, obscures "the living reality of the women and men subsumed under it" and erases "the socioeconomic and political context within which it unfolds."[4] Hence a contrapuntal reading of the feminist project in Islam is indispensable if one is not to isolate any analysis from the global currents that both inform it and could, in turn, be influenced by it. Since neither global capitalism nor a male-dominated and historically entrenched version of Islam is conducive to a genuinely liberating Islamic culture, the feminist project faces the monumental task of contesting both orthodoxies simultaneously and dialectically.

The feminist question in Islam is necessarily implicated in the cross-currents of several contestatory discourses and ideologies, including women versus the patriarchy within Islamic communities, the secular West versus Islam, the West's acceptance of certain forms of Islam over others, the specificity of the Islamic feminist project, and the various ideological tendencies within Islamic thought itself. Therefore, a careful articulation of an Islamically progressive agenda —democratic, antipatriarchal, and anti-imperialist—might provide the impetus for a new revolutionary paradigm.[5] This new Islamic consciousness, firmly rooted in usable traditions but uncompromisingly universal in outlook, can redefine the very meaning of Islam without abandoning the parameters of the faith. Syncretically arranged and engaged in permanent dialogue with the progressive agendas of other cultures, its ultimate goal is a culturally "polycentric" world founded on economic socialism and gender equality. This conception of Islam alone can legitimate feminism in the Islamic world by posing a formidable challenge for clerical, orthodox Islam, which has stubbornly refused to extend more freedoms to women and minorities. It also must confront the existing global capitalist system, which has no intention of reducing poverty or creating a more humane and egalitarian civilization.[6] Because capitalism is structurally incapable of creating equality, committed feminists need to look beyond mere reformism and toward radically different, indigenous, and pluralistic alternatives. A progressive Islam, empowered by the equal status and dynamic contributions of women, and extending full rights to minorities, is therefore one way to break away from Eurocentric structures and redynamize progressive non-Western traditions in a genuinely multicultural world.

The West's crusade against Islam has been joined by Westernized Muslim writers such as the Moroccan Tahar ben Jelloun, who has attempted to depict Islam as a reactionary force that has set back or destroyed the freedoms of women and writers and eclipsed the traditions of non-Arab peoples. Ben Jelloun's treatment of gender in *The Sand Child* and *The Sacred Night*,[7] for instance, earned him the pres-

tigious Goncourt literary prize and persuaded American publishers
to make his fiction available to English-speaking readers for the first
time. The novels are about gender repression and sexual mutilation
in an obdurately unenlightened Islamic society. In *The Sand Child,*
Hajji Ahmad Suleyman, an aging patriarch with seven daughters, in
an attempt to save his honor and protect the inheritance of his children from his two scheming brothers, decides that his next newborn
will be a boy, regardless of the actual sex of the baby. His name will be
Ahmed. A daughter is then born into this fate, at a time of nationalist
struggle for independence, suggesting that the anticolonial resistance
is informed by a strong patriarchal ideology. The boy's circumcision
is faked, and as the girl begins to reach puberty her chest is "ban-
daged with white linen, pulling the bands of cloth so tight that [she]
could hardly breathe. It was absolutely vital that no breasts should
appear" (24). Ahmed goes through all sorts of social contortions to
hide her femininity (including a fake marriage) before she lifts the
veil on her true identity and enters yet another universe of violent
repression.

   Ben Jelloun's improbable tale of the grotesque seemingly confirms
the West's suspicion that Islam is hostile to women and inhospitable
to their demands for change and freedom. In fact, John Erickson has
stated that "nowhere in Maghrebian literature is the problem of sexuality more graphically explored, with all of its ties to much more
extended social and political problems, and linked more indissolubly
with literary revolt" than in *The Sand Child.* Ben Jelloun, according
to Erickson, sets out to undermine the "structuring values in Islamic
societies."[8] It is true that Ben Jelloun would have liked his female
protagonist to be "held back by no religion" and to move freely from
"myth to myth"; however, as a longtime resident of France, the author knows that immigration to the West is not necessarily a solution
for the oppressed and persecuted girl. Indeed, his later novel *Les yeux
baissés* does problematize the migration of a Berber girl from a High
Atlas village to Paris, presenting an even bleaker picture of the predicament of Muslim women within existing global arrangements.[9] Fleeing her old, murderous aunt, the young Moroccan woman finds little
relief in the gray, cold, noisy, and crowded French metropolis, where
she joins her immigrant father. She awakens to her sexuality and

begins to flirt with a handsome Portuguese boy, but she also loses her religious convictions and is shocked by her discovery of anti-Arab racism. Unable to return to the confining village culture she left behind and condemned to remain the Other in France, the young girl struggles throughout the novel to construct a positive identity, her eyes downcast ("les yeux baissés") mostly out of oppression, not respect. The net of oppression has been enlarged to include the cruelties of tradition, state neglect, immigration, and the damaging legacy of colonialism. Ben Jelloun's "veiled narrative" enables him, however, to avoid closure, leaving the predicament of Muslim women unsettlingly suspended.

I cite the case of Ben Jelloun's recent fiction to illustrate the complex impact feminism has had on certain Muslim novelists. Are women to be given their rightful place in the canon only if Islam is depicted in the broadest Orientalist strokes?[10] Is it possible to champion women's rights while extricating progressive Islam from the deadwood of orthodoxy and the biased interpretations of much of Western scholarship? Islam has been used in so many contradictory ways that one cannot accept, as both orthodox jurists and Orientalists have, a monolithic definition of this religion (Said has warned us against this repeatedly). During the Arab world's struggle for independence, for instance, the nationalist bourgeoisie used Islam to rally the masses for the liberation of their occupied land and to preserve capitalism (or, in other instances, state socialism). This form of Islam was obviously infused with a patriarchal spirit (a problem that has afflicted many a revolutionary movement in the twentieth century),[11] although its anti-imperialist thrust was unmistakably liberating. And it was imperialism that, paradoxically, "created the objective basis for both the development of women's struggles and the integration of women into the more general national struggle against colonialism."[12] But if women were temporarily liberated from the shackles of a stifling Islamic orthodoxy by imperialism, they were eventually recontained by a new Islamic consciousness that refused to grant them more rights, despite their heroic struggle to preserve the sanctity of Islam itself. The new nationalist regimes were thus ensnared by more contradictions, for they had copied the colonial model of the nation-state, subscribed to a multitude of international organizations controlled by former colonialists, and accepted their neocolonial status while perpetuating a stagnant, apolitical, and mostly reactionary version of Islam. Such a complicated situation, with a variety of discourses (some legitimated by the state to suit its needs), has made an accurate reading of the Islamic sociopolitical context difficult and can be approached only from a dialectical position that recognizes the specificity and historicity of Islamic cultures and the impact of global capitalism on them.

The prominent feminist-sociologist Fatima Mernissi, however, has implicitly accepted the capitalist model of human relations, as she eschews the cautionary approach and indeterminate position of Ben Jelloun's fiction to champion a bourgeois notion of democracy and individual liberties as the foundations for any Arab nation that aspires to genuine sovereignty and development.[13] Mernissi agrees that the situation of women in Morocco must be understood in relation to both the cataclysmic changes affecting that country and the redistribution of social space in it, and she keeps the distinct histories of West and East firmly in mind, especially those regarding the treatment of women.[14] She also understands that colonialism has had the unintended effect of suppressing the legitimate struggle of women by subsuming it in an uncritical Islamic ideology of resistance. In the final analysis, however, Mernissi is clearly in favor of a bourgeois definition of human rights and democracy. In *La peur-modernité*, she repeats the familiar Orientalist thesis that only a secular modernity can free Arabs from their long and deadly paralysis, although she avoids blaming Islam itself. She even admits that Islam is the "symbolic capital" of the wretched and the voice of the proletariat in the struggle against the beneficiaries of international capitalism (in the modern Arab state poor children go to the Qur'anic school while upper-class children attend kindergarten).[15] Thus the oppressed continue to derive from Islam a powerfully inspiring impulse for justice. Yet Mernissi dismisses this Islamic legacy as dated in the contemporary era and suggests, instead, that it must give way to a secular civil society, democratically organized, that protects individual freedoms. For the lack of democracy leads to a host of social ills, including immigration to the "very paradoxical" West (78).

Mernissi's reflections on the position of women throughout much of Islamic history imply that democracy and individual freedoms were abolished with the advent of Islam, when the Prophet Mohamed destroyed polytheism in Mecca and replaced it with an uncompromising (but benevolent) monotheism. Describing democracy as a form of *shirk* (disbelief through associating another deity with Allah), she calls for the reestablishment of the culture of polytheism that had reigned in Arabia in the pre-Islamic period and thus, in a striking parallel with Rushdie's *Satanic Verses,* redefines the Jahiliya as an exciting era of discussion and human rights. According to Mernissi's metaphor, Muslims are on a crusade to veil anything that threatens their faith, whether it be Western democracy, history (associated here with polytheism and powerful goddesses), or simply any form of change. Islam is depicted as fundamentally antihistorical and antifeminist, a religion that has totally eradicated the Jahiliya from consciousness. In fact, Islam has even launched the new patriarchal calendar of the *Hijra* (170–71), which, like the Qur'anic school, has relevance only to those who are poor and abide by the faith; for it is Western time that regulates transactions in the global village. Mernissi still (intuitively) believes in an Arab take-off (196) and criticizes the West's essentialization of Muslim women despite the latter's remarkable accomplishments in the past few decades (206, 247–48 n 10); however, her methodology desacralizes the Qur'an by reducing it to a mere historical document in *Le harem politique,*[16] and by showing that it was produced in a series of human negotiations in which God always intervened—rather diplomatically—on behalf of the Prophet. For her, adopting secularism means further demystifying the transcendental process of revelation and solving all social issues through the powers of human agency, not by an uncritical resort to the male-constructed texts of Islam.

Mernissi's rereading of Islamic history—a project she considers necessary to demystify the regnant but dubious misogynist myths—can be remarkably perceptive and invigorating. If parliaments in Islamic countries are harems that exclude women from any meaningful political participation and that allow men to decide the fate of women, their roots are in the beginnings of the caliphal state, legitimized by the aristocratic principle of *bay'a* (pledge of allegiance), and in which the caliph is "veiled" from the people he governs, the *'amma* (a rather derogatory word for the masses of people, akin to what the French call "le petit peuple").[17] Through brilliant etymological connections, Mernissi stretches the symbolism of the veil to include the realm of politics, demonstrating with astonishing perspicacity the erosion of political freedoms with the consolidation of the early empires based on ethnic and gender exclusions. (Arabhood and maleness were initially indispensable criteria for the position of caliph, but though the Arabhood requirement would eventually be contested, the criterion of maleness never was.) The caliphal state (symbolized by the Friday sermon [*khotba*] and the inscription of the name of the caliph on coins) was thus to become an exclusively masculine domain, although women were allowed to rule in specific instances. However, this practice contradicted the Prophet's insistence on converting the mosque—outside prayer time—into a democratic, public space and using the Friday *khotba* as a sort of brief public report on the affairs of the state (123–27). With the advent of the caliphal state, this mosque-based popular democracy was gradually drained of its content (130, 132) and transformed into an oppressive institution for women, who were—in clear violation of the Prophet's practice—discouraged from attending mosques (136). The closing of the mosque and the veiling of women therefore amount to the closing of the political arena to democratic participation and the veiling of resistance to authoritarianism (140–41). Restoring women into the political arena thus becomes the necessary condition for the restoration of the long-eclipsed democratic spirit in Islam.

While Mernissi's reinterpretation of Islamic history does indeed challenge the unimaginative, orthodox stranglehold of the still powerful *'ulama* (religious scholars), she, like the male elites she questions, remains conspicuously silent on the bases of power at the dawn of the new millennium. If the *'ulama* are the co-opted intellectuals of feudal, patriarchal regimes in the Islamic world, late capitalism has created its own set of privileged intellectuals and theories, which, I contend, have not been sufficiently examined by Muslim feminists or Western scholars writing on feminism in the Islamic world. When Mervat Hatem, after surveying scholarship on Middle Eastern women, called Mernissi "very weak" because of her "largely unsuccessful" attempt to link "the textual with the historical" and "the sexual with the economic,"[18] she should have specified the context she was referring to, since Mernissi is, in fact, quite capable of historicizing Islamic texts. Mernissi's failure to understand "the material and social systems of particular epochs" is less likely an ideological strategy (as is the case with the *'ulama* who obfuscate meanings to marginalize women) than the result of the enormous task of conceptualizing a method to examine the various interlocking factors of oppression synchronically. Like many Muslim scholars, she states that "progressive persons of both sexes in the Muslim world know that the only weapon they can use to fight for human rights in general, and women's rights in particular, in those countries where religion is not separate from the state, is to base political claims on religious history."[19] But Hatem's suggestion that Mernissi fails to account for gender within a Marxist reading of social formations is true: by associating capitalist individualism with women's liberation, Mernissi privileges an economic system that creates precarious social spaces and imbalances that only exacerbate intellectual rigidities.[20] While Mernissi has strategically fought for the integration of women into a more democratized political process, it is now equally crucial to move beyond the false essentialization of women as ideologically neutral and examine how socioeconomic systems enhance or reduce the freedoms of both sexes in an increasingly globalized capitalist environment.

The struggle in the Islamic world today is, in fact, over democratizing decision making and wresting the state from the hands of regimes that have ossified religion and turned it into a tool of political control. Even the Islamists who now openly challenge the legitimacy of the state do not seem to object to democratic political structures, provided that they do not hinder the application of Islam.[21] In other words, despite their lack of clearly articulated readings of canonical texts and the history of Islamic societies generally, and their inability to outline a coherent vision of the future, many revivalist movements share the same general aspirations of liberating Muslim people from the dependencies imposed on them in the modern period. The widespread fear that Islam cannot open genuine spaces for democratic practice cannot be justified by historical precedent. Mernissi herself has shown—despite her occasional privileging of the pre-Islamic period—that a popular form of mosque-centered democracy existed during the Prophet's time and that it was the caliphal political system (borrowed from major pre-Islamic civilizations) that violated the early Islamic principles. Hence, depending on how it is done and from which ideological perspective, the recovery of an Islamic past, thoroughly cleansed of the residue of centuries of male-dominated interpretations, can be useful to women fighting for freedom in the Islamic world. Some of the feminists previously mentioned (such as Mernissi) have already taken the step of unveiling and studying the pages of history, and it is now the task of other Muslim and socialist feminists to build on these monumental efforts.[22]

Nawal El Saadawi's feminist and "contrapuntal" critique of Arab patriarchy was, in fact, remarkably comprehensive two decades ago, when she subjected all grand narratives to uncompromising critique without using the mantle of "culture" to disguise distinct power relations: imperialists are imperialists, and pathological Muslim men who find satisfaction in the mutilation of women's bodies are just that.[23] Like Mernissi, she implies that the orthodox version of Islam enshrined in the *Shari'a* has curtailed the freedoms and power enjoyed by women not only during the Jahiliya but also during the early stages of Islam, when women like 'Aisha, the youngest of the Prophet's wives, exercised a high degree of authority and independence (125–31). Undoubtedly, legalized clerical Islam privileged the male through the sanction of men's polygamy and the insistence on women's monogamy (which could mean the legalization of prostitution for the benefit of men); it also adopted some Christian motifs, such as the separation of body and soul, which El Saadawi views as one of the greatest afflictions of the human race, for it associates sexuality with sinfulness and tends to emphasize a cult of virginity that not infrequently leads to frigidity (149–50, 120–21). Women have thus come to be associated with *fitna* (chaos) and pleasure, which are "contradictory, and in terms of logic, mutually exclusive conceptions" (137), but which seem to have conditioned Arab men's ambiguous attitude and inhibited their adequate examination of the tragedy of women in their cultures (165, 167). The Arab man's honor, as Ben Jelloun dramatically illustrates in *The Sand Child* and *The Sacred Night,* still depends on the compliance and domination of women, although the patriarchal family is increasingly weakened by the mod-

ern state, which renders many precolonial practices and other concepts of honor impractical (207).²⁴

El Saadawi's indictment of the unholy global alliance of Western
imperialism and reactionary Islamic jurisprudence and customs to
maintain the inferior status of women is, however, complex enough
to allow for a progressive Islamic agenda. She calls on Western feminists to understand that "in underdeveloped countries, liberation
from foreign domination often still remains *the* crucial issue" and
that women in the Arab world are more interested in it than in freedom of speech and belief, "male chauvinism," or copying the social
models of affluent Western societies: "In its essence, the struggle
which is now being fought seeks to ensure that the Arab peoples take
possession of their economic potential and resources, and of their
scientific and cultural heritage so that they can develop whatever they
have to the maximum and rid themselves once and for all of the control and domination exercised by foreign capitalist interests. They
seek to build a free society with equal rights for all and to abolish the
injustices and oppression of systems based on class and patriarchal
privilege" (ix–x). Thus El Saadawi took the unfashionable stance of
seeing the Islamic revolution in Iran as essentially liberating and as
reminiscent of an "early Islam [that] laid the first foundations of
what might be called Primitive Socialism," which would later be
eclipsed by a successive line of rulers, beginning with 'Uthman Ibn
'Affan, the Third Righteous Caliph and leader of the Ummayad dy-
nasty and ending with a variety of imperialist rulers and their agents
in the Arab world (iii). Given El Saadawi's insistence on preserving
Arab people's "cultural heritage" free from the declulturing tendencies of capitalism, she calls for (and applies) a methodology that
would "visualize the links between the political, economic and social
remoulding of society, and the cultural, moral, psychological, sexual
and affective remoulding of the human being" (xvi). It is not possible, El Saadawi argues, "to separate the sexual and emotional life of
people, and their economic life," for "any separation is artificial and
will lead to ideas that are incomplete, shallow and distorted" (182).²⁵

An example of the shallow debate that has characterized the question
of feminism in Islam is the issue of the veil as a token of women's

repression; for the Western media, the picture of the veiled woman visually defines both the mystery of Islamic culture and its backwardness.[26] Despite its close association with Islam, the veil is in fact an old eastern Mediterranean practice that was assimilated by Islam in its early stages of expansion. In the two suras in the Qur'an that refer to the veil, not only is there no specific mention of veiling the face but certain parts of the body are in fact assumed to be visible.[27] Women in pre- and early-Islamic Arabia actively contributed to social and economic life; it was the gradual absorption of other civilizations into the world of Islam that eclipsed the "ethical vision" of the new religion—a vision that is "stubbornly egalitarian, including with respect to the sexes."[28] From the birth of Islam in Arabia to the rise of the Abbasids, the position of women seemed negotiable; however, as Islam expanded, non-Arab prejudices against women were written into Islamic law (many theologians who later developed and interpreted the *Shari'a* were of non-Arab stock),[29] and the egalitarian message of early Islam was conveniently forgotten. It was this "legal and social vision of establishment Islam [that] gave precedence to women's obligations to be wives and mothers."[30] Even the few misogynist elements in the *hadith* may have been influenced by Muslims' contact with Christian asceticism, especially since Islam, unlike the belief widespread in Christendom for so long, never asserted that "women have no soul."[31] It was the ancient Middle East, not Arabian customs and early Islamic practices, that provided the prototype for the harems adopted by the Abbasids and later dynasties.[32] Leila Ahmed argues that had the earlier "ethical voice" been heard, "it would have significantly tempered the extreme androcentric bias of the law, and we might today have a far more humane and egalitarian law regarding women."[33]

Still, the erosion of women's rights, enforced by a male-constructed law, did not silence or immobilize women entirely; nor were men equally content with the subordinate status of their female partners. Mernissi has written an entire book about women who rose to political leadership despite the odds against them, and Ibn Battuta, the renowned Moroccan traveler from Tangier, was impressed by the large number of women who still attended prayers in the mosque when he was in Shiraz.[34] Indeed, Afsaneh Najmabadi has convincingly demonstrated that many Iranian women (especially those from the upper class) were learned and cultured well into the modern period and that our imagining premodern Iranian women as illiterate and silent (because veiled) is a modernist distortion of traditional women's real lives. Because the orality of premodern culture required a homosocial setting where no male presence was allowed, Muslim women told their own uncensored stories, completely unconcerned with the prudish repressive values that were later ushered in with modernity.[35] Muslim women in Islamic Spain of the eleventh and twelfth centuries (who were admittedly freer than their counterparts in the East) displayed an astonishing measure of erotic freedom in their public poems and their own personal lifestyles.[36]

Even the premodern veiled women of polygamous harems were both sexually and economically freer than their European contemporaries. When Lady Mary Wortley Montagu traveled to Turkey in the eighteenth century, she wrote that she "never saw a country where women may enjoy so much liberty, and free from all reproach as in Turkey."[37] Indeed, as late as the nineteenth century, English women continued to report on the superiority of Turkish women in almost every sphere of social life, including hygiene, economics, and legal rights. In her *Women of Turkey, and Their Folklore* (1893), the first complete ethnographic study of women in the Middle East, Mary Lucy Garnet praised Muslim women and launched a bitter attack on Christian misogyny, "the Liberal state," and "the movement for universal suffrage"; she even made an astonishing critique of John Stuart Mill, who, in his *Subjection of Women,* failed to distinguish among the status of women in various cultures.[38]

The harem didn't prevent Egyptian women from conducting business and international trade within the Islamic ecumene prior to Western encroachment. Allied with the 'ulama, women exercised sufficient control over their lives "to go to courts and sue, for divorce, for business deals, for unpaid loans, i.e. for exactly the same things as men (except that men could repudiate their wives and women had to sue for divorce)." There is also evidence that some women beat their husbands and appeared "unveiled in public." With the Westernization of social institutions under Mohamed 'Ali, however, the major trade routes "to and from the Hijaz, Syria and the rest of the Ottoman

Empire" were reoriented toward Europe, eroding Muslim women's access and economic independence.[39] Similarly, although traditional, veiled women told stories with what might be considered today pornographic content while making copious references to Islamic texts to bolster their arguments, this discursive freedom was veiled by modern women who sanitized their descriptions with the help of the exalted language of science and frequent references to European writers and women. Iran's anxiety to catch up with the West led to the establishment of a new educational system privileging science and including "courses on home management, education of children, hygiene, fine arts and crafts, and [in some instances, French] cooking." The chaste woman was to become the one who propelled her country into the future, erasing obsolete traditional practices and relating to her husband the way European and American women did: "The woman of modernity, thus crafted through the construction of a veiled language and a disciplined de-eroticized body, as well as through the acquisition of scientific sensibilities, could now take her place next to her male counterpart in public heterosocial space. Instead of being envisaged as a threat to social order, her very disciplined language and body became the embodiment of the new order. Unlike her traditional Other who was scripted not only illiterate but crudely sexual, a shrew if not a whore, she could now be imagined unveiled." This hollow conception of freedom advanced by women trapped in the discourse of modernity would, ironically, be taken at face value by the Islamists in the post-1970s period, when the veil was mistakenly revalorized as the true symbol of chastity.[40] And although women's general condition has deteriorated since the advent of the caliphal state, one must make a similar effort to differentiate and sort out the good men (such as the Andalusian and Moorish philosophers Ibn al-'Arabi [1165–1240] and Ibn Rushd [1126–98]) who, in contrast to the proverbially harsh 'Umar ibn al-Khattab (the second of the four Righteous Caliphs) and the influential Khorasan-born scholar-philosopher, Abu Hamid Al-Ghazali (1058–1111), strongly argued for the emancipation of women.[41]

Hence, within the temporal and spatial world of Islam, the position of women and male attitudes toward them were determined by a variety of social factors, not least of which was ethnicity. Despite these variations, however, the fact remains that women—until the shock of European imperialism unleashed new agendas and turned them into a contentious topic of debate—had been increasingly confined in private spaces and harems and could only socialize in certain circumstances, such as in the *hammams* (public baths). It is rather tragic that the emergence of the status of women as an issue of major social concern would be ensnared by the reigning discourses of modernity and its antithetical defensive Islamic response. Often, both discourses fail to register the subtle nuances of history, and both demonstrate an inadequate grasp of the centrifugal forces that have been shattering world cultures in the modern period.

Muslim women's entrapment in a false debate may well have started, Leila Ahmed contends, with the publication of Qasim Amin's book *Tahrir al-mar'a* (The liberation of women) in 1899. Amin, who was unabashedly apologetic for European genocidal wars and colonialism, used the pretext of the veil, as the British had done before him, to launch an assault on Islam, despite Victorian England's own patriarchal attitude toward British women. The book was subsequently suspected of playing into the hands of British colonialism and its designs on Islam, and it prompted a strong defense of the veil and other un-Islamic practices as irrevocably indigenous. The publication of Amin's book and the reaction to it became a "precursor or prototype" of the ensuing debate that mired the feminist agenda in larger and more confusing issues of cultural and political sovereignty:

> Amin's book then marks the entry of the colonial narrative of women and Islam—in which the veil and the treatment of women epitomized Islamic inferiority—into mainstream Arabic discourse. And the opposition it generated similarly marks the emergence of an Arabic narrative developed in resistance to the colonial narrative. The veil came to symbolize in the resistance narrative, not the inferiority of the culture and the need to cast aside its customs in favor of those of the West, but, on the contrary, the dignity and validity of all native customs coming under attack—the customs relating to women—and the need to tenaciously affirm them as a means of resistance to Western domination.[42]

European hostility and Orientalism, then, fundamentalize Islam into a defensive orthodoxy and largely dictate the cultural agenda of the Muslim peoples, since "it is Western discourse that in the first place determined the new meanings of the veil and gave rise to its emergence as a symbol of resistance."[43] The process of Western hegemony stimulates reactionary tendencies within Islamic cultures and delays women's emancipation from the clutches of clerical Islam. Because the most privileged and Westernized classes in Arab society eagerly surrendered to the cultural imperialism that was an integral part of the colonial process, the disinherited masses resorted to Islamic doctrine, even the most obscurantist practices, as a form of resistance to the perceived onslaught on their identity. Positions were thus dangerously polarized and hardened.

That it was Egyptian and Iranian upper-class women who first condemned native customs as backward, proclaimed the superiority of the West, and uncompromisingly equated unveiling with liberation is not only historically ironic but also revealing of the class structure of the Islamic world today. Many upper-class women who advocate unveiling may only be interested in conforming to trends in international fashion (since it is not clear that Western dress has any practical value besides its symbolism), which, like the veil of old, is inaccessible to the poor. While the class appropriation of veiling has shifted from the upper classes to the lower ones, the meaning and symbolism of a woman's dress in the Islamic world today is still determined by regional attitudes, inherited legacies, and the negotiation of identity within the hegemonic structures of capitalism. In any case, whether veiled or not, women's conditions are determined not by the clothes they wear but by the degree to which they manage to forge an identity for themselves outside the (often male-constructed) discourses of modernity or religious authenticity.

When, on January 8, 1936, Reza Shah Pahlevi (r. 1921–41) decreed compulsory unveiling in public places, associating Muslim women's traditional attire with residual backwardness, he mindlessly "inflicted pain and terror" on many women accustomed to the symbolism of the veil.[44] Although unveiling women was then seen as a symbolic act of the nation's resolve to catch up with modernity, the oil-based "sultanistic state" of Muhammad Reza Shah, no longer relying on its traditional base of support among social elites, simply resorted to repression in order to accomplish the same goal of modernization. Under this regime, women's rights became royal grants.[45] The revolt against the dictatorial powers of the late Shah was thus accompanied by a general repudiation of the icons of Western culture, once again leading nativists to associate veiling with the fight against imperialism. As Iran has tried to come to terms with the challenge of the West for more than a century, and as state ideologies of emancipation have shifted from nationalist modernity to sultanistic authoritarianism to "the moral purification of a corrupt society,"[46] women's status has been determined largely by the confrontation between the changing images of a hegemonic West and a defensive Islam. This larger conflict has complicated the agenda for Muslim women, and in this seemingly interminable civilizational tension Muslim feminists find themselves caught, as Leila Ahmed eloquently puts it, between the two "opposing loyalties" of sex and culture, "forced almost to choose between betrayal and betrayal."[47]

Decreeing veiling or unveiling, however, does not make women willingly transform themselves overnight, en masse, for the sake of new ideologies.[48] Like the many women today who have resisted veiling and continue to read it from a modernist perspective, some early Islamic feminists resisted the ideologies of modernity by arguing for a gradualist approach. Claiming that it was still premature to do away with the veil, given men's unenlightened attitudes and upper-class women's interest in (Western) fashion only, feminists such as Malak Hifna Nassef (1886–1918) focused on promoting education and abolishing polygamy.[49] If this discourse of Islamic "female affirmation"—widely shared by influential Islamic organizations such as the Muslim Brethren—is still, according to Ahmed, "mostly unchronicled,"[50] it may be because the dominating currents of Western feminism partake in many of the assumptions of Western secularism and Orientalist legacies, as well as other liberal bourgeois values (such as a dehistoricized notion of human rights and an implicit acceptance of the bourgeois political apparatus as a reliable mechanism for negotiating the grievances of the exploited).

In its reappearance in the past two decades, however, the veil has acquired a new symbolism and cannot be read within the set of symbolic earlier binarisms described by Najmabadi. In countries where the veil is not mandated, many women choose it both as a reaction to the failed bourgeois nationalist program of the postindependence era (although there is still a great deal of male coercion) and as part of the mainstream, middle-class rejection of the secular ideologies that have dominated public life. Veiling cannot, in these historical circumstances, "be constructed as regressive" and must be seen as the younger women's recuperation and affirmation of their heretofore marginalized identity. Islamic dress is "the uniform of arrival," the latest stage in a long struggle against colonialism and the postcolonial elites who, although politically secular, continue to impose a false Islamic orthodoxy on the people they govern.[51] The veil is a reminder that most Islamic societies are still part of the global neocolonial order and that the collective process of liberation through the recuperation of a mutilated identity is far from complete. The response the veil elicits is thus largely a symbolic statement about continuing class struggle in the Islamic world: hence Leila Ahmed's call for the same multilayered, anti-imperialist position already practiced by feminists such as Nawal El Saadawi.

This feminist position, however, requires an examination of the validity of secularism as a project in the Islamic world and, as El Saadawi recently argued, the demystification of a new hegemonic terminology that includes such words as *democracy, human rights,* and *civil society.*[52] While establishing a secular political structure finally may not be problematic (for as long as it remains a technical matter and does not infringe on basic Islamic values it is not likely to elicit much resistance), the secularization of the Revelation and of the Prophet's life have been universally rejected, if not condemned by the Islamic world (as the case of Rushdie amply demonstrates), and cannot be the basis of any emancipatory social movement in the Arab and Islamic worlds. Secular structures fit badly in cultures in which human agency is constantly negotiating its boundaries with those of the Revelation, in which accommodation to divine intent is a fundamental principle. But this is precisely the agenda of secular elites in remolding Islamic countries, and, because of it, a new form of Orientalism has emerged to equate the re-Islamization of secularized discourses with extremism. I began this book by questioning the validity of secularism as a global project, although it is well known that the concept is the intellectual product of a specific moment in European history. Moreover, even fewer scholars have examined the imperialist connotations of the epistemology of secularism that Abdulwahab al Masseri has cogently exposed:

> Secularism is not a separation between religion and the state, as propagated in both western and Arab writing. Rather, it is the removal of absolute values—epistemological and ethical—from the world such that the entire world—humanity and nature alike— becomes merely a utilitarian object to be utilized and subjugated. From this standpoint, we can see the structural similarity between the secular epistemological vision and the imperialist epistemological vision. We can also realize that imperialism is no more than the exporting of a secular and epistemological paradigm from the western world, where it first emerged, to the rest of the world.[53]

At a time when the reigning ideology of capitalism has desacralized all of human life for the sake of a destructive acquisitiveness, the need to open up noncapitalist spaces is more urgent than ever. The insistence on establishing an alternative social imaginary makes Islam appear as the perennial threat it has always been, especially since it has become quite clear that the nationalist secularist model of the postindependence period has utterly failed to emancipate the people and is now seen as a dismal failure.[54] Even in Turkey, the oldest secular Muslim society, the ideology of secularism continues to exist only because it is enforced by the military.[55]

Dominant Western secular ideologies could be questioned and resisted where viable traditions of social organization can lay the framework for a more humane and egalitarian society. If Islam is increasingly seen as the enduring example of this alternative, then a vigilant resistance to the sort of monolithism persistently denounced by Edward Said and to the partriarchal extremism that seeks to subvert the progressive and prophetic essence of Islam must continue to guide all attempts at emancipatory reform. For Islam is primarily a cosmopolitan culture that, since its inception, has preached the sort of ethnic and religious tolerance that many Western societies are still trying to achieve,[56] although it has long failed to eradicate certain social and political inequities based on class, gender, and religion. In fact, the upheaval that Islam underwent with the advent of European colonialism may have strained social relations further and exacerbated un-Islamic patriarchal practices, for colonial subjects were bewildered by two worldviews and could only escape the resulting confusion either by embracing one or the other, or by vacillating in the middle and never formulating a position of their own.

The institutionalization of the nation-state (an outcome of a secular epistemology) is in itself a form of cultural aggression against Islam and other cultures that share in the communal traditions of kinship and honor. Furthermore, the nation-state has had catastrophic effects on much of the Third World, where thousands of culturally autonomous communities were tyrannized by dictatorships and parasitic bureaucracies, often financed and upheld by metropolitan centers. Indeed, no agency has succeeded in oppressing the peoples of the Third World more successfully than the state, with its wide-reaching apparatuses of social and political control and its affiliation with international organizations designed to further the conquest of the poor through debt and other economic schemes. The case of the Arab Gulf states, in all their mythical splendor, is a concrete illustration of this new world order in which natural wealth, if not carefully managed by scrupulous financiers, leads inexorably to dependency and erodes the simple but self-sufficient economies that once granted autonomy to these societies.[57] The rejection of certain Western secular models in the age of late capitalism is consequently a survival imperative for Muslim people, not just a fanatical reaction to "progress."

Yet, despite its enduring strengths, Islam is now incontestably challenged by the universalized ideology of modernity and cannot resist its interpellating discourses simply by rationalizing the *Shari'a* or by proving the infallibility of the Qur'an in the Revelation's consistency with modern scientific discoveries.[58] The resumption of *ijtihad* and the differentiation of the ethico-religious from the existing socioeconomic (in the granting of equal divorce rights and the elimination of polygamy) appear to be necessary steps in creating a more equitable and inclusive public space for Muslim women. The restoration of what John Esposito calls "the dynamic relationship of *ijtihad* and *ijma* [consensus],"[59] which to me suggests innovation within tradition, is an equally urgent undertaking to avoid other superficial configurations and can only be achieved through an indigenous and progressive educational system, not the bifurcated one that has disoriented students and alienated the ruling elites from the people they govern. Esposito contends that "Islamic history, if correctly understood, has a lesson for the conservatives and reformers. It offers a picture of a dynamic, changing, adaptive religious tradition. A fuller appreciation of the real as well [as] idealized Islamic past can provide the understanding and means or methodology for Islamic responses to the challenge of modernity as Muslims once more repeat the process of Islamization—to develop a viable political, legal, and economic model of society and to draw on all available data and practices, but to do so in light of the *Qur'anic* principles and values."[60]

Esposito's recommendation, however, may well entail a critical reading of the *Shari'a* itself, which has been the basis of gender relations and classical family law and has also been codified and jealously guarded by conservative religious scholars (*'ulama*) since the tenth century. Despite the undeniable progressive elements in early Islam (acknowledged by El Saadawi, Ahmed, Mernissi, Walther, and others), the *Shari'a*, largely unquestioned to this day, has continued to enforce the prevailing traditional roles of women. This may be why Mernissi anticipated that social struggles in the Arab world will be over civil rights.[61] The problem is that proponents of this political alternative assume that bourgeois democracy (a participatory or parliamentary system that implies the existence of classes vying for political control) is inherently liberating, even though the ideology of pluralism can be manipulated to contain oppositional and democratic forces in much of the Third World.[62] Arguing for civil rights as a reliable basis for a legitimate feminist movement in the Islamic world today not only dismisses the weight of tradition and culture (and thus paradoxically partakes in the same antihistoricism of which Islam is accused) but also discourages any attempt to conceptualize and build genuine movements of resistance to what Von Laue called the "global revolution of Westernization."

The proposition that religion and state be separated is a tenuous one in the world of Islam, for its impact would be superficial and would benefit—as it has until now—only those superficially Westernized elites who have maintained patriarchal regimes in the Arab world and beyond. Still, Arab states have not been able to adhere fully to the text of the 1948 Universal Declaration of Human Rights (UDHR) because the tension between, on the one hand, Islamic teachings and the religious principles of the *Shari'a* and, on the other, the legitimization of individual human rights in a secular framework of social relations proved, in the long run, to be irresolvable. In her detailed study of major Islamic documents dealing with human rights issues, Ann Elizabeth Mayer concludes that, despite the fact that Islam initially provided unprecedented rights to women, all the Islamic documents dealing with human rights fail to elevate women to an equal status with men and fail to meet the basic standards of the UDHR and the Convention on the Elimination of All Forms of Discrimination against Women (CEDAW).[63] To the extent that Mayer suspects patriarchal, neocolonial regimes of concocting these "schemes" in order to stifle dissent (163, 177) and to legitimize, through the deceptive use of modern terminology, the archaic Islamic tenets of the *Shari'a,* her argument remains persuasive. However, when she avoids any meaningful discussion of either the last eight articles in the UDHR dealing with economic rights or the utter failure of Western capitalist societies to implement other "human rights" documents such as the International Covenant on Economic, Social, and Cultural Rights (1966), she privileges the monadic, nebulous individual supposedly free from physical coercion by the state but trapped in an economic system that distorts the meaning of humanity, freedom, and happiness.

I am not implying that the political is absolutely and mechanistically determined by the economic (a margin of autonomy always exists,[64] but whether it works in the interests of the working class and the poor is still not clear). I too think that expanding the sphere of political freedom is still strategically indispensable, but to regard this as an end in itself, or to assume that political rights (freedom to vote, etc.) will be translated into better social conditions is an unproven proposition, especially in this advanced epoch of capitalism characterized by relentless corporate warfare on the working classes and by the accelerated depletion of natural and life-sustaining resources. Marx himself preferred democracy to other political systems, but he had no doubt that freedom of contract under postslavery capitalism was still a form of enslavement. In *The Holy Family* (1845), he explained this paradox succinctly: "The *slavery of civil society* is *in appearance* the greatest *freedom* because it is in appearance the fully developed *independence* of the individual, who considers as his *own* freedom the uncurbed movement, no longer bound by a common bond or by man, of the estranged elements of his life, such as property, industry, religion, etc., whereas actually this is his fully developed slavery and inhumanity."[65] This tension between freedom and exploitation is precisely the reason Marx thought capitalism irredeemable, and envisioned communism as the most civilized system of human relations.

If the crisis of the Muslim is one of identity, the solution does not lie in accepting a bourgeois definition of the human, but in examining the historical and cultural background of the prevailing (Western) capitalist equation of the individual with what Suad Joseph called in a different context an "autonomous, contract-making self," where the "self" is conceived of as property.[66] Mayer herself, who makes detailed and legalistic (i.e., textual) comparative analyses of Islamic and Western laws, concludes that the current notion of international human rights is based on "Western traditions of individualism, humanism, and rationalism and on legal principles protecting individual rights."[67] The indifference to Islamic law in the drafting of international human rights documents was probably prompted by the West's assumption of its own superiority and by the fact that "Islam is overwhelmingly the religion of Third World countries" (39). Although for Mayer the topic of Islam is still mired in historical antagonisms—the secondary literature on human rights is too weak to elucidate the issues and "dealing with Islam is like stepping into a minefield" (14)—she is convinced that "Islam is not the cause of the human rights problem endemic to the Middle East" (xvii). However, instead of tackling the epistemological and ontological differences that fuel the tension between the Islamic and Western views of society and the individual, she devotes most of her book to criticizing mostly obscure officially sponsored documents for failing to be consistent

with the international laws ratified by Islamic governments. There is
no mention of the complicity of Western governments in supporting
undemocratic regimes and no examination of the unequal distribution of power at the United Nations; in short, Mayer's legalistic approach in comparing texts (although this is a strategy she uses to
enlarge the sphere of freedoms in Islamic societies) turns her book
into an ahistorical analysis that does not elucidate the tensions between the West and Islam.

For instance, Mayer fails to examine how the notion of the "individual" in Islam is inextricably tied to the spiritual and socioeconomic welfare of the community, as Mahmood Monshipouri has
shown: "The atomized and 'private' individual, abstracted from the
social and political context of his or her surroundings, is a product of
the rationalizing aspects of modernization and the spread of science
and technology."[68] Or, as al Masseri further explains, the "individual,"
according to the model propagated by Western capitalism, is

> a set of abstract needs defined specifically by monopolies, advertise-
> ment and fashion companies, and by several entertainment indus-
> tries. In this context, the individual is no more than a unit reduced to
> a receptor of heavy instructions from public institutions that have no
> individuality and no value other than augmenting profit. These in-
> stitutions resemble an absolute state that has appointed itself as an
> absolute power and that has remodelled individuals so that they
> could play the roles or perform the functions assigned to them. To
> talk of human rights (in the abstract) is, therefore, to continue the
> original assault on the intermediary institutions that began in the
> Renaissance and left humanity completely naked before the state and
> its institutions.[69]

Although Monshipouri dismisses the pressure of the West on Islamic societies as a simplistic form of cultural imperialism that rests
on "the amorphous assumption of value diffusionism," he proposes
that only an internal evolution that emphasizes economic rights is
likely to work. Such a system would be consistent with the aspirations
of Third World peoples, expressed in the New International Economic Order (NIEO), and with the fundamental precepts of Islam.
"Muslim perspectives on universal human rights," he points out,

"have traditionally revolved more around themes of social justice than of individual freedoms." Indeed, like many Marxists who have advocated a synthesis of civil and economic rights, Monshipouri argues for an entente between Islam and the secular West: "In the final analysis, just as the Islamic views and traditions on certain fundamental human rights ought to evolve in keeping with the modern world, so too the Western liberal traditions (those belonging to the Lockean praxis) must be complemented by necessary additions compatible with the global evolution of economic rights."[70]

Muslim identity, as Dwyer's interview with mostly Muslim Arab intellectuals revealed (see chapter 2), is often privileged over individual rights. Since, in Islam, "the conceptual basis [of rights] is teleological and their ethical foundation theological,"[71] the boundaries of individual freedom are determined not by secular law but by divine decree. Even the idea of freedom itself is defined by Mahmoud Mohamed Taha in transcendental terms as being primarily secure in one's innermost being.[72] The rights to autonomous identity and self-determination have solidified the Arab states' position—despite their varying degrees of involvement in the reigning international order—toward the Western-inspired human rights charter precisely because bourgeois democracies assume the sovereignty of the individual, not the community.[73] The incompatibility of Islamic principles and secular assumptions, together with the Third World's resistance to Western hegemonic aims, complicated the 1993 Conference on Human Rights in Vienna, although minorities and particularly women seem to have benefited from an expanded definition of rights.[74] It is perhaps not surprising, given the current definition of human rights in the West, that women would emerge as beneficiaries while entire peoples do not have the right to determine their own cultural and economic agendas.[75]

For this reason, neocolonialists will continue—partly through the agency of individualism—to discredit non-Western conceptions of rights, and the debate over feminism in Islam will continue to be implicated in larger ideological struggles. But remembering that gender and gender difference are products of history, and are "reproduced through complex moralities, idioms and structures,"[76] may allow the feminist agenda to take center stage now and not wait, as

Iranian feminist Nayereh Tohidi cautions us against, until "the days after the revolution," or the time—which has yet to dawn—when ideological and cultural binarisms (colonizer/colonized) are dismantled. To chart out an acceptable "cartography" of struggle, feminists need to engage Dorothy Smith's "relations of ruling" strategy, which designates a totalizing approach to the multifarious but interlocking practices of power.[77] (However, I still do not think that Tohidi's Western secular model of social relations is ultimately effective in Islamic societies.)[78]

Gender hierarchies were more fluid in the precolonial period.[79] To claim that Islam is essentially undemocratic and "patriarchal" is ideologically suspect, because it freezes the history of Muslim peoples and downplays the impact of imperialism on gender relations in Islamic countries.[80] The recent popularity of civil society as "the new analytical tool that will unlock the mysteries of the social order" has not only obscured the cultural foundations of this concept in European Reason and Christian Revelation, it also dangerously posits the duplication of very specific cultural evolutions in Western Europe and the United States in parts of the world that have undergone different historical experiences and whose populations respond to different markers of identity. It assumes the inevitability of capitalism as a system of social relations, since "it was in the modern era, with the nascent capitalist economy and the freeing of the individual from traditional and communal ties, that the problem of squaring individual and social goods and desiderata achieved a new saliency. The modern ideas of civil society developed by Locke, Ferguson, Smith, and Hutcheson (and, and to some extent, Shaftesbury) were all attempts to posit a solution to the new problem of the social order that emerged at the end of the seventeenth century."[81] Moreover, the notion of civil society "is based on a gendered distinction between public [male] and private [female] domain," and "is now being challenged in the West by feminists and people of color." Consequently, "its uncritical application to Third World countries and the uncritical use of the relative existence of components of civil society as measures of 'modernity' or progress are highly problematic."[82]

While women are inevitably caught up in the "political-cultural battleground" of Muslim societies, and all "political and cultural projects are gendered,"[83] there is no reason to believe that secularized discourses are indispensable for the emancipation of women from a male-dominated Islam. The case of Algeria is a glaring instance of how secular modernization in the postindependence period has been primarily mimetic, restricted to a vacuous political discourse, since the Family Code, based on the precepts of the *Shari'a*, has continued to regulate gender and family relations. Cherifa Bouatta and Doria Cherifati-Merabitine present the *moudjahidates* (women who valiantly fought for independence) as symbols of the Algerian woman who was betrayed by the promise of the revolution.[84] But contrary to Bouatta's implication, it was the postcolonial secular system that permitted the marginalization of women by maintaining the supremacy of men. Women were to be legitimated as equals not through secular legislative measures (although the Algerian Constitution affirmed women's equality) but through their heroic struggle against French imperialism. If they were able to conquer previously closed (because sacralized) spaces, it was because the regressive codes of a failed patriarchal Islam had so clearly failed to defend the country.[85] In other words, it was the national struggle against imperialism that brought women out of their confined, privatized social spaces into the public sphere, where their contributions would be crucial for the liberation of Algeria. It is not clear at all that the modernist project embraced by the secular elites immediately after independence included a concrete agenda for the relinquishing of male privilege and the sharing of social and political responsibilities with women.[86] And that has been so not because of a deliberate conspiracy but because of the contradictory nature of the Algerian society in the postcolonial period. Political will, in this case, has not been able to eradicate a more profoundly entrenched culture of Islam and kinship. And it is partly this irresolvable contradiction that has thrown Algeria in its current impasse.

The failure of both modernist ideologies and clerical Islam indicates the need for a third way that is both indigenous and progressive, a way that was charted out by Mahmoud Mohamed Taha in his still largely unread manifesto *The Second Message of Islam*. Taha's argument is serious and, if widely discussed, might provoke a debate rooted in what John Esposito calls "a consistent Islamic rationale."[87] Taha and his disciple Abdullahi Ahmed An-Na'im, however, go further than any mainstream reformist to call for the total elimination of the *Shari'a* (since it is inherently inegalitarian and patriarchal and cannot be altered beyond certain limits) and the creation of a new law based on Meccan Revelation (i.e., before the Prophet's flight [*hijra*] to Yathrib, later Medina, an event that inaugurated the Islamic calendar, and that, in Mernissi's view, set back the freedoms of women and reinstated them at point zero in history). Although extremely controversial, such an arrangement would not necessarily be un-Islamic, for the *Shari'a* is "a situational, not a transcendental law."[88] If the Revelation could adapt to the specific historical period of Arabia's transition into a new Islamic order, then it makes little intellectual sense to canonize the interpretations of orthodox *'ulama* into an antihistorical immutability. Both Taha and An-Na'im use the method of *naskh* (abrogation) to retrieve the earlier, abrogated verses of the Meccan Revelation, which (unlike the later, ethnic-specific messages revealed to the Prophet during the process of *umma*-building) are more egalitarian and universal in spirit.[89] Taha's "Second Message" is an Islamically derived critique of both the stagnation of Islamic scholarship and the failure of "industrialized Western civilization . . . to reconcile the needs of the individual with the needs of the community." The first message of Islam was the preparatory phase (including the gentle censorship of certain unacceptable practices and the implicit maintenance of others) for the eventual emancipation of all peoples through a revolutionary reading of the Qur'an. This, according to Taha, is the only solution for enlightened Muslims who reject both orthodox interpretations of Islam and the corrosive program of Western secularism. As An-Na'im says in the introduction to Taha's book, the best way to combat the obscurantism of Islamic extremism today is not through an equally irrational recourse to secular ideology but through reforms that "would make Islam a viable modern ideology." Taha's conception of the "Good Society" as economically socialistic, politically democratic, and founded on the equality of men and women is both consistent with Islamic principles and the only way out of the cultural impasse facing Muslims today.[90]

In his book on civil rights and international law in Islamic societies, Abdullahi An-Na'im states, at the outset, that the reconstructed *Shari'a* should be based on the same Islamic foundations, since "Islamic identity" is "essential for the political viability of the proposed reforms." An-Na'im even reads the actual Islamic resurgence as an expression of "the right to self-determination," including the (misguided) attempt to reinstate the *Shari'a* as the binding law in social relations. Yet the historical *Shari'a* is proving too inflexible to meet the legitimate aspirations of women within the political framework of the nation-state (whose existence An-Na'im takes for granted, for it seems that the concept "is now firmly and irrevocably established throughout the Muslim world"), which means that the *Shari'a*, not being divine, must be challenged from within an Islamic context if women and religious minorities are to enjoy their constitutional rights as citizens and members of a nation-state. Adopting the "principle of reciprocity," or the golden rule that "one should treat other people as he or she wishes to be treated by them," as the "common normative principle" of universal standards of human rights will help extend "those rights to which human beings are entitled by virtue of being human" to historically marginalized segments of the population.[91] Since the *Shari'a*'s sanction of slavery and discrimination on the grounds of religion and gender conflict with these basic principles, Islam is harmed by its continued unmodified implementation.

Although I am not sure I agree with An-Na'im's premise that the nation-state will (or should) endure as a form of political and social organization in the Islamic world and elsewhere, I share his criticism of Western governments for not laying the groundwork for the execution of the lofty principles they preach and for refusing to eradicate the conditions of inequality, within both their metropolitan centers and semi-colonies. Any agenda that seeks the emancipation of women in the Islamic world must examine the implications of its program at a variety of interlocking levels if it is not to be co-opted by the dehumanizing effects of the global capitalist system. In this case, a positive sense of identity works to ensure continued resistance to the destructive effects of commodity culture.[92]

Now, then, is the time to dispel the entrenched belief that the religion of Islam acts as a barrier to women's fulfillment outside men's arbitrary control, and to acknowledge that it is a male-manipulated interpretation of Islam, often encoded in an unexamined *Shari'a*, that has allowed Orientalist prejudices to persist in the West and among Westernized Muslim elites.[93] A thoroughly redefined Islam, in dynamic relation with other cultures, must be preserved as a viable alternative to both Westernization and extremist religious practices, both of which ultimately threaten the Islamic cultures that sustain the identities of women and men equally. While the term *Islam* itself may evoke strong (mostly negative) reactions among Westernized Muslims, feminism must still be understood as "a mode of intervention into *particular* hegemonic discourses" and not as a universal response to an assumed universal patriarchy.[94] The common denominator of victimization that certain Western feminists have ascribed cross-culturally erases the complexities, pluralities, and historical specificities of different cultures; its monolithic assumptions are therefore akin to those of Orientalism. This is why "sisterhood cannot be assumed on the basis of gender" but "must be forged in concrete historical and political practice and analysis."[95] Moreover, as Lazreg has put it, "to think of feminism in the singular is sociologically inappropriate."[96]

The egalitarianism inherent in what Leila Ahmed calls "the ethical voice of Islam" is one reason "Muslim women frequently insist, often inexplicably to non-Muslims, that Islam is not sexist. They hear and read in its sacred text, justly and legitimately, a different message from that heard by the makers and enforcers of orthodox, androcentric Islam."[97] This voice needs to be retrieved through a progressive reading of the *Shari'a* and the resurrection of *ijtihad* as the basic core of a dynamic Islamic scholarship. The Prophet's wives (despite the highly publicized portions of Rushdie's *Satanic Verses*, which may appear to be outrageously demeaning to women) could stand as a new model of womanhood in Islam, for it is now well known that several of his wives challenged male supremacy and, as widows, took an active interest in public and political affairs. Several, such as 'Aisha, Umm Salama, and Umm Habiba, were renowned for their "intellectual qualities," and 'Aisha is said to have been one of the principal sources of 2210 *hadiths*.[98] In short, once it becomes clear that "there is a general thrust towards equality of the sexes in the

Quran [*sic*]" and that several verses, such as the (in)famous one on polygamy were "contextual" justifications, not "normative" ones, and that therefore their "applicability must be seen as dated, not for all times to come," a progressive reform can proceed simultaneously with the harnessing of energy needed to resist the increasing marginalization of the world of Islam and the Third World generally. And because the Qur'an intervenes rather ambiguously in the social sphere,[99] the forms of social relations would be negotiable if men were to be guided (forced?) back to the true spirit of Islam, long frozen into a debilitating orthodoxy.

This process has begun in parts of the Islamic world. Even in the Islamic Republic of Iran, a country governed by a male clerical elite, there is now a thriving intellectual debate over how to challenge repressive laws from within the Islamic tradition itself. Incredible as it may sound, "no other group has been as determined and resourceful in challenging the various economic, social and cultural obstacles that have been placed in its way as have been Iranian women under the Islamic Republic."[100] Emerging Islamic feminists in Iran are challenged "to maintain a delicate balance between reclaiming a national identity, reaffirming progressive elements of the indigenous culture, and the struggle to create a democratic, just, and coherently developed society."[101] Interestingly, this approach, as Ziba Mir-Hosseini has demonstrated, can be more effective in societies where Islamic identity itself is secure, "where Islam is no longer part of the oppositional discourse in national politics." Following her illuminating study of the feminist journal *Zanan*, Mir-Hosseini concludes that distinctions between the *Shari'a* and the temporal laws of the government, a new separation of realms (state versus religion), is opening up new spaces of Islamic opposition to the very government that rules in the name of Islam. Paradoxically, "what made such a shift possible is the Islamic Republic's ideological understanding of Islam, which opens the way to challenging the hegemony of the orthodox interpretive process."[102] Once the fundamental identity and cultural worldview of Muslims is no longer threatened by non-Muslim hegemonic ideologies, textual interpretation is deployed by progressive Islamic elements to challenge the clerics that now rule in the name of a revolutionary, anti-imperialist Islam. Having entered educational institutions and the workforce in unprecedented numbers, many Iranian women, wearing the Islamic dress, have submitted their candidacy for high political office (including the presidency), and many have joined ranks with other Muslim reformers who are calling for no less than the dismantling of the theocratic state, the cornerstone of the ruling regime's ideology.[103] Indeed, the scope of the Islamic feminist movement is so large and thoroughly revolutionary that it may well be one of the best platforms from which to resist the effects of global capitalism and contribute to a rich, egalitarian polycentric world.

When the Moroccan writer Leila Abouzeid captured the hypocrisy of the postcolonial ruling classes in her novella *Year of the Elephant* by exposing the predicament of Zahra, a traditional guerrilla fighter against French colonialism who is repudiated by her husband upon independence for a younger, more modern woman, she made her protagonist seek strength in tradition and Islam, not in some ill-digested and amorphous ideology of modernity without resonance among the people.[104] Contrary to Tahar ben Jelloun's suggestion in *The Sand Child* and *The Sacred Night,* Abouzeid defines Morocco's nationalist movement of resistance to colonialism as a liberating epoch for women; it is modernized national elites who have subverted this potentially egalitarian project by pursuing the mirage of Westernization in the postcolonial era. Despite her profound disillusionment, Abouzeid's protagonist, Zahra, continues to pray, wear the *djellaba,* and, as a committed revolutionary, to wait for the day when the world's cultures are finally able to negotiate their destinies in their own vocabularies.

Conclusion

Indispensable Polycentricity

What we can do is destroy the myths which, more than money or weapons, constitute the most formidable obstacles in the way of the reconstruction of human societies.
—Cornelius Castoriadis, *Philosophy, Politics, Autonomy*

The late Cornelius Castoriadis brought many useful reminders to scholars attached to mythical certainties, especially those who have frozen the West into an unchanging cultural essence. He not only shows through his vast erudite reading of ancient Greek texts that Greek democracy rested on the ability to question all social dogmas, including self-generated ones, but his readings also reveal that ancient Greeks were the first to develop an interest in "others," a feature that he doesn't hesitate to characterize as fundamentally Greco-Western. "As far as we know," he states, "only two societies, the Ancient Greek and the Western European, have developed a genuine interest in others *as* others and attempted to attain a knowledge and an understanding of their ways of being."[1] Knowing the other *as* other, without deploying this knowledge for self-serving uses, such as conquest, meant that the world must be seen as one in its diversity. The Greek project of "autonomy" ensured against ethnic complacencies by including the realms of geography and historiography into the larger realm of philosophy. The ancient Greeks understood that the *eidos* of a society (the unique and irreplaceable spirit of a culture in history)² is unrecoverable, "that each social-historical form is truly and genuinely singular," and that "language bears and conveys the whole of the life of a society and a substantial part of its 'history.'" Hence translations or even philosophical speculations about different cultures are stamped with inescapable prejudices. Such a limitation, however, should not dissuade scholars from trying to know others, only to understand that "an essential lacunarity" in their work is an inevitable by-product of the unbridgeable gaps that separate cultures.

Reexamining the etymological roots of prevailing cultural paradigms and readopting the Greek principles of autonomy ("unlimited interrogation" of everything and anything) will inevitably complicate the certainties that fuel the clash-of-cultures thesis. In ancient Greece, concepts were never sealed and frozen for the rest of history, but were kept in a fluid state of incompleteness; the "adoration of the *fait accompli* [was] unknown and impossible as an attitude of the mind [*esprit*]," and only began to appear in the new political climate of the Stoics. Thus the recovery of "autonomy" as a project could help reawaken scholars to the limitations of prevailing prejudices perpetuated by unchanging discourses (Orientalism, culturalism, and secularism) and encourage the reimagining of new forms of otherness, new diversities capable of sustaining world cultures in a postcapitalist phase of human development.

Muslims, including many *mujtahids* (creative scholars), are also challenged to conceive of such a world if they want their religion to have any global relevance in the future. The much exalted notion of *ijtihad*, while certainly indispensable, does not, in and of itself, guarantee the articulation of an Islamic project firmly committed to global polycentricity, since any intellectual effort remains inescapably trapped—whether consciously or not—within the ideological parameters that inform it. Though many social issues (such as women's freedom and the rights of minorities) need to be addressed without doing violence to the *eidos* of Islamic societies, no progressive Islamic outlook is finally credible without taking into account the economic forces that have shaped world cultures in the last few centuries and that imperil the cultural foundations of all societies in this new millennium. The unending saga of the modern conflict between the

presumed homogeneous entities of the West and Islam is shaped by
the emergence of capitalism and cannot be understood without taking this context into consideration. It would be impossible to understand the rise of Eurocentrism (the belief that European "values" are
the culmination of history and that "others" are backward and need
European intervention or knowledge) if the world-shattering event
of the rise of Europe following the conquest of America in 1492 is not
acknowledged. The Eurocentric diffusionist geography has polarized
the world into an all-competent inside (Greater Europe) and empty
outside (Others). Hence others need European know-how, even if
that means direct intervention or neocolonial models of modernization.[3] Such a belief has been necessary to justify the colonization of
peoples since that auspicious date, for it was the exploitation of the
American continent that decidedly catapulted Europe onto the world
stage as a major economic and later industrial power. The relative
parities that had prevailed among the three continents until then
(and which, according to Eric Wolf, extended into the late eighteenth
century) were now permanently broken in favor of Europe and its
extensions overseas. Beginning in 1492, Europe began to move from a
sluggish, protocapitalist economy to a capitalist revolution because
the huge amounts of American wealth infused into its economy eventually undercut competing industries in the eastern hemisphere. Pre-
cious metals, plantation economies, extra European labor, and the
expansion of European trade in extra European colonies allowed for
the "centration of capitalism in Europe" (197). European colonialism
prepared the ground for both the bourgeois (Glorious) and Industrial revolutions, further strengthening global polarizations and establishing the uneven development inherent in the capitalist mode of
production (206).

The world cultures that had been connected through trade in the
precapitalist or tributary period were overwhelmed by the capitalist
mode of production based on the exploitation of labor for the transformation of natural resources into commodities and were gradually
integrated into the emerging global system.[4] Displaced European
peasants and farmers, indentured Chinese and Indians were added to
African Americans who had just been liberated from slavery to seek
their fortunes as wage laborers in an industrial system that requires

flexibility to maximize its rates of profit. At a time when tough Euro-American anti-immigration laws continue to be implemented, it helps to remember that "an estimated 50 million people [mostly dispossessed workers, peasants, and squeezed-out cultivators] left Europe permanently between 1800 and 1914" (363). The United States absorbed most of these immigrants and created, in the process, new social conditions that have become the subject of intense debates in recent years. The various nationalities, ethnic groups, and even races (if one is willing to accept such a notion) that have made the United States a plural society, and that now constitute the main actors in the still unsettled multicultural debates, are all effects of the earlier phases of capitalism.[5] As with the various "post-al" theories, to leave out the analysis of capitalism as a system of social relations and the displacement of international labor in the process of capital accumulation from any meaningful discussion of identity politics in the United States is to overlook the true force behind ethnic diversity and ignore the major centrifugal element in American demographics. In *Europe and the People without History,* Eric Wolf concludes that

> Capitalist accumulation thus continues to engender new working classes in widely dispersed areas of the world. It recruits these working classes from a wide variety of social and cultural backgrounds, and inserts them into variable political and economic hierarchies. The new working classes change these hierarchies by their presence, and are themselves changed by the forces to which they are exposed. On one level, therefore, the diffusion of the capitalist mode creates everywhere a wider unity through the constant reconstitution of its characteristic capital-labor relationship. On another level, it also creates diversity, accentuating social opposition and segmentation even as it unifies. Within an ever more integrated world, we witness the growth of ever more diverse proletarian diasporas. (383)

I raise the issue of multiculturalism and culture wars to highlight the culturalist component of these debates and to differentiate my notion of multiculturalism or cultural polycentricity from mainstream definitions. The assumed identities that motivate many of these social groups are often reimagined in the aftermath of displacement or rewritten to account for new power relations. The conquest of America and the rise of Atlantic Europe, for instance, created the need to rewrite history and relegate the frontiers of the European peninsula to the realms of barbarity and Oriental despotism. The geographical location of Greece posed a challenge that could only be surmounted by dissociating Greece from its natural and cultural environments. Since Egypt, Mesopotamia, and Persia were the Orient, Greece had to be (dis)Oriented and inscribed into the new geography of the West. "In this process of construction," wrote Samir Amin, "one cannot establish any opposition between Greek thought (in order to make it the ancestor of modern European thought) and 'Oriental' thought (from which Greece would be excluded). The opposition Greece = the West/Egypt, Mesopotamia, Persia = the East is itself a later artificial construct of Eurocentrism."[6]

It is probably not a coincidence that the works of ancient Greece were discovered by Europe only after the fall of Constantinople in 1453 (on the eve of the discovery of America), since much of what the Arabs had translated and later transmitted to Europe was the product of an already "Christianized Hellenism." The Arabs "only became acquainted with Socrates, Plato, and Aristotle through Plotinus" (41–42). Thus both Christianity and Islam are "heirs of Hellenism and remain, for this reason, twin siblings, even if they have been, at certain moments, relentless adversaries. It is probably only in modern times—when Europe, from the Renaissance onward, takes off on the road toward capitalism—that the Mediterranean boundary line forms between what will crystallize as the center and periphery of the new worldwide and all-inclusive system" (26).

Despite long-standing theological disagreements, the cultural affinities between Islam and Christianity could play a significant role in dispelling modern prejudices and establishing a better society for the future, especially if both religions are stripped of their orthodox, conservative dogmas and reinvigorated with a progressive spirit that takes into account resilient global diversities. One simply cannot find hope in the expansionist agenda of a Eurocentric modernity, since it is premised on an unnegotiable intolerance of Others and a polarizing, wasteful, and unsustainable economy. The problem, as Amin argued, "is not one of management, but resides in the objective necessity for a reform of the world system; failing this, the only way out is through the worst barbarity, the genocide of entire peoples or a worldwide conflagration." Amin then goes on to charge Eurocentrism

> with an inability to see anything other than the lives of those comfortably installed in the modern world. Modern culture claims to be founded on humanist universalism. In fact, in its Eurocentric version, it negates such universalism. For Eurocentrism has brought with it the destruction of peoples and civilizations who have resisted its spread. In this sense, Nazism, far from being an aberration, always remains a latent possibility, for it is only the extreme formulation of the theses of Eurocentrism. If there were an impasse, it is that in which Eurocentrism encloses contemporary humanity. (114)

The invention of villainy is not merely the relic of a prehistoric atavism; like the sort of Orientalism critiqued by Edward Said, it performs a vital ideological function in the capitalist economy. Whether the threatening "alien" force is Islam or communism, demonizing others solidifies the status quo and benefits the ruling classes. The "apocalyptic rhetoric" of the Cold War and the U.S. call to "roll back" communism were, as Eric Hobsbawm argued, ideological devices for bolstering American expansionism abroad and controlling domestic political and economic agendas. The discourse of anticommunism was useful for harnessing political votes, raising taxes, repressing dissent, and expanding the ever lucrative arms markets and the defense economy. The superpowers had long known that nuclear war was not an option, and spheres of influence were mostly demarcated; the U.S.-sponsored "apocalyptic *tone*" only racked "the nerves of generations."[7]

One is tempted to apply the same analysis to the unending suspicions that have marked the West's relations with Islam, since, according to Annemarie Schimmel, "among all the religions which Christianity had to confront and deal with, Islam was both misunderstood and attacked most intensely. For more than a millennium Islam seemed to be a major threat—if not the major threat—for the people of Europe, and this feeling has contributed to the fact that Islam and those who confessed it, the Muslims, were regarded as arch enemies of Christianity and western civilization."[8] In the era of capitalist expansion, however, these old antagonisms have less to do with theological disputes; the project of demonizing Muslim others meets various interwoven ideological needs, including the control of Third World resources and persuading citizens of Western societies, through manipulated differentiation and consent, that they are members of a superior civilization.

Manufactured cultural biases and antagonisms deflect people's attention from the more pressing issues facing humanity as a whole and energize the real powers undermining world cultures and "imagined communities." Although power relations and configurations have shifted dramatically in the last few decades, the languages of politics and scholarship still operate on dated assumptions whose effect is to freeze live histories into immutable and misleading stereotypes. One can understand how people without sufficient access to academic scholarship continue to believe that nations and cultures as they imagine them are real; but how does one account for the persistence of such beliefs in whole fields of academic study, despite a continuous barrage of information telling us that the world is being dramatically reconfigured by the rising powers of multinational organizations and extraterritorial bodies and laws? Will apologists for the West ever be able to separate commercially packaged cultural products from the Western heritage they seek to defend? Can Muslims realistically go back to an unmodified Golden Age of Islam, even if one accepts that such an age ever existed? If the answer to the last two questions is difficult, if not impossible, what, then, are the options?

I have tried to argue that a solution to the actual impasse is the rereading of the past and the present within the new global realities engendered by capitalism, and the imagining of a post-Eurocentric, postcapitalist world in which cultures live in constant progressive dialogue with one another. I suppose that the disincentives for such an undertaking are powerful, not least because of the tendency of dominant institutions to dismiss such alternatives as utopian or subversive; yet one cannot ignore the dysfunctions of capitalism without basically resigning oneself to some impending global nightmare. Since the real world is structured along economic imperatives that relegate most Islamic countries to the periphery or to the neocolonial status shared by most poor or technologically marginal countries, cultural disputes that don't take the global situation into account appear as gestures of empty nostalgia or expressions of false consciousness. Nativism, whether it takes on the polished look of academic sophistication, crude racist statements, or xenophobic legislation, expresses a sense of displacement that is real; however, the widespread feeling of alienation that fuels such attitudes is not caused by cultural or ethnic differences but by the relentless penetration of capital into every sphere of human life.

Ironically, while the demise of labor privileges and the lowering of real wages in advanced capitalist countries continue to endanger already precarious social balances and fuel xenophobic populist reactions, the multinational corporations that impose injurious bargains on national governments continue to rearrange the world's geography and scoff at national or cultural pride. "The global system of trade and production is fast constructing a new functional reality for most everyone's life, a new order based upon its own dynamics and not confined by the traditional social understandings. People may wish to turn away from that fact, but there is essentially no place to hide, not if one lives in any of the industrialized nations."[9] Motorola's personnel policies, for instance, make "the preoccupation of American politics with race and cultural superiority [seem] ludicrous, out of touch and perhaps dangerous" (84).

In its broad outlines, the only concern of the global financial system is to force governments in advanced capitalist centers to abandon their broader social responsibilities and define fiscal policy as hypervigilance against inflation, and coerce peripheral governments into providing cheap labor and lax social regulations. While social bases are crumbling (partly because of the unreliability of capital, diminishing revenues from taxation to pay interest to creditors [such as bondholders], the relentless destruction of finite natural resources, and the degradation of human life generally), many nations have surrendered to their own ethnocide and found refuge in antiquated antagonisms. Indeed, if social indicators have any significance at all, they reveal that economically advanced nations have already "entered a prefascist social condition that will ripen in various ugly ways if the market's imperatives prevail, if commerce and finance refuse to compromise their objectives" (364).

What otherwise justifies continued investment in the arms industry and growing defense budgets in the United States (despite testimonies from intelligence agencies that the United States faces no major threats),[10] if the interests of the global ruling classes are spread out across the world, and corporations rely on the small, already saturated international market—including China's growing middle class—to sell their goods and services? The danger to the global economic system is not Confucianism or Islam but the growing numbers of unemployed workers made redundant by automation in the advanced industrialized centers,[11] and the billions of dispossessed people in the Third World who have no hope at all. It would be hard to justify the arms race in the dated language of nationalism, unless one understands that imagined hostilities are deliberately deployed to obfuscate the real threat of capitalism to human cultures. Because economic globalization will be—if it already isn't—confronted by the classical challenge of how to maintain or expand the rate of profit while introducing automation and slashing decently paid jobs, "the surplus of gifted, skilled, undervalued, and unwanted human beings," on the one hand, and billions of excluded people in poor countries, on the other, are the real "Achilles heel of this emerging global system."[12]

This new millennium, as in the earliest phases of capitalism, is already marked by the widening gap between poor and rich, both internationally and within the borders of increasingly defensive nation-states (see the introduction for the latest report on the widening income gaps in the United States). We now live in a world in which the "three richest people in the world have assets that exceed the combined gross domestic product of the 48 least developed countries" and the "world's 225 richest individuals, of whom 60 are Americans with total assets of $331 billion, have a combined wealth of over $1 trillion—equal to the annual income of the poorest 47 percent of the entire world's population." These figures, taken from the 1998 United Nations Human Development Report, provide even more alarming insights into global inequalities. As the poor are abandoned to their diseases and multinational pharmaceutical corporations concentrate their research on lifestyle remedies, it is not really surprising to learn that Americans spend more on cosmetics than is needed "to provide basic education for everyone in the world." Even more telling is to learn that Europeans spend more on ice cream than "the estimated annual total needed to provide clean water and safe sewers for the world's population," and that both Americans and Europeans spend more money on pet food "than the estimated annual additional total needed to provide basic health and nutrition for everyone in the world."[13] In Europe itself, while the per capita share of the joint national income in the European Community "has increased by 80 per cent from 1970 to 1990," the ranks of the unemployed are swelling with technologically displaced labor, and those who are still employed are seeing their real incomes shrinking. The undermining of adequate wages that sustain a mass-consumer base, together with demographic explosions in the periphery, are exerting intolerable pressures on fragile ecosystems and already disintegrating societies.[14] That is why Hobsbawm concluded his book on the (short) twentieth century with a sober warning that the present economic system "cannot go on *ad infinitum*" and that the world has no option but to change if it wants to avoid the twin risks of "explosion and implosion."[15]

When I question the ideology of "human rights" that is now deployed by major industrial countries to pressure authoritarian countries such as China, my critique doesn't call for abandoning the project of protecting human dignity (quite the contrary) but seeks to highlight the inexplicable contradiction of seeking to liberate people from political tyranny while condemning them to a painful existence of unending economic struggle and misery. If one-fifth of the world's population already consumes 86 percent of its resources, and if a projected 8 out of 9.5 billion people will be living in developing countries by 2050,[16] it is structurally impossible to create the conditions for the democratic ideals envisioned by the defenders of human rights.

Noting that the Universal Declaration of Human Rights is a "badly crafted" and redundant document, Winin Pereira has convincingly shown how all the document's lofty rights are canceled out by the Eurocentric systems imposed on the world's indigenous peoples.[17] The rights to life, democracy, development, food, health, employment, and education are all undermined by the global capitalist system. The propagation of an industrial model of education impoverishes people's lives and cultures and leaves children vulnerable and dependent on the very system that excludes them.

> Western countries which pride themselves on their high levels of literacy have actually produced a majority of citizens who choose to read only newspapers (a skill which requires a reading age of about eight years). Those who can acquire information about the latest sex scandal or the most horrific crime or royal divorce are deemed to be "literate"; [*sic*] an achievement which shows up favourably in the United Nations Development Index. Whereas the wisdom, the vast stores of orally transmitted knowledge of a person in the Two Thirds World shows up simply as "illiteracy" and is therefore deemed to be "underdeveloped." Just which one is the more competent functional human being is not in doubt. (114)

This formal educational system is part of a "covert operation . . . waged against childhood [considered in the West as "a time of gilded inutility"] to ensure children will grow dependent on a market system from which they will later have neither the resources nor the imagination to escape" (140, 142). Such a system also favors confining nuclear families over extensive, polycentric, and dynamic ones, and sets out to fix the population problem by providing false promises of a better life to the poor. The whole debate over population explosions has served to mask the rich nations' patterns of wasteful consumption, since it is primarily metropolitan capitalist nations that consume most of the world resources. And while the rich continue to exhaust the world's resources, the traditions of frugality, asceticism, self-reliance that were once the gift of religions and other cultural traditions are being destroyed by globalization:

> Under the new economic colonialist regime cultural rights continue to be overruled, in particular the rights to the maintenance of traditional husbandry and medicinal and sustainable industrial systems. These are reviled as superstitions or as archaisms unfit to survive in the modern world. The elimination of cultural systems which promote a frugal use of resources and a sustainable life-style is essential to the promotion of the market economy, so that those who adhere to the older principles can be converted into faithful hyperconsum-

ers. By this destructive invasion, the most harmonious beautiful and intricate cultural practice must inevitably go down before the right to sell hamburgers and colas. (124)

Studying the issue of human rights in Islam, Heiner Bielefeldt agrees that to have meaning, human rights must be seen as "operating in response to concrete experiences of injustice in the modern world, such as political oppression by an absolutistic state, exploitation of workers in the market economy, colonialism, and imperialism."[18] Relying on John Rawls's notion of an "overlapping consensus" that entails limited normative demands, Bielefeldt argues that human rights "can potentially be connected with more comprehensive doctrines or cultural values, insofar as they refer to the principle of human dignity which itself might facilitate a critical mediation between the normative requirements of human rights on the one hand and various religious or cultural traditions on the other." In any case, because "the scope of human rights is limited" to the "political and legal aspects of human coexistence," they should not be seen as opposed or superior to cultural and religious traditions. And so Bielefeldt recommends that people from the West adopt a self-critical analysis of their own culture "in order to overcome the various forms of ideological appropriation of human rights" (593), detach themselves "from the idea that these rights are simply individualistic claims that are detrimental to communitarian solidarity" (600), refrain "from building human rights into an ideology of general progress modeled on the patterns of Western civilization," and finally "not confuse human rights monitoring with demands for the introduction of a Western-style market economy" (615–16).

Economists such as David Koren and Serge Latouche, both of whom had worked as consultants for international organizations promoting development in the Third World before they became critics of the international economic system, have, in different ways, attributed the actual impasse to the philosophies of the European Enlightenment. For Latouche, the economic has become the substitute of "culture" in the West, since the utilitarian project at the core of modernity not only reduces the complex facets of life to economic advantage, it also moralizes such endeavors and invites newcomers to reject their sustainable traditions in the futile attempt to catch up with modernity. Discarding human solidarities and ancestral values as liabilities in the calculus of profitability, all life is desacralized, including human bodies, which could now be debited "piece by piece" and sold "on the retail market."[19] Led by alienated elites, encouraged by the vociferous dogmas of development, and coerced by international financial organizations, poor countries, including Islamic ones, ignore the "infinitely more human" values of their traditions and lose sight of the fact that the "grand society" of capitalism is the most polarizing and inhuman society in the history of the world. Not only that, but as I have repeatedly suggested, the poor countries that subscribe to such schemes only prolong their dependence while corporations, unmoved by human suffering and the tensions they create, deplete the already scarce resources of disadvantaged nations.

Convinced that Western societies, with their contractual relations, voluntary associations, and their pursuit of a happiness quantified by material possessions and the satisfaction of artificial needs is unable to provide alternatives, Latouche locates hope in what he calls the "archipelago of the informal," the "informal nebula" that refuses to play by the rules, and which poses a "fundamental challenge" to the mainstream ideology of development.

> The informal is an enormous nebula which expresses the seething chaos of human life in all its dimensions, with its horrors and its marvels. Employment within the informal is estimated to furnish between 60% and 80% of urban jobs in most Third World towns. As the informal connects also with the countryside, and as it is not limited to jobs alone, it would not be excessive to imagine that the informal nebula involves billions of human beings and encompasses situations of extreme contrast. Without closing our eyes and painting the entire picture rosy, we may assert that we are witnessing a rebuilding of social bonds sufficient to justify some hope. (47)

Composed of the three or four billion people who have been outcast from "the great banquet table of the consumer society," these Others survive by "reactivating solidarity networks and reinventing a lost mode of social interaction. The networks of reciprocity and the logics that permit their persistence and proliferation derive from a *re-*

embedding of the economic within the social." Invariably described by mainstream economists and experts in negative terms, Latouche nevertheless considers the informal sector, the "*other* of the grand society" as an original form of "resistance to mimetic development." "The existence of a sphere full of vitality and creativity, born in the rupture, developing on the margins and protected by its difference, constitutes the first outline and the hope of a genuine '*alternative*' *society* and not an *other* development." The castaways reinvent a new *sociality* through syncretism and through the revalorization of solidarity as "a form of true wealth" (36, 50, 130–31, 144, 145, 188–218).

Because Latouche's bet on the informal nebula precludes the possibility of integrating the sectors that elude state regulation into the capitalist system, and because he doesn't address the motivating sources for the solidarities he rightly champions, his argument overlooks the strength cultural traditions could play in reinforcing alternatives to the reigning global system. David Koren connects change with a new spirituality that allows humans to see themselves as part of an unfolding universal Consciousness; William Greider hopes for a yet-to-be-defined "global humanism."[20] These attempts to reach for a generic spirituality neglect the fact that cultural diversity subsists precisely because indigenous people draw from the strength of their local traditions, not from the abstract values of universal theories. In other words, there is an inviolable element of tribality in organic solidarities (unlike the contractual ones criticized by Latouche) without which such solidarities cannot exist in the first place. The challenge is not to invent a superficial universal spiritual alternative to the various parochial fundamentalisms besetting the world today but to remove the stresses and antagonisms that constrict the sphere of what Geoffrey Hartman called generosity or tolerance and lead to such culturalist excesses. If informed by an awareness of the interdependence of the world's cultures and peoples and the threat of global capitalism to the survivability of all cultures, new progressive cultural identities, able and willing to change within the broad parameters of their traditions without being traumatized by the humiliating forces of imperialism and subjugation, could emerge as viable alternatives for the building of a more harmonious multicultural world.

Although they do not formulate a viable spirituality for our culturally diverse planet, most progressive economists and scholars agree on the fundamental necessity of the world's "outcasts" to delink from the global capitalist system.[21] Samir Amin has consistently argued for this solution as the only alternative poor countries have for rescuing their populations from further dependency and for building sustainable models of development. He thus adds a small but important correction to the linear view espoused by traditional Marxists, the one that posits that the entire world will have to be homogenized by the forces of capitalism before a genuinely global working-class consciousness emerges to reclaim ownership of the mode of production and usher in a socialist state. For Amin, the main feature of "really existing capitalism" is not the long-term process of gradual homogenization but the constant "polarization" of the world into centers and peripheries (not necessarily nations), which generates "unequal development" and makes the project of "catching up" a mere and dangerous illusion. While economic delinking from the global capitalist system does not entail "autarkic withdrawal" from the world, it means a revalorization of a culture's own internal dynamics and the rejection of a Eurocentric hegemony that refuses to postulate any alternatives to its own biases. "Internal factors take on a decisive role in societal evolution only when a peripheralized society can free itself through delinking from the domination of international value. This implies the break-up of the transnational alliance through which the subordinated local comprador classes submit to the demands of international capital." Unless one accepts Europeanization as the inevitable outcome of history, delinking is, in reality, the "only realistic course of action."[22]

Although Amin expects economic delinking to take place within more or less defined cultural or historical boundaries (Arabs, Africa), the cultural—except for his important critique of culturalist, Orientalist, or Eurocentric theses—remains peripheral to his argument. To be sure, he does argue that a critique of economic laws that appear as objective and natural in the capitalist period ("economism") is necessary for a "truly universalist perspective" enriched by the contributions of all peoples; but the cultural forces that are supposed to contribute to such a project are left mostly unexamined. He says little about the role of Islam (in the case of Arabs), although he recognizes that Islamic fundamentalism is a "veritable symptom of the global crisis of our society," a fundamentalism that is, in any case, less aggressive than the one promoted by the "religion of the market."[23] If Islamic fundamentalism expresses the need for delinking (xv), it still lacks the universalist view necessary for the project of polycentricity.

To argue that Amin's diagnosis of Islamic fundamentalism is correct, however, doesn't relieve progressive multiculturalists and Muslims from theorizing possible uses of the Islamic religion and its legacies. People cannot simply will their identities, memories, pasts, and histories away; to try to do so would only exacerbate tensions and lead to Kemalist policies that have kept Turkey in a perpetual state of social tension. The religion of Islam is the vital core of Islamicate societies, despite the massive encroachment of secular economism and the proliferation of other Eurocentric practices in social and political institutions. Islamists or fundamentalists are right to insist that to continue to favor postcolonial dependencies over indigenous legacies amounts to the tacit support of Western hegemony, but their weakness is in their inability to theorize a progressive view of Islam that responds to the world's new challenges and doesn't simply propose the duplication of laws and practices that prevailed in social conditions irreproducible in the present. Historical conditions or what Castoriadis called the "*eidos*" of an Islamic community that lived more than a thousand, five hundred, or even fifty years ago cannot be recuperated, even by Muslims speaking the same language and using the same religious and literary texts. It is these ruptures or lacunas that necessitate a progressive *ijtihad* and make self-critique indispensable for all peoples, cultures, and religions, including Christianity, Judaism, and even secular democracy (for the latter, Castoriadis would use the term "autonomy").

Many intellectuals rightly recommend *ijtihad* to temper the excesses of oppressive Islamic regimes and zealots, but who recommends *ijtihad* as the necessary cultural practice to revitalize Islamic traditions in order for Muslims to delink from the global capitalist system, reduce the sphere of dependency, and launch a new dialogue with other cultures based on reciprocity, not hegemony? A new Islam that revises or simply scraps outdated practices of the *Shari'a*, provides equal rights and opportunities to women and religious minorities, and encourages the faithful to think globally and multiculturally could still be opposed by the dominant powers, if this new vision of Islam also resists the corrosive practices of late capitalism. Such a progressive Islam is likely to be demonized for the same reasons Marxism and socialism have been in the past.

The experience of liberation theology in Latin America is instructive in this regard. This progressive Christian movement was precipitated by the failure of the dominant economic and political systems to include the poor and protect them from the injustices perpetuated by oppressive governments. Choosing to highlight the progressive tenets of Christianity, liberation theologians redefined Jesus as an activist championing socially oppressed classes and fighting against injustice and exploitation. The notion of poverty was enlarged to include not only all historically marginalized peoples, including women, but also the evangelically poor (i.e., those who have no solidarity with the socioeconomically poor and the persecuted).[24] Though seemingly a threat to the Vatican, such a movement is still deeply rooted in Christian traditions and is revolutionary only to the extent that it makes use of Marxism and Marxist analysis without confining itself to Marx's atheistic vision or its mission exclusively to the proletariat. Moreover, liberation theology is well within the papal tradition that has repeatedly expressed strong reservations about capitalism and that has occasionally suggested that a certain form of socialism is indeed closer to the ideals of Christianity. It may be well to remember that in his commemoration of the fortieth anniversary of Pope Leo XIII's "Catholic social doctrine" issued in 1891, Pope Pius XI stated that

> Socialism inclines toward and in a certain measure approaches the truths which Christian tradition has always held sacred; for it cannot be denied that its demands at times come very near those that Christian reformers of society justly insist upon. . . . It can even come to the point that imperceptibly these ideas of the more moderate Socialism will no longer differ from the desires and demands of those who are striving to remold human society on the basis of Christian principles.[25]

In his encyclical *Populorum Progressio* (March 26, 1967), Pope Paul VI took an even more radical stand as he condemned colonialism, neocolonialism, and the inequities produced by the capitalist system for the tensions and tragedies suffered by the poor. "When whole populations destitute of necessities live in a state of dependence barring them from initiative and responsibility and all opportunity to advance culturally and share in social and political life, recourse to violence, as a means to right these wrongs to human dignity, is a grave temptation." Paul VI asked people to participate in their own development, to "become artisans of their destiny," and called for immediate reform if the world is to avert worse tragedies.[26] Expanding on this spirit, liberation theology simply highlights the Christian traditions of social justice while separating itself from a rigid secular Marxism.[27]

Still, Marxist analysis, as Ernst Bloch, the German philosopher had argued, remains indispensable for the recovery of the Christian (or any religious) socialist tradition. Even Paul Tillich, whose socialist commitments were tempered after he immigrated to the United States, continued to believe that socialism is "the only possible economic system from a Christian point of view."[28] Tillich's reservations about traditional socialism anticipate liberation theology's cautious borrowing from Marxism. For Tillich, socialism's failure has been its propensity to confine itself in mechanistic straightjackets and overlook holistic strategies that take into account people's traditions and cultural aspirations.[29] Although I agree with Tillich's approach, I think his views tend to reduce the complex views of Marx, as Engels explained in a letter to J. Bloch in 1890:

> According to the materialist conception of history the determining element in history is *ultimately* the production and reproduction in real life. More than this neither Marx nor I have ever asserted. If therefore somebody twists into the statement that the economic element is the *only* determining one, he transforms it into a meaningless, abstract, and absurd phrase. The economic situation is the basis, but the various elements of the superstructure . . . also exercise their influence upon the course of historical struggles and in many cases preponderate in determining their *form*. There is an interaction of all three elements in which . . . the economic movement finally asserts itself as necessary.[30]

Although Marx wrote relatively little about religion and his views were never seriously elaborated, his atheism was premised on a "genetic fallacy," or the mistaken belief that "God excludes human freedom."[31] To be sure, the economic is primary in Marx's analysis, but Marx didn't claim that communism would resolve all human contradictions and reinvent human nature—he simply suggested that communism would unleash the human potential suppressed by the alienating effects of capitalism. As Marsden argued, "the idea that communism involves a *total* transformation of human nature stands or falls on the textual evidence of Marx's own corpus, which provides no basis for such an argument" (175).

What is remarkable in the case of liberation theology is the fusion of various traditions and the disappearance or, at least, the blurring of cultural boundaries. One is not tempted to nationalize Marx and Christianity, but to see both as dynamic components in the human legacy, interacting critically with each other and with the indigenous peoples whose ancestors were once grievously massacred by other Christians, and inadvertently providing a model of progressive interaction envisioned in a culturally polycentric world. The dialogue is about how to free human beings from dangerous economic systems and restore their dignity; it is not a contest for domination or a struggle for cultural purity. It is hard to predict the future of this dialogue, but "if a deeper relationship develops between popular Marxist and Catholic movements," L. S. Stavrianos thinks that "the implications for Latin America, not to speak of the entire Third World, are tantalizing. What the end result of those implications might be is impossible to say."[32]

Both liberation theology and a progressively defined Islam could address the injustices of the modern capitalist system and provide alternatives to failed Eurocentric models for social, economic, and political arrangements. As Sohail H. Hashimi recently argued, "The challenge of shaping a 'culturally authentic' response to a world shaped and dominated by the West is not unique to Muslims; it is indeed the challenge facing all of the formerly colonized peoples who comprise the Third World. The Islamic revival is in fact incomprehensible if divorced from the broader phenomenon of 'Third Worldism.'"[33] Because God's vision of justice and dignity triumphs over worldly ambition and human power permeates the texts of both religions, one cannot fight the spirit of Christianity and Islam without removing the egalitarian and prophetic messages embedded in them. What then does one do with these religions? Should they be erased, annihilated, subjected to a new holocaust in order to cleanse the world from their excesses? Even if that were to happen—even if Islam, let us say, were to be completely conquered and defeated, as has been the wish of many since the Crusades—could one realistically expect the existing capitalist system to create better social and economic conditions for the rest of humanity? With the challenge of prophetic, egalitarian traditions (progressively interpreted religious traditions, Marx's communism, etc.) removed from the stage of history, would the West and its extensions finally be able to enter the utopian world of posthistory and live in the eternal bliss of mundane economic calculations?

There is nothing in current economic and political trends to indicate that such an outcome is possible, even if xenophobia and cultural arrogance were to be stretched to genocidal extremes. Blaming cultural differences for the traumatic displacements engendered by the economic system will continue to inflame destructive passions and exacerbate the global human predicament. The Asian economic crisis of the late 1990s led several countries that had been on the path of capitalist development to accuse the West of colonialism, and Indonesia even organized collective Muslim prayers for a solution to the crisis. Instead of wrestling with the real issues undermining long-term economic survivability, the Indonesian government resorted to simplifying, scapegoating, and myth-making formulas to explain the crisis and avoid facing the failure of Indonesian leaders to imagine a mode of development delinked from capitalist dependency and its false promises of helping the country achieve parity with the West.[34]

What we need is a revolutionary concept that accommodates global diversities and moves beyond traditional antagonisms to formulate a clearheaded and sober vision of a world united by fragile bonds and threatened by capitalist excess. The World Health Organization now reports that scarcity and superabundance have led to a world of malnourished people, especially as traditional diets have been replaced by corporate (mostly junk) food loaded with fats and sugars. The direct and indirect costs of obesity in the United States—not counting the $33 billion spent on dieting regimes and the emotional toll of social exclusion—have been estimated to cost $118 billion annually, a sum large enough to "constrain or even unravel a nation's development gains."[35] This paradoxical example of loss and impoverishment within a culture of abundant material wealth shows that no one ultimately wins under the iron laws of existing capitalism—rich bond and stockholders, superpowers, and workers in advanced capitalist economies are all condemned to share this finite planet with its legions of castaways. The winners might find it difficult to reconsider their positions (since people and institutions do not normally relinquish their privileges), yet it has become unquestionably clear that, under current arrangements, today's advantage for the rich may be tomorrow's liability for the whole world. As early as 1930 John Maynard Keynes had speculated that technological innovation would gradually liberate humans from economic necessity to pursue, for the first time in human history, more creative and fulfilling lives. Keynes predicted that the love of money for its own sake would appear as a "somewhat disgusting morbidity, one of those semi-pathological propensities which one hands over with a shudder to the specialists in mental disease. All kinds of social customs and economic practices, affecting the distribution of wealth and of economic rewards and penalties, which we now maintain at all costs, however distasteful and unjust they may be in themselves, because they are tremendously useful in promoting the accumulation of capital, we shall then be free, at last, to discard."[36] Yet more than seven decades after Keynes's prediction, the dictates of profit have grown bigger, the dream for a more enlightened human civilization is diminishing, and the social conditions that had created the conditions for the violence of the earlier decades of the twentieth century are gradually being reinstated amid a widespread historical amnesia.

It is this ominous prospect that justifies a reevaluation of the world's indigenous traditions, including Islam. Only a progressive multiculturalism that accepts the unnegotiability of differences and the opaqueness of otherness, and is uncompromisingly critical of the dominant logic of capitalism, can diffuse the tensions that continue to be inflamed by ahistorical scholarship. The call for a polycentric world liberated from the absolutism of capital doesn't entail the support of a particular political camp or a specific theological view; just as many critics of capitalism during the Cold War were also opposed to Soviet communism, one could be critical of both capitalism (and its ideological manifestations) and a reactionary view of Islam.

More broadly, this book tries to challenge secular academics to include the world's nonsecular expressions as equally worthy of consideration and valid alternatives, and Muslim scholars to rethink their attachments to texts and canons that have obscured the egalitarian and viable legacies of Islam. The modern world's problems, Hodgson rightly suggested, "will probably be truly solved only in common, even while each people must face them as best it can for itself within the conditions set by its own situation." For the Islamic community, this implies reassessing the *Shariʿa* and overcoming its sense of exclusivity "without sacrificing its formative discipline," and entering a "dialogue with contemporary culture common to all communities . . . without sacrificing its integrity."[37] Muslims "must find ways of understanding and renewing [their] experience of the Qurʾân as a vehicle of the inward life at the same time as they renew their response to the Qurʾân as a guide to social relations" (440). For this transformation to be successful, the codes of the *Shariʿa* must be restored to their historicity and be seen as particular events stamped by the ideological struggles of their time. Just as earlier Islam incorporated aspects of the "Irano-Semitic prophetic tradition," especially the Jewish one, contemporary Muslims need to rethink their values along new global realities. The private beliefs of non-Muslim progressive scholars should not be censored by religious scholars, as many Muslims tend to do in the case of Marx. Indeed, adopting a universal vision rooted in Islamic traditions may help Muslims "overcome the cultural dislocations of our time" and illuminate the "human conscience in a technicalistic world" (440). As Hodgson concluded in his landmark study of Islam, all peoples and cultures, not just Muslims, "have a stake in the outcome; even those who explicitly or even militantly reject any religious tradition" (438–39, 441).

The proliferation of an academic terminology celebrating a hybridity caused by traumatic dislocations has effectively transformed symptoms of a global crisis with potentially apocalyptic proportions into virtues to be promoted as intellectual ideals in the postcolonial world. John Gray, the Oxford political scientist who has highlighted the contradiction of the conservative Right that simultaneously upholds traditional values and promotes capitalism, sees no hope for cultural diversity under such a regime:

> In societies whose traditions are not individualist the penetration of the free market means a major rupture in the transmission of culture. A global free market, if it could be constructed, could be built only on the ruins of the world's diverse cultures. It would mean the universal triumph of western individualist values whose compatibility with any kind of social stability, even in their cultures of origin, is more than doubtful. The social backlash against the free market in its global form is likely to be as powerful as that against laissez-faire in the late nineteenth-century England. The overwhelming likelihood is that the late modern project of a global market will fail as other utopian projects have failed.
>
> Long before it fails, however, this late modern universalist project may inflict incalculable and irreparable damage on all other cultures.[38]

Faced with such a bleak outcome, Gray joins Latouche in arguing for re-embedding the economic in the social (183), yet he offers only an elusive solution premised on a reformed and more humane capitalist system. I argue that the world's cultures—alien as they may appear to the elites in rich countries—must be allowed their own autonomous spaces to grow, from which they can contribute to the polycentricity that has become indispensable for human survival. To me, the most realistic strategy for all indigenous and Hispanicized peoples of the Americas, members of Asian and African cultures, and displaced minorities is to reexamine critically their traditions and memories, even while they are affirming them against capitalist homogenization. One needs to ask whether it is still possible to rearticulate totalizing narratives of hope and transcendence, not in the sense of moving away from and beyond history—that, we all know, is impossible—but in the sense transcendence has been defined by Terry Eagleton, as "the historical action of projecting oneself beyond the limits and pressures of a particular settlement into a wider perspective."[39] The question, as I emphasized earlier, is no less urgent for those who have taken up the defense of the West at precisely the same time Western culture has become increasingly difficult to define. For it may well be that what is celebrated as the Western heritage has become, under the relentless process of corporate commodification, nothing more than a series of symbols and icons, if not consumer products, deployed to bolster the spirit of a nationalism that has been stripped of its loftier visions of human solidarity and reduced to the endless defense of "interests."

Harvey Cox has recently given us a powerful insight into how the rhetoric of older gods who reigned over a finite and sacred world has been transferred to the newly coined theology of what he calls The Market. Reading through the business sections of influential newspapers and periodicals, Cox detected the elements of "an entire theology" whose "celestial pinnacle is occupied by The Market," a god whose "divine attributes . . . are not always completely evident to mortals but must be trusted and affirmed by faith." Unrestrained by the competing institutions that had kept it in check, The Market reverses the Catholic concept of mysterious "transubstantiation" and redefines it as the endless process of a desacralizing commodification. Through its omnipotence, The Market miraculously transforms the once sacred land, the human body, or even entire villages with their lakes, businesses, and historical monuments into mere "purchasable items." Finding more analogies and indications that The Market has become the undisputed God of the present, Cox begins to wonder "whether the real clash of religions (or even civilizations) may be going unnoticed," since it has now become clear that "for all the religions of the world, however they may differ from one another, the religion of The Market has become the most formidable rival, the more so because it is rarely recognized as a religion." In this radically new theological climate, Cox realizes that "disagreements among the traditional religions become picayune in comparison with the fundamental differences they all have with the religion of The Market." Yet these religions, seemingly unable to measure or resist The Market's overwhelming powers, "eventually settled for a diminished but secure status."

Though tucked away in the pages of the *Atlantic* under the section Notes and Comment, Cox's essay is a powerful appeal to all human cultures to find ways to unshackle themselves from this insatiable deity—aptly represented as a bull or bear in money and stock markets—that needs infinite expansion to reign. With such a god at the helm of the new millennial human civilization, Cox, a "keen supporter of ecumenism," sees no possibility of theological compromise—so radically at odds is this deity with previous conceptions of the world and the humans inhabiting it. Confronted with this rather unusual theological impasse, Cox hopes for "a rebirth of polemics," as he seeks to awaken us to the millennial decisions and epic struggles awaiting the world's cultures.[40] In this titanic confrontation, nothing could be more promising than weaving strong bonds of human solidarity, nourished by a common vision of justice, dignity, and compassion, across the world's rich, resilient, and time-tested religious traditions. The divisive and corrosive powers of capitalism may yet be contained and replaced with the promise of unbounded human possibility in a culturally and religiously polycentric world.

Notes

Preface

1 It is both amusing and telling to know that Barthes was half asleep in a bar when he had these epiphanous realizations. See Roland Barthes, *The Pleasure of the Text,* trans. Richard Miller (New York: Hill and Wang, 1975), esp. 49, 66–67. For a discussion of Barthes's celebration of the non-sentence, that which cannot accede to the sentence, and the pleasurable "writing aloud" that falls outside the sentence, see Homi K. Bhabha, *The Location of Culture* (New York: Routledge, 1994), 180–85.

2 See Michel Foucault, *Politics, Philosophy, Culture: Interviews and Other Writings, 1977–1984,* ed. Lawrence D. Kritzman (New York: Routledge, 1988), 324, 265.

Introduction: Villainies Veiled and Unveiled

1 Daniel Pearl, "In Iran's Holy City, Islamic Factions Fight for Soul of a Nation," *Wall Street Journal,* 11 August 1999; Ahmed Arif, "Islamic Principles of Justice, Equality," *Wall Street Journal,* 26 August 1999. More than a month after the article and letter were published, the *New York Times* reported that the supreme leader of Iran, Ayatollah Ali Khamenei, stunned Iranians by praising President Khatami's devotion to Islam and its principles. Though such a gesture may have surprised many Iranians and observers, the *Times* explained that the reformist Khatami still wants "a more tolerant Islamic state, not Western-style secularism in which the Muslim faith is relegated to the private domain." See John F. Burns, "Ayatollah Tries to Defuse Rage of Hard-Liners," *New York Times,* 2 October 1999, New England edition. Islam

continues to confound those who rely on Western political terminologies. When the Muslim cleric Aburrahman Wahid was elected
president in Indonesia, the Western media found itself compelled to
explain to an audience used to the general stereotype of Islam as a
violent and oppressive religion that Islam can indeed accommodate
human rights and free trade. Even more perplexing was the fact that
President Wahid was opposed by Islamic parties (Seth Mydans, "In
Indonesia, Islamic Politics Doesn't Mean Religion," *New York Times,*
10 October 1999, sec. 4). The *Times,* however, published the article
under a rubric titled "Secular Rules," revealing yet again the syntactic
lacunas that separate the worldviews of Islam and secularism.

2 I am modifying Michel Foucault's use of the complex concept of "heterotopia" to use it only in the sense that a heterotopia "is capable of
juxtaposing in a single real place several spaces, several sites that are in
themselves incompatible." See Michel Foucault, "Of Other Spaces,"
Diacritics 16 (spring 1986): 25.

3 I refer to amorphous cultural constructs such as the "West" and "Islam" only strategically. In re-creating the familiar argument opposing
the "West" to other invented homogeneous cultural entities such as
"Islam," I am assuming that the fairly well-known limitations of such
essentialist categories are kept in mind. By the same token, I do not
want to occlude those core features that have contributed to the belief
in real or imagined cultural traditions and the differences that distinguish them from one another. Let us assume for now that the
"West" refers to a somewhat identifiable cultural-economic matrix
that includes mostly Europe and its colonial extensions. The native
populations of America and those, such as Africans, who were forced
into exile occupy a more complex place within the Western social
order, as do the working classes and political minorities. The West is a
secular and ideological concept born out of Europe's long history of
"encounters" with different cultures and histories. In this chapter, and
in other parts of the book, I continue to allude to the arbitrariness and
ahistoricity of such notions.

4 Edward Said's *Orientalism* (New York: Vintage, 1979), by now a popular book in various academic fields, remains the most comprehensive
critique of Orientalism as a project in the Euro-American academic
tradition.

5 See Owen Chadwick, *The Secularization of the European Mind in the
Nineteenth Century* (1975; rpt. Cambridge: Cambridge University
Press, 1990); Eric Hobsbawm, *The Age of Revolution: Europe, 1789–1848*
(1962; rpt. New York: Barnes and Noble Books, 1996), 234–47.

6 Nikki R. Keddie, "Secularism and the State: Towards Clarity and Global Comparison," *New Left Review* 226 (November–December 1997): 21–40. When Ruedy claims that secularism "possesses native Islamic roots," what he probably means is that the *'ulama* have had different views on the relationship between religion and politics (as the political struggle in Iran continues to indicate). Epistemologically, however, secularism, like many of the modern *isms,* is a quintessentially European concept and, as such, is charged with the ideologies of its beginnings. See John Ruedy, ed., *Islamism and Secularism in North Africa* (New York: St. Martin's Press, 1994), xvi.

7 Commenting on the Iranians, Foucault said: "They don't have the same regime of truth as ours, which, it has to be said, is very special, even if it has become almost universal. The Greeks had their own. The Arabs of the Maghreb have another." This inaccessible "regime of truth" is what may have irritated even progressive elements in the West, since the "Iran affair and the way it has taken place have not aroused the same kind of untroubled sympathy as Portugal, for example, or Nicaragua. . . . in the case of Iran, I soon felt a small, epidermic reaction [that] was not one of immediate sympathy." What Foucault diagnosed as "a sort of unease when confronted by a phenomenon that is, for our political mentality, very curious" is what has been left out of theoretical inquiry. See "Iran: The Spirit of a World without Spirit," in Foucault, *Politics, Philosophy, Culture,* 211–24.

8 Geoffrey H. Hartman, *The Fateful Question of Culture* (New York: Columbia University Press, 1997), 181, 192. Hartman's book is endlessly fascinating, no less so for relegitimizing the practice of literary studies, and even more so the art of poetry and literature in general.

9 In an illuminating essay, José Rabasa argues that whenever cultural encounters are unequal, dialogue becomes a form of conquest, since the Other is humanized and given chivalrous attributes only to be conquered and appropriated. Indeed, dialogue with the Other may simply be impossible, since "referents can never be recognized as long as two different contexts or discourses mediate their significance." See José Rabasa, "Dialogue as Conquest: Mapping Spaces for Counter-Discourse," in *The Nature and Context of Minority Discourse,* ed. Abdul R. JanMohamed and David Lloyd (New York: Oxford University Press, 1990), 197.

10 Eric Hobsbawm, *The Age of Extremes: A History of the World, 1914–1991* (New York: Pantheon Books, 1994), 453–55. Hobsbawm's otherwise magisterial work still characterizes the Iranian revolution in surpris-

ingly simplistic terms, as the revolution becomes merely an attempt to
return to the early Islamic period.

11 See Robert D. Kaplan, "The Coming Anarchy," *Atlantic*, February 1994,
44–76.

12 Ibid., 46, 54, 73–75. The use of explosive Third World class structures
as metaphors for the emerging social conditions in developed nations
is a rather revealing phenomenon. Michael Lind thinks that the major
threat to the United States is "Brazilianization," which separates races
primarily by class. "Behind all the boosterish talk about the wonders of
the new American rainbow is the reality of enduring racial division by
class, something that multicultural education initiatives and racial
preference policies do not begin to address" (Lind, *The Next American
Nation: The New Nationalism and the Fourth American Revolution*
[New York: Free Press, 1995], 216).

13 Samuel P. Huntington, "The Clash of Civilizations?" *Foreign Affairs* 72
(summer 1993): 22–49. Many people responded to the provocative
argument in the essay. Richard E. Rubenstein and Jarle Crocker criticized Huntington for overlooking "exogenous factors," such as the
failure of "existing systems to satisfy people's basic needs," including
"identity bonding, security, meaning and development." Traditions are
not static monoliths; their survival, in fact, attests to their "plasticity"
and adaptability to new conditions. Huntington's paradigm doesn't
help explain intracivilizational conflicts in sub-Saharan Africa, for
instance; "pan-nationalist militancy . . . is not a spontaneous growth
but a response to political subordination, cultural humiliation, and
blocked economic development." A system that would prevent civilizational clashes is therefore yet to be born (Rubenstein and Crocker,
"Challenging Huntington," *Foreign Policy* 96 [fall 1994]: 113–28). For a
sample of international responses to Huntington's 1993 essay, see the
World Press Review, February 1994, 24–26. Huntington eventually elaborated his ideas in *The Clash of Civilizations and the Remaking of the
World Order* (New York: Simon and Schuster, 1996) and continued to
use his "clash of civilizations" thesis to explain Russia's conflict with
Muslim Chechnya and the futility of flattening Grozny ("A Local Front
of a Global War," *New York Times*, 16 December 1999, New England
edition).

14 Matthew Connelly and Paul Kennedy, "Must It Be the Rest against the
West?" *Atlantic*, December 1994, 76, 79, 82.

15 In reviewing Huntington's "clash" essay, Samir Amin reiterated his
long-held belief that by positing cultures to be outside history (i.e.,
unaffected by processes of change) culturalism erases even Europe's

medieval cultures, which certainly did not think of themselves as capitalist. If anything, capitalism empties cultures of their content. The difficulty with Amin's critique is that it can't fully escape from the economistic abstractions that often ignore the liberatory possibilities of cultures and religion. For this reason, Arif Dirlik stipulated a "Marxist culturalism" that centers the Other in an inalienable present of struggle. Dirlik's epistemological compromise is useful, but he avoids theorizing the reconfiguration of an acceptable cultural strategy that is not merely romantic. See Samir Amin, "Imperialism and Culturalism Complement Each Other," *Monthly Review* 48 (June 1996): 1–11; Arif Dirlik, "Culturalism as Hegemonic Ideology," in JanMohamed and Lloyd, *Nature and Context of Minority Discourse*, 394–431.

16 J. M. Blaut has demonstrated that there was nothing exceptional about Europe's social institutions to permit the continent to forge ahead of contemporaneous cultures, and eventually to equate non-Europeanness with backwardness, if the conquest of the American continent in 1492 is not taken into account; for it is this colonialist—even genocidal—venture that definitely tilted the balance in favor of Europe in the international economy. When Europe rose, after 1492, "this reflected not some quality of 'Europeanness,' but the immense wealth which came into Europe as a result of colonialism in the sixteenth century and thereafter." See J. M. Blaut, *The Colonizer's Model of the World: Geographical Diffusionism and Eurocentric History* (New York: Guilford Press, 1993), 135.

17 The Age of Catastrophe, i.e., "from the outbreak of the First World War to the aftermath of the Second," was the culmination of a long series of wars among European nations. See Hobsbawm, *Age of Extremes*, 6–7. The refusal of French citizens to accept draconian fiscal policies to meet low inflationary standards required for economic integration in the European Community in 1999 led to the victory of socialists and communists in the 1997 legislative elections and the demise of the moderate right. The fear of American commercialism in Europe, especially in France, is a recurring event and is often described by American commentators as typical European anti-Americanism. Hence American thought cannot conceive of an Americanness separate from the business interests of major U.S. corporations; American identity thus blends into the ethos of trade and becomes the physical embodiment of capitalism itself. It is probably for this reason—the successful and complete fusion of capitalism with Americanness—that the House Un-American Activities Committee was set up during the McCarthy era to charge communists with cultural treason.

18 The rise of social science disciplines (sociology, political science, and even anthropology) are, in a very real sense, attempts to specialize knowledge away from the indispensable connections necessary for a more coherent comprehension of human societies, especially after 1492. Specializations are major obstacles to the sort of perspective that has made Marx an enduring but "hidden interlocutor in much social science discourse" (Eric Wolf, *Europe and the People without History* [Berkeley: University of California Press, 1982], 20; see esp. the introduction).

19 The common use of the adjective *Islamic* to refer to civilizations or cultures shaped, in varying degrees, by the religion of Islam is theoretically confusing, if not outright misleading, as the late Marshall G. S. Hodgson argued in the introduction to his magnum opus, *The Venture of Islam*. For Hodgson, the adjective *Islamic* is best restricted to the pure religious practice; the more accurate *Islamicate* refers not only to the religion of Islam but also "to the social and cultural complex historically associated with Islam and the Muslims, both among Muslims themselves and even when found among non-Muslims." Although this eminent scholar made a compelling argument for the need to coin new terminology to deal with the history of "Islamdom," older prejudices continue to determine the questions asked by, and consequently the outcomes of, scholarship on Islam. See Marshall G. S. Hodgson, *The Venture of Islam: Conscience and History in a World Civilization*, vol. 1, *The Classical Age of Islam* (Chicago: University of Chicago Press, 1974), 59.

20 Huntington, *Clash of Civilizations*, 144.

21 Of course, Huntington was writing before December 1999 when the European Community formally accepted Turkey's bid for membership. Still, one of the conditions for Turkey's eventual inclusion in the European Union is the establishment of democratic institutions that protect political freedoms and respect the human rights of Kurds and Muslim activists. But how can the Turkish military open up the political system and still keep the secular system that it has so jealously guarded for decades? Indeed, Turkey's membership in the European Community is now increasingly viewed by nationalist elements as a dangerous move that might weaken the secular foundations of the state and alter power relations. See Warren Hoge, "Turkey Is Invited to Apply for Seat in European Union," *New York Times*, 11 December 1999, New England edition; and Stephen Kinzer, "Debate Rages among Turks over Steps toward Union," *New York Times*, 23 March 2000, New England edition.

22 Huntington's characterization of Fatima Mernissi's position is, to put it simply, inaccurate. Mernissi's voluminous body of feminist work could be defined as a sophisticated attempt to educate Muslims about the value of individualism and freedom from obscurantist collective (patriarchal) tyranny. I address the ideological assumptions of this effort in my larger discussion of the politics of feminism in the Islamic world.

23 Bernard Lewis, "The Roots of Muslim Rage," *Atlantic,* September 1990, 60, 48.

24 Huntington, *Clash of Civilizations,* 207.

25 Jonathan Riley-Smith, *The Crusades: A Short History* (New Haven, Conn.: Yale University Press, 1987), xxviii–xxix.

26 See Bernard Lewis, *Semites and Anti-Semites: An Inquiry into Conflict and Prejudice* (New York: Norton, 1986), esp. chaps. 1, 2, 3.

27 Ibid., 120–21. For a thorough examination of the history of Jews in Islam, see Bernard Lewis, *The Jews of Islam* (Princeton, N.J.: Princeton University Press, 1984). In a later book Lewis clarified that even though the term *Judeo-Christian* "designates a genuine historical and cultural phenomenon," the expression is still new, and "in earlier times would have been found equally offensive on both sides of the hyphen." Lewis also reminds his readers that Christianity and Islam espouse certain common theological views that both religions do not share with Judaism. And all three monotheistic religions have more in common than one is led to believe from the culturalist thesis. "Compared with the other great religions of the world, the differences between [Judaism, Christianity, and Islam] seem insignificant, the resemblances overwhelming." See Bernard Lewis, *The Multiple Identities of the Middle East* (New York: Schocken, 1998), 113–14.

28 William H. McNeill, the eminent historian of the West, describes world history since 1500 "as a race between the West's growing power to molest the rest of the world and the increasingly desperate efforts of other peoples to stave Westerners off" (quoted in Daniel Pipes, *In the Path of God: Islam and Political Power* [New York: Basic Books, 1983], 97).

29 Huntington, *Clash of Civilizations,* 310.

30 The cases I highlight below may be dated by the time this book is published, but the pattern of social bifurcations and exclusions, generalized stress and violence, and various other pathologies will most likely continue unmodified under the present structures of global capitalism.

31 Richard J. Barnet and John Cavanagh, *Global Dreams: Imperial Corporations and the New World Order* (New York: Simon and Schuster, 1994), 13–22.

32 Ibid., 196–97, 200–204, 220. The aggressive marketing of cigarettes is eerily reminiscent of the British and, to a lesser extent, U.S. illegal opium trade in China in the early decades of the nineteenth century.

33 Quoted in Barnet and Cavanagh, *Global Dreams,* 325, 332–33.

34 See David C. Koren, *When Corporations Rule the World* (West Hartford, Conn.: Kumarian Press, 1995), 158, 160–75, 185–93. Hobsbawm wrote that "never was the word 'community' used more indiscriminately and emptily than in the decades when communities in the sociological sense became hard to find in real life—'the intelligence community', 'the public relations community', the 'gay community'" (Hobsbawm, *Age of Extremes,* 428). The same applies to the word *culture,* which is now used to describe what are merely contingent practices, lifestyles, and workplace habits. For an insightful analysis on the use of the term, see Hartman, *Fateful Question of Culture,* esp. 21–59.

35 In *The Wealth of Nations* (1776), Adam Smith wrote: "It is to prevent this reduction of price, and consequently of wages and profit, by restraining that free competition which would most certainly occasion it, that all corporations, and the greater part of corporate laws, have been established." And elsewhere: "People of the same trade seldom meet together, even for merriment and diversion, but the conversation ends in conspiracy against the public, or in some contrivance to raise prices" (quoted in Koren, *When Corporations Rule the World,* 56, 222).

36 Koren, *When Corporations Rule the World,* 58–59.

37 Already in 1992, Flora Lewis, a senior columnist of the *New York Times,* was writing that European nations have to decide whether "democracy and the free market economy are compatible," since no government can regulate the "fluid mass" of the complex "global economy" (Lewis, "The End of Sovereignty," *New York Times,* 23 May 1992). The pervasive image of helpless and disempowered governments in this latest stage of capitalism is, however, exaggerated. The expansion of capitalism still relies heavily on state intervention, and it is doubtful whether the consolidation of capital could ever be achieved without it. Antisocial measures such as the deregulation of industries and the unceasing attack on social programs only illustrate the government's historic alliance with the capitalist ruling class. On this subject, even Adam Smith sounds like Marx: "Civil government, so far as it instituted for the security of property, is in reality instituted for the defence of the rich against the poor, or of those who have some property against

those who have none at all" (quoted in Koren, *When Corporations Rule the World*, 75).

38 Koren, *When Corporations Rule the World*, 229–47; James Brooke, "Slavery on the Rise in Brazil, as Debt Chains Workers," *New York Times*, 23 May 1993. Around 200 million illegal immigrants, mostly young women from poor countries, are often exploited, dehumanized, and treated as slaves, including in European countries. See Thierry Parisot, "Quand l'immigration tourne à l'esclavage," *Le Monde diplomatique*, June 1998, 20–21.

39 Nathaniel C. Nash, "Poor Peru Stands By as Its Rich Past Is Plundered," *New York Times*, 25 August 1993; John Dorfman, "Getting Their Hands Dirty? Archaeologists and the Looting Trade," *Lingua Franca*, May–June 1998, 29; Barbara Crossette, "Iraqis Hurt by Sanctions, Sell Priceless Antiquities," *New York Times*, 23 June 1996, sec. 1. In Cambodia, temples are also being dismantled and looted. See Seth Mydans, "Raiders of Lost Art Loot Temples in Cambodia," *New York Times*, 1 April 1999, New England edition.

40 James Brooke, "Kidnappings Soar in Latin America, Threatening Region's Stability," *New York Times*, 7 April 1995; Sam Dillon, "Security: A Growth Industry in Mexico," *New York Times*, 15 October 1998, New England edition; Sam Dillon, "Mexican Arrested in a String of Kidnappings," *New York Times*, 26 February 2000, New England edition; Seth Mydans, "Kidnapping of Ethnic Chinese Rises in Philippines," *New York Times*, 17 March 1996, sec. 1.

41 "Murderous Pirate Attacks Are on the Rise," *New York Times*, 3 February 1999, New England edition.

42 John Noble Wilford, "Among the Dying Species Are Lost Tribes of Mankind," *New York Times*, 2 January 1994, sec. 4; Leda Martins and Patrick Tierny, "El Dorado, Lost Again?" *New York Times*, 7 April 1995.

43 Elizabeth Olson, "Free Markets Leave Women Worse Off, Unicef Says," *New York Times*, 23 September 1999, New England edition; Michael Specter, "Traffickers' New Cargo: Naïve Slavic Women," *New York Times*, 11 November 1998, sec. 1. For the prostitution of East European women in Western Europe after the collapse of the Iron Curtain, see Yves Géry, "Trafic de femmes en provenance de l'Est," *Le Monde diplomatique*, February 1999, 10.

44 Judith Miller and Paul Lewis, "Fighting to Save Children from Battle," *New York Times*, 8 August 1999, sec. 1; Joseph P. Fried, "Women Plead Guilty in Baby Smuggling Case," *New York Times*, 16 July 1999, New England edition.

45 Claire Bisset, "La marche des enfants rebelles," *Le Monde diplomatique,*
    June 1998, 21; James Petras and Tienchai Wongchaisuwan, "Thailand:
    Free Markets, AIDS, and Child Prostitution," *Z Magazine,* September
    1993, 35–38. The same authors point out that the modern "sex industry
    developed along with U.S. military bases in Thailand during the Indo-
    china war, expanding rapidly after a treaty, signed in 1967, allowing
    U.S. soldiers in Vietnam to come on 'rest and recreation' leave to
    Thailand" (35).

46 See David Cay Johnston, "Gap between Rich and Poor Found Substan-
    tially Wider," *New York Times,* 5 September 1999, sec. 1. For an earlier
    report in the same newspaper, see Keith Bradsher, "Widest Gap in
    Incomes? Research Points to U.S.," *New York Times,* 27 October 1995.

47 Susan Chira, "Study Confirms Worst Fears on U.S. Children," *New
    York Times,* 12 April 1994.

48 See Robert Pear, "Researchers Link Income Inequality to Higher Mor-
    tality Rates," *New York Times,* 19 April 1996; Tamar Lewin, "Parents Poll
    Shows Child Abuse to Be More Common," *New York Times,* 7 Decem-
    ber 1995.

49 Matthew L. Wald, "Total Cost of U.S. Nuclear Arms Is Put at $5.48
    Trillion," *New York Times,* 1 July 1998, New England edition; Tim-
    othy L. O'Brien, "Gambling: Married to the Action, for Better or
    Worse," *New York Times,* 8 November 1998, sec. 4.

50 See James Sterngold, "Life in a Box: Japanese Question Fruits of Suc-
    cess," *New York Times,* 2 January 1994, sec. 1; Stephanie Storm, "In
    Japan, Mired in Recession, Suicides Soar," *New York Times,* 15 July 1999,
    New England edition; Stephanie Strom, "Tradition of Equality Fading
    in New Japan," *New York Times,* 4 January 2000, New England edition;
    Sheryl WuDunn, "Child Abuse Has Japan Rethinking Family Auton-
    omy," *New York Times,* 15 August 1999, New England edition. News of
    crumbling Russia are frequent, but one published article reminded me
    of the indigenous peoples who drowned their defeat in alcohol once
    they had been successfully conquered. See Michael Specter, "Deep in
    Russian Soul, a Lethal Darkness," *New York Times,* 8 June 1997, sec. 4.
    For an article on the United Nations Development Program report, see
    Paul Lewis, "Road to Capitalism Taking Toll on Men in the Former
    Soviet Bloc," *New York Times,* 1 August 1999, sec. 1.

51 See, for instance, John Rockwell, "The New Colossus: American Cul-
    ture as Power Export," *New York Times,* 30 January 1994, sec. 2.

52 Paul Kennedy, *Preparing for the Twenty-first Century* (New York: Ran-
    dom House, 1993), 32–33.

53 "World Bank Says Hunger Can Be Cut in Half," *New York Times,*

30 November 1993; Warren E. Leary, "Billions Suffering Needlessly, Study Says," *New York Times*, 2 May 1995.

54 The U.S.-Mexican border is one example of a thriving economic zone that is creating its own separate culture. "With 11 million people and $150 billion in output, it is an economy larger than that of Poland and close to the size of Thailand's." But this output is generated in an environment of inequality where "a low-wage economy [is] nestled against a prosperous giant," an arrangement that is "becoming a model for other regions split by wage or technology gaps." See the special report on the U.S.-Mexican border in *Business Week*, 12 May 1997, 64–74.

55 See Benjamin R. Barber, "Jihad vs. McWorld," *Atlantic*, March 1992, 53–63.

56 See *The Foucault Reader*, ed. Paul Rabinow (New York: Pantheon, 1984), 245; Michel Foucault, *Power/Knowledge: Selected Interviews and Other Writings, 1972–1977*, ed. Colin Gordon (New York: Pantheon, 1980), 119.

57 In his theoretically groundbreaking book on the phenomenon of Islamism, Bobby Sayyid argues that the sort of unmediated Islamism inaugurated by Khomeini provincializes the West and gives substance to Fanon's statement that "the European game has finally ended" and that "we must find something different." See Bobby S. Sayyid, *A Fundamental Fear: Eurocentrism and the Emergence of Islamism* (London: Zed, 1996), 151, 129, 150–51. I find Sayyid's sophisticated analysis inspiring, but I don't think that provincializing the West can be successfully achieved if Muslims don't theorize their emplacement within global capitalist structures. Economic dependency speaks louder than the most strident discourses of cultural authenticity; in fact, the tone of the latter is usually determined by the excesses of the former.

1. Can the Postcolonial Critic Speak?
Orientalism and the Rushdie Affair

1 Huntington, "Clash of Civilizations?" 31. The fear of Islam is being played out in dramatic ways on the European stage. Turkey, as we have seen, is being kept out of the European market partly because of its dominant religion, Islam. And ethnic cleansing was applied to Bosnians because they were Muslim. Susan Sontag suspected that the reason why very few artists—and for that matter, intellectuals—expressed concern about Bosnia is because the term *Muslim* is a "turn-off." The

New York Times later made the same suggestion. On the exclusion of Turkey from the European Community, see Scott L. Malcomson, "Heart of Whiteness," *Voice Literary Supplement,* March 1991, 10–14. Susan Sontag's interview appeared on the *MacNeil/Lehrer Newshour,* 3 August 1993. Finally, see Roger Cohen, "West's Fears In Bosnia: 1) Chaos, 2) Islam," *New York Times,* 13 March 1994, sec. 4.

2 Arif Dirlik, "The Postcolonial Aura: Third World Criticism in the Age of Global Capitalism," *Critical Inquiry,* no. 20 (winter 1994): 331, 356, 329, 339, 353.

3 Ibid., 340.

4 Frantz Fanon, *The Wretched of the Earth,* trans. Constance Farrington (New York: Grove Weidenfield, 1968), 245.

5 Dirlik, "Postcolonial Aura," 334 n. 6.

6 Fanon, *Wretched of the Earth,* 189.

7 Gayatri Spivak, Edward Said, Akeel Bilgrami, Ibrahim Abu-Lughod, Eqbal Ahmad, Agha Shahid Ali, "Antithetical to Islam," *New York Times,* 17 February 1989, letter to the editor.

8 "Who Needs the Great Works?" *Harper's,* September 1989, 47–48.

9 One must continue to stress the gross violations of basic human rights (complex as this concept may be) in much of the Third World, and the Arab and Islamic worlds in particular. This pervasive condition has crippled intellectual inquiry and co-opted many scholars; but although they must be held accountable, these Third World regimes should be situated within larger global configurations defined by the extraterritoriality of capital and the reduction of most governments into guardians of (foreign) investments. Third World nations in the era of capitalist globalization are being reduced to police states selling themselves as "stable" societies that provide cheap and semi-skilled labor to foreign investors. Even regions in the First World have begun to act like Third World countries, offering big incentives and "parks" for industries willing to relocate.

10 Gayatri Chakravorty Spivak, "Can the Subaltern Speak?" in *Marxism and the Interpretation of Culture,* ed. Cary Nelson and Lawrence Grossberg (Urbana: University of Illinois Press, 1988), 295–96, 308.

11 Gayatri Chakravorty Spivak, *The Post-Colonial Critic: Interviews, Strategies, Dialogues,* ed. Sarah Harasym (New York: Routledge, 1990), paperback back cover. Christopher Miller struggles at length with the "paradox" of using the mediation of the Western methodological device of anthropology to study African literature. He finally chooses the dialogic gesture to reduce the impact of ethnicity (Anglo-Eurocentrism) and relativize his beliefs; and he rightly notes that "unless the

Western critic attempts to suspend—to hold at least in temporary abeyance—the systematic criteria and judgements that emanate from Western culture, ethnocentrism will persist forever." Miller is well aware that leaving Africans alone might put him "out of business" altogether, as Weber states; but, like Spivak, he goes on to defend his undertaking as best as he can. Linda Alcoff also struggled with this issue, although she offers a somewhat modified approach to this dilemma. Alcoff calls on speakers to (1) exercise restraint (since speech is mastery); (2) "interrogate the bearing of our location and context"; (3) be accountable for their utterances; (4) treat discourse as an "*event* which includes speaker, words, hearers, location, language, and so on." The difference here is accountability. See Christopher L. Miller, *Theories of Africans: Francophone Literature and Anthropology in Africa* (Chicago: University of Chicago Press, 1990), 65, 28, and esp. chaps. 1, 2; Linda Alcoff, "The Problem of Speaking for Others," *Cultural Critique*, no. 20 (winter 1991–92): 5–32. But to define the context of our speech risks to become an infinitely regressive procedure if we don't begin from the simple assumption that we are speaking from within an academic apparatus thoroughly informed by the dominant capitalist ethic.

12 Spivak, *Post-Colonial Critic,* 94, 37, 135, 115.

13 Abdul JanMohamed, "Worldliness-without-World, Homelessness-as-Home: Toward a Definition of the Specular Border Intellectual," in *Edward Said: A Critical Reader,* ed. Michael Sprinker (Oxford: Basil Blackwell, 1992), 97, 105.

14 Edward Said, "Criticism/Self-Criticism," *Lingua Franca,* February–March 1992, 37–43. What the black historian may have intuitively objected to in Said's presentation has been documented and clarified by Aijaz Ahmad. Ahmad has shown how Said has been thoroughly subjected to the very Orientalist tradition he has denounced in *Orientalism*. According to Ahmad, the "high humanism" of this tradition is what prompts Said's beliefs in the liberal virtues he often invokes. Said seems "transfixed by the power of the very voice" he criticizes. Ahmad further notes that the categories of Orientalism and "third world female subaltern" are perfectly suitable for privileged Third World intellectuals who nevertheless need "documentary proof that they have always been oppressed." See Aijaz Ahmad, "Orientalism and After: Ambivalence and Cosmopolitan Location in the Work of Edward Said," *Economic and Political Weekly,* 25 July 1992, 98–116. That Said's sensibilities are more Western than Arab is evident in his musical taste. In a 1999 interview, Said stated his preference for the "classics" and admitted that he had no interest in other musical traditions. "For me,"

Said told his interviewer, "music is still Western classical music. Arab music is not my thing." See Emily Eakin, "Look Homeward, Edward," *New York,* 27 September 1999, 51.

15 Edward Said, *Culture and Imperialism* (New York: Knopf, 1993), 332. In his moving memoir, *Out of Place* (New York: Knopf, 1999), Said explains that such a position is the only he could finally adopt, traversed as he is since birth with irreconcilable cultural dissonances. Although Said's "unhoused" self has helped him enlarge the scope of his theorizing, his privileged intellectual outlook has not been able to erase the sense of loss that has haunted him throughout his life.

16 Said, *Culture and Imperialism,* xxvi–xxvii.

17 See Edward Said, "The Phony Islamic Threat," *New York Times Magazine,* 21 November 1993, 62–65.

18 Akeel Bilgrami, "What Is a Muslim? Fundamental Commitment and Cultural Identity," *Critical Inquiry* 18 (summer 1992): 821–42.

19 Said, *Culture and Imperialism,* 200, 221–22.

20 John Tomlinson, *Cultural Imperialism* (Baltimore, Md.: Johns Hopkins University Press, 1991), 11.

21 Anne McClintock, "The Angel of Progress: Pitfalls of the Term 'Post-Colonialism,'" *Social Text,* nos. 31–32 (1992): 84–98; Ella Shohat, "Notes on the 'Post-Colonial,'" *Social Text,* nos. 31–32 (1992): 103.

22 The same has been true of dominant multicultural theories in the United States. George Yúdice has shown how U.S. multiculturalism, based on identity politics, universalizes its project and obliterates post-colonialist struggles against [U.S.] imperialism. Seen in this light, U.S. multiculturalism ends up, wittingly or not, serving transnational capital's interests (co-opting indigenous resistance through the dissemination, via powerful and well-endowed media, of one particular version of identity). See George Yúdice, "We Are *Not* the World," *Social Text,* nos. 31–32 (1992): 202–16. Coca-Cola Company, whose major income is outside the United States, has already "banished" words such as "domestic" and "foreign" from its vocabulary and is therefore ahead of many cultural and educational institutions. See Roger Cohen, "For Coke, World Is Its Oyster," *New York Times,* 21 November 1991.

23 In *The Wretched of the Earth,* Fanon writes scathingly about Westernized intellectuals who "take up a fundamentally 'universal standpoint'" (218–19). Moreover, the Westernized intellectual often fails to "measure the real situation which the men and the women of his country know" (223). Fanon himself had adopted a universalist position in *Black Skin, White Masks;* his transformation may indicate his closer identification with the "wretched."

24 Dirlik, "Culturalism as Hegemonic Ideology," 406.

25 See Stanley Fish, "Boutique Multiculturalism, or, Why Liberals Are Incapable of Thinking about Hate Speech," *Critical Inquiry* 23 (winter 1997): 378–95.

26 François Burgat, *The Islamic Movement in North Africa* (Austin: University of Texas, Center for Middle Eastern Studies, 1993), 6.

27 John L. Esposito, *The Islamic Threat: Myth or Reality?* (New York: Oxford University Press, 1992), 199–200, 202. In the United States, once the secular model displaced the religious foundations of the university in the nineteenth century, the spiritual dimensions of life were virtually excluded from the curriculum. "Academic fundamentalism is the issue," wrote Page Smith, "the stubborn refusal of the academy to acknowledge any truth that does not conform to professorial dogmas." In this world, "certain ideas are simply excluded, and woe to those who espouse them. Such individuals are terminated, lest their corruption spread to others." See Page Smith, *Killing the Spirit: Higher Education in America* (New York: Penguin, 1990), 5.

28 Edward Said, *Covering Islam: How the Media and the Experts Determine How We See the Rest of the World* (New York: Pantheon, 1981), 8, 136, 154.

29 Akbar Ahmed, *Postmodernism and Islam: Predicament and Promise* (London: Routledge, 1992), 87. This is not to suggest that Greek philosophy was not without its developed sense of tolerance and self-doubt. The point here is simply to contrast the effects of the Greek humanist legacy with those of the Semitic (religious) one.

30 See Fredric Jameson, *The Political Unconscious: Narrative as a Socially Symbolic Act* (Ithaca, N.Y.: Cornell University Press, 1981), 252.

31 For Lyotard, the text is also an "event" (81), but it is an "event" that is blissfully unrepresentable (since this assumption prevents the oppressiveness of totalities and activates differences). No wonder, then, that Fredric Jameson reads a certain despair in Lyotard's theory, perhaps prompted by the failure of the Left in France. See Jean-François Lyotard, *The Postmodern Condition: A Report on Knowledge,* trans. Geoff Bennington and Brian Massumi, foreword by Fredric Jameson (Minneapolis: University of Minnesota Press, 1984).

32 Krishan Kumar, *From Post-Industrial to Post-Modern Society: New Theories of the Contemporary World* (Oxford: Blackwell, 1995), 132, 135, 146, 147–48.

33 Alex Callinicos, *Against Postmodernism: A Marxist Critique* (New York: St. Martin's Press, 1990), 168, 169. David Harvey also indicates that postmodernism doesn't happen in a "social, economic or political

vacuum" but in a growing corporate culture that has commodified artistic and cultural production and managed to get rid of the stricter canons of modernist aesthetics and replace them with infinite variations. Although the postmodernist movement seems to be confined to the realm of the aesthetic, Harvey notes that "changes in the way we imagine, think, plan, and rationalize are bound to have material consequences." Yet "postmodern philosophers tell us not only to accept but even to revel in the fragmentations and the cacophony of voices through which the dilemmas of the modern world are understood." See David Harvey, *The Condition of Postmodernity: An Enquiry into the Origins of Cultural Change* (Oxford: Basil Blackwell, 1989), 63, 115, 116.

34 Spivak, *Post-Colonial Critic,* 11–12, 45, 51, 53, 68.

35 This should be a concern for Westerners, too, especially those struggling to expand freedom of speech in Third World countries. The "corporate takeover of public expression" is the subtitle of Herbert Schiller's book on the vanishing spaces of public expression and the rise of corporate discourse in the West. The ramifications of the corporate monopoly over speech in the United States are yet, in my view, to take their rightful place in cultural and literary studies. See Herbert Schiller, *Culture Inc.: The Corporate Takeover of Public Expression* (New York: Oxford University Press, 1989); and Edward Herman and Noam Chomsky, *Manufacturing Consent: The Political Economy of the Mass Media* (New York: Pantheon, 1988). Of course, corporate control of the media and cultural enterprises has intensified since the publication of Schiller's book in 1989. In such conditions, the preoccupation with freedom of speech risks becoming a vacuous expression that, among other things, reflects the false consciousness of intellectuals living under the iron laws of capitalism.

36 Tomlinson, *Cultural Imperialism,* 11.

37 Bill Ashcroft, Gareth Griffiths, and Helen Tiffin, *The Empire Writes Back: Theory and Practice in Post-Colonial Literatures* (London: Routledge, 1989), 160.

38 See Said, *Culture and Imperialism;* and Walter Rodney, *How Europe Underdeveloped Africa,* rev. ed. (Washington, D.C.: Howard University Press, 1981). For an illustration of how Western financial organizations continue to drain the Third World generally of its resources, see *Race and Class* 34 (July–September 1992).

39 The creation of missionary schools and Western universities in the Middle East is part of this pattern. The American University of Beirut (AUB), for example, consciously aims at producing a Westernized Arab

leadership. See Robert D. Kaplan, "Tales from the Bazaar," *Atlantic,* August 1992, 46. La Francophonie is a continuation of colonialism through language, despite the obvious benefits of learning, and even mastering, a second language.

40 Quoted in Akbar Ahmed, *Discovering Islam: Making Sense of Muslim History and Society* (London: Routledge, 1988), 126. The mélange that postmodern and postcolonial theories sometimes celebrate may suggest that global intermixing has grown out of a natural process of globalization and not a deliberate strategy of colonialism carefully orchestrated by the imperialists in the nineteenth century.

41 Ngũgĩ Wa Thiong'o has worked tirelessly to emphasize the primacy of language in reconstructing a cultural imaginary. In *Moving the Center: The Struggle for Cultural Freedoms* (Portsmouth, N.H.: Heinemann, 1993), which builds on many of the arguments in *Decolonising the Mind: The Politics of Language in African Literature* (Portsmouth, N.H.: Heinemann, 1986), Ngũgĩ shows that the African elites have been designed to perpetuate neocolonial structures while the peasants and the masses, through their marginalization, preserved native customs and languages. The cultural control of the Third World (dissemination of certain ideas, inventing a mutilated consciousness, false self-perceptions, etc.) are an integral part of the imperialist project, because this generalized cultural confusion weakens resistance (51, 54). The writer in the neocolonial state must therefore side with the people (74) and make an attempt to restore African languages, despite the loud cynical cries of the Europhones (21).

42 Ashcroft, Griffiths, Tiffin, *Empire Writes Back,* 108; Tim Brennan, "Rushdie, Islam, and Postcolonial Criticism," *Social Text,* nos. 31–32 (1992): 258–76.

43 Ali Mazrui, "Satanic Verses or a Satanic Novel?" *Third World Quarterly* 12 (January 1990): 116–39.

44 Hobsbawm, *Age of Extremes,* 242.

45 See, for instance, Youssef Ibrahim, "The Arabs Find a World in which They Count Less" *New York Times,* 5 April 1992, sec. 4. All Muslim states, despite the impression of prosperity that a few countries may convey, are part of the Third World. The combined economic output of eight of the largest Islamic economies—Turkey, Indonesia, Iran, Malaysia, Pakistan, Bangladesh, Egypt, and Nigeria—amounts to "less than that of Italy." See Stephen Kinzer, "Third World's Answer to Group of 7," *New York Times,* 14 June 1997, New England edition.

46 Mazrui, "Satanic Verses or a Satanic Novel?" 118.

47 Dirlik, "Postcolonial Aura," 348.

48 Mark Edmundson, "Prophet of a New Postmodernism," *Harper's*, December 1989, 62, 68.

49 Qadri Ismail, "A Bit of This and a Bit of That: Rushdie's Newness," *Social Text*, no. 29 (1991): 123.

50 Aamir Mufti, "Reading the Rushdie Affair: An Essay on Islam and Politics," *Social Text*, no. 29 (1991): 107.

51 Salman Rushdie, *Imaginary Homelands* (London: Granta, 1991), 16, 13–14, 15. The prophetic dimensions of this last sentence (written in 1982) have been tested by history. The irony in the whole Rushdie tragedy is that, dangerously satirical though it might be, *The Satanic Verses* is not necessarily or even intentionally blasphemous. The uproar was mostly fueled by nonliterary polemics, not by a close reading of the novel.

52 Salman Rushdie, *Is Nothing Sacred?* (London: Granta, 1990), 7, 9, 14.

53 Spivak, *Post-Colonial Critic*, 20–21.

54 Dirlik, "Culturalism as Hegemonic Ideology," 398.

55 Mazrui, "Satanic Verses or a Satanic Novel?" 136.

56 Lisa Appignanesi and Sara Maitland, eds., *The Rushdie File* (Syracuse, N.Y.: Syracuse University Press, 1990).

57 Mahmoud Mohamed Taha, *The Second Message of Islam*, trans. Abdullahi Ahmed An-Na'im (Syracuse, N.Y.: Syracuse University Press, 1987), 6, 112, 129, 153; my emphasis.

58 See Tomlinson's analysis of Cornelius Castoriadis's critique of modernity in *Cultural Imperialism*, 164.

59 Before the eruption of the Gulf War on January 17, 1991, Bernard Lewis explained to a Jewish audience in Israel that secularism arose out of a conflictive Christian history. He said that "secularism in its modern political connotation, the idea that religion and authority, church and state are distinct and different and therefore ultimately separable, is in a profound sense Christian." The long history of schism and heresy in Christendom has no parallels in Jewish and Islamic histories. "There is nothing," said Lewis, "in Islamic history remotely comparable with such epoch-making Christian events as the Christological controversies, the schism of Photius, which split the Greek and Latin churches, the Reformation, the holy office of the Inquisition and the bloody religious wars of the 16th and 17th centuries which in effect compelled Christians to secularize their states and societies in order to escape from the vicious circle of persecution and conflict. Muslims encountered no such problem and therefore required no such solution." See Bernard Lewis, *Secularism in the Middle East* (Rehovat, Israel: Weizmann Institute of Science, 1991), 3–36.

60 See Kevin Dwyer, *Arab Voices: The Human Rights Debate in the Middle East* (Berkeley: University of California Press, 1991); Burgat, *Islamic Movement in North Africa,* 73.

61 Dwyer, *Arab Voices,* 215.

62 Appignanesi and Maitland, *Rushdie File,* 194.

63 Mazrui, "Satanic Verses or a Satanic Novel?" 126.

64 The film and television industries in Egypt have been used to undermine Islamist groups, proving, once again, that art, often dependent on patronage, is almost always political. See Chris Hedges, "Battling the Religious Right: The Celluloid Front," *New York Times,* 18 April 1994.

65 Many Arab and Muslim writers and intellectuals have written in favor of Rushdie, and their statements were published in book form, initially in France. They wrote in support of his freedom to speak, although not everyone listed seems to have read *The Satanic Verses.* Some even used the occasion to launch attacks on the patriarchy or to advance their own agendas for a project of secularization in the Islamic world. In my view, only two writers stand out for the depth and historical perspectives of their analyses. Mohamed Arkoun, a prominent Islamic scholar in France, while insisting on Rushdie's right to freedom, placed the controversy in the larger context of the West's repudiation of the spiritual, a West that, "under the cover of a defense of 'freedom of expression,' in fact seeks to debase Islam and prove that all the old talk about the civilizing mission of the European colonial powers is and has always been fundamentally valid. . . . Thus, merely to protest against the intolerance of Muslims alone means covering over with a veil of silence some things that represent a decisive aspect of the whole battle that has involved Rushdie." Amin Maalouf, the famous author of *The Crusades through Arab Eyes,* reminds the reader that "a billion Muslims have the impression of living in a foreign, hostile, indecipherable universe," that such conditions engender grave dilemmas that, unless resolved, will probably lead to even greater dramas. See *For Rushdie: Essays by Arab and Muslim Writers in Defense of Free Speech* (New York: Brazillier), 47, 217.

66 Salman Rushdie, "In Good Faith," *Newsweek,* 12 February 1990, 52, 53.

67 Mufti, "Reading the Rushdie Affair," 111.

68 See Fredric Jameson, "Postmodernism and Consumer Society," in *Postmodernism and Its Discontents,* ed. E. Ann Kaplan (London: Verso, 1988), 13–29.

69 Fatima Mernissi has noted the general "malaise" that affects both the highly educated and the most impoverished members of the Third World with a sense of "self-depreciation," leading them to immigrate

to "the very paradoxical West" ("un Occident très paradoxal"). See Fatima Mernissi, *La peur-modernité: Conflit Islam démocratie* (Paris: Albin Michel, 1992), 78.

70 Salman Rushdie, *The Satanic Verses* (New York: Viking, 1989), 490, 507.

71 Rushdie, *Imaginary Homelands*, 431.

72 Ahmed, *Postmodernism and Islam*, 121.

73 Rushdie, *Imaginary Homelands*, 377.

74 Edward Said first visited the United States at the age of sixteen; Spivak arrived in the same country at the age of nineteen, and has been a resident alien since 1966. See Edward Said, "Palestine, Then and Now," *Harper's*, December 1992, 47; Spivak, *Post-Colonial Critic*, 75.

75 Hobsbawm, *Age of Extremes*, 15.

76 "Where nothing is sacred, every belief becomes revisable," notes Ahmed in *Postmodernism and Islam* (13). The persistence of the "sacred" in even the most revolutionary regimes, such as the Sandinista one in Nicaragua, is testimony that no utopian project of society can easily dispense with it. Rigoberto López Pérez, the Nicaraguan poet who sacrificed himself to rid his country of dictatorship, is now endowed with a shrine. "The creative or spiritual, and its product the sacred, needs to receive scientific recognition as a valid expression of human life." See John Bretlinger, "Socialism and the Sacred," *Monthly Review* 44 (October 1992): 27–43. Terry Eagleton also argues that "deeply persistent beliefs" must be taken seriously, for they are the real expression of the people whom many of us seek to emancipate (Eagleton, *Ideology: An Introduction* [London: Verso, 1991], 12–13).

77 The educator Henry Giroux has used the metaphor of borders to conceptualize a progressive form of multicultural education. "Borders elicit a recognition of those epistemological, political, cultural, and social margins that distinguish between 'us and them,' delineate zones of terror from locations that are safe, and create new cartographies of identity and difference. The concept of borders when defined as part of a politics of cultural difference can be used heuristically to make problematic specific authorial positions secured in monolithic views of culture, nationalism, and difference." See Henry A. Giroux, "Post-Colonial Ruptures and Democratic Possibilities: Multiculturalism as Anti-Racist Pedagogy," *Cultural Critique*, no. 21 (spring 1992): 23.

78 See "Looking Back from 2992," *Economist*, 26 December 1992–8 January 1993, 17–19.

79 For a reassessment of U.S. military strategies in relation to the Islamic threat, see interview with Alain Joxe in *Le Monde*, 22 December 1992; and Alain Joxe, "Humanitarisme et empires," *Le Monde diplomatique*,

January 1993, 1, 6–7. For the U.S. flexible military strategy in the post–Cold War era, especially in relation to the Third World, see Daniel B. Schirmer, "Access: Imperialist Expansion in the Post Cold-War Era," *Monthly Review* 45 (September 1993): 38–51.

2. Millennium without Arabs?

1 In her chapter titled "On Becoming Arab," Leila Ahmed questions and resists the Arabness imputed to her by contending ideologies and shows how Egypt became an "Arab" country (*From Cairo to America— A Woman's Journey* [New York: Farrar, Strauss and Giroux, 1999], 243–70). She notes that in 1913, when an Arab conference was organized in Paris, "an Egyptian who was attending as an observer asked permission to speak [but] was refused on the grounds that the floor was open only to Arabs." It was only later, Ahmed goes on to note, that Egypt became consciously Arab. "It was as if we had become Arab, and all the region had actually become Arab (when, once, only Arabia had been Arab), because the Europeans saw us as Arabs—all of us as just Arabs. And because to serve their own political interests and in pursuit of their own ends—the dismantling of the Ottoman Empire, the acquisition of new colonial territories, retaining control of territories under their mandate—it was strategically and politically useful to them, in this particular era in history, to define us, and to have us define ourselves, as Arabs. And gradually we had all complied, imagined this, correctly or not, to be in our own interest, too" (266).

2 *Time* (special issue: *Beyond the Year 2000: What to Expect in the Millennium*), fall 1992, 36–37.

3 Christopher Lasch, "Is Progress Obsolete?" *Time*, fall 1992, 71.

4 See Samir Amin, "Culture and Ideology in the Contemporary Arab World," *Rethinking Marxism* 6 (fall 1993): 26.

5 There is, of course, no indication that the incomparably vast oil reserves of the Middle East are about to run out in the near future. In fact, the West's reliance on Middle Eastern oil is growing and is profitable to both Western oil companies and states. Not only that, but if this trend continues, even American companies may be allowed to operate in blacklisted countries—such as Iran, Iraq, and Libya at the time of this writing—to further develop and exploit their oil fields. See Michael Field, *Inside the Arab World* (Cambridge, Mass.: Harvard University Press, 1995), 21; and Agis Salpukas, "Still Looking to the Persian Gulf," *New York Times*, 26 March 1995, sec. 4.

178 Notes to Chapter Two

6 Abdellah Laroui, *Islam et modernité* (Paris: Editions la Découverte, 1987), 171–79.

7 Mohamed 'Abid al-Jabri, *Naqdh al-'aql al-'arabi* (Critique of the Arab mind), vol. 1, *Takween al-'aql al-'arabi* (Formation of the Arab mind) (Casablanca: Al-markaz athaqafi al-'arabi, 1991), 56–95.

8 Issa J. Boullata, *Trends and Issues in Contemporary Arab Thought* (Albany: State University of New York Press, 1990), 45. It would be interesting to decide whether such a work constitutes what Edward Said called a good example of Orientalist influence on Arab thinking and scholarship. In *Orientalism,* Said stated that "there is some reason for alarm in the fact that [the influence of Orientalism] has spread to 'the Orient' itself: the pages of books and journals in Arabic (and doubtless in Japanese, various Indian dialects, and other Oriental languages) are filled with second-order analyses by Arabs of 'the Arab mind,' 'Islam,' and other myths" (322). To me, what Al-Jabri is doing seems closer to what Said does in his book on Orientalism: i.e., analyze instituted discourses that have framed "Arab" and Muslim thinking and scholarship for more than a millennium. Here the Other is, in some ways, oneself.

9 Bernard Lewis, *The Arabs in History* (1950; rpt. New York: Harper Torch Books, 1967), 15.

10 Maxime Rodinson, *The Arabs,* trans. Arthur Goldhammer (Chicago: University of Chicago Press, 1981), 25.

11 Ibid., 26.

12 Hodgson, *Venture of Islam,* 1: 326; vol. 2, *The Expansion of Islam in the Middle Periods* (Chicago: University of Chicago Press, 1974), 119–20, 350, and n. 352. The *Shari'a,* initially an evolving process, "was both more and less than what is now usually regarded as law," and could even be adapted to *'urf* (local customs) as the juridical procedure known as *'amal* in Morocco indicates. See Albert Hourani, *A History of the Arab Peoples* (Cambridge, Mass.: Harvard University Press, Belknap Press, 1991), 161–62. Lately, with the fundamentalizing of Islam, the *Shari'a,* once again, emerges as a profoundly controversial issue, deployed by Islamists to counter Western hegemony and dismissed or criticized by secular (Arab) intellectuals as either dated or incoherent.

13 Hodgson, *Venture of Islam,* 1: 249–73, 344. The *'ulama,* even those who laid out the foundation of Islamic jurisprudence and law, were often engaged intellectuals at odds with the state. The Imams Abu Hanifa (700–767), Malik ibn Anas (710–795), Mohamed ash-Shafi' (767–820), and Ahmed ibn Hambal (780–855) were often persecuted; Abu Hanifa

even died in prison. See Akbar S. Ahmed, *Discovering Islam: Making Sense of Muslim History and Society* (London: Routledge, 1988), 48–49.

14 Hourani, *History of the Arab Peoples*, 223.

15 Technicalization defines the "great Western transmutation" that erupted in Europe between the sixteenth and eighteenth centuries. All aspects of social life underwent a radical transformation; individualism gradually replaced the communal life of "agrarianate" societies, and innovation was institutionalized. This force would create a permanent wedge between what has come to be called "Europe" and the rest of the world. "The Western Transmutation, once it got well under way, could neither be paralleled independently nor be borrowed wholesale. Yet it could not, in most cases, be escaped. The millennial parity of social power broke down, with results that were disastrous almost everywhere." The advent of this Technical Age created a "development gap [that] has from the beginning, divided the world into two sets of peoples who have been inescapably bound up with each other, yet found it bafflingly hard to comprehend each other. It is this bafflement that is expressed in Kipling's 'East is East and West is West and never the twain shall meet.'" See Hodgson, *Venture of Islam*, vol. 3, *The Gunpowder Empires and Modern Times* (Chicago: University of Chicago Press, 1974), 200, 202–3.

16 Benedict Anderson reminds us that the "non-arbitrariness of the sign" was important in sacral cultures, since "ontological reality is apprehensible only through a single, privileged system of re-presentation." This accounts for the still prevailing belief that the Qur'an is untranslatable. See Benedict Anderson, *Imagined Communities: Reflections on the Origin and Spread of Nationalism* (1983; rpt. London: Verso, 1991), 12, 14.

17 Ibid., 18–19, 77, 90–91, 159. Anderson suggests that the saturation of the limited Latin readers market led publishers to conspire with the "lexicographic revolution": "The coalition between Protestantism and print-capitalism exploiting cheap popular editions, quickly created large new reading publics—not least among merchants and women, who typically knew little or no Latin—and simultaneously mobilized them for politico-religious purposes" (40).

18 If imperialism is seen as the logical outcome of vernacular nationalisms (remember that market considerations were never removed from the definite displacement of Latin as a sacred language), then we don't need to account for the United States's successor role to European imperial rule. The entire American continent may be seen as the colony of settled lexicographic communities from Europe. The absolute hege-

mony of Spanish, English, Portuguese, and French mean that conquistador cultures banished the possibility of a significant indigenous nationalism and only revived pre-Hispanic languages when the danger of successful resistance could no longer be considered. The creole triumph would eventually mean that indigenous languages would survive in marginalized tribes and be made available only to specialized scholarship and "museumization." Anderson is right to add this crucial fact of creole nationalism in the Americas in his revised edition. The creole elites who fought Spain for independence used pre-Hispanic symbols only for differentiation; otherwise, they remained loyal to their lexicographic affiliations (see 192).

19 Anderson, *Imagined Communities*, 75 n. 23. Expatriate Levantine Arabs in Tangier were among the pioneers of the Moroccan nationalist struggle for independence. See Mohamed 'Abid al-Jabri, "Al-harakatu asalafiya wa al-jama'at a-diniya al-mu'asira fi al-maghrib" (The Salafi movement and contemporary religious groups in Morocco), in *Al-harakatu al-islamiya al-mu'asira fi al-watan al-'arabi* (Contemporary Islamic movements in the Arab world) (Beirut: Center for Arab Unity Studies, 1987), 189–235.

20 Turkish nationalism had a profound effect on and further encouraged Arab nationalist tendencies. See Hourani, *History of the Arab People*, 319. For a brief essay on the reciprocal Otherness of Turks and Arabs, see Henri Laurens, "Naissance du monde arabe," *Qantara* (magazine des cultures arabe et méditerranéenne), October–November–December 1995, 36–38.

21 Anderson, *Imagined Communities*, esp. the chapter "Official Nationalism and Imperialism," 83–111, 140.

22 Quoted in Theodore Von Laue, *The World Revolution of Westernization: The Twentieth Century in Global Perspective* (New York: Oxford University Press, 1987), 14–15.

23 See Anderson, *Imagined Communities*, 116–22. New colonial secular pilgrimage patterns (displacing traditional Islamic ones) are often the hallmark of Arab and African colonial and postcolonial literature. One of the poignant episodes in these novels is the educated native's voyage to the metropole and the identity crisis he or she undergoes. An interesting topic to explore would be a study of the literature of the two types of pilgrimages (colonial/secular, traditional/Islamic) in the Islamic world.

24 European languages and nationalism had the same effect on African (post)colonial history and culture.

25 Maxime Rodinson, *Marxism and the Muslim World,* trans. Jean Matthews (New York: Monthly Review Press, 1981), 208.

26 Rodinson, *Arabs,* 98.

27 Ibid., 160.

28 Rodinson, *Marxism and the Muslim World,* 209.

29 In the latest revised edition, Anderson puts more emphasis on the colonial state as the "immediate genealogy" (*Imagined Communities,* 163) of Third World nation-states. The census and the map rearranged peoples and geographies while archaeology (the "museumization" of the past) and print capitalism helped disseminate—through books, postcards, and various other paraphernalia—the new identity of the nation. Postindependence states continued "this form of political museumizing" (182–83) in their efforts to solidify their sovereignty.

30 E. J. Hobsbawm, *Nations and Nationalism since 1780: Programme, Myth, Reality* (1990; rpt. Cambridge: Cambridge University Press, 1992), 137. Unlike in Europe, the notion of territorial sovereignty was, even in the fragmented postcaliphal age, insulting to Muslim rulers. See Bernard Lewis, *The Muslim Discovery of Europe* (New York: Norton, 1982), 202.

31 Field, *Inside the Arab World,* 29–30. The term *Middle East* was invented in 1902 by a U.S. naval officer, Alfred Thayer Mahan (1840–1914), to designate the geographical area between the Arabized provinces of the Ottoman empire and India. It was quickly popularized by a (London) *Times* reporter in 1903. As late as 1915, Mark Sykes (1879–1919), Kitchener's representative in Arab lands, was still referring to Turkey, Syria, Palestine, Mesopotamia, and the Arabian peninsula as "historical and ethnographical provinces" of the future "Turkish Asia" to replace Ottoman rule. His plan would later be refined in a memo written jointly with François Georges-Picot, a French diplomat. The plan (1916) stipulated, among other things, the protection of Christianity and the encouragement of Jews to consider settling Jerusalem. See Roger Adelson, *London and the Invention of the Middle East: Money, Power, and War, 1902–1922* (New Haven, Conn.: Yale University Press, 1995), 22, 123–26.

32 William Ochsenwald, "Ironic Origins: Arab Nationalism in the Hijaz, 1882–1914," in *The Origins of Arab Nationalism,* ed. Rashid Khalidi et al. (New York: Columbia University Press, 1991), 189–203. It must also be remembered that when Arab nationalism emerged in the twentieth century, it was primarily an urban movement. See Hobsbawm, *Age of Revolution,* 139.

33 Said Bensaid, "*Al-Watan* and *Al-Umma* in Contemporary Arab Use," in *The Foundations of the Arab State,* ed. Ghassan Salamé (London: Croom Helm, 1987), 149–74; Iliya Harik, "The Origins of the Arab State System," in Salamé, *Foundations of the Arab State,* 20–21; Bahgat Korany, "Alien and Besieged Yet Here to Stay: The Contradictions of the Arab Territorial State," in Salamé, *Foundations of the Arab State,* 49.

34 Ghassan Salamé, "Le nationalisme arabe: mort ou mutation?" in *Le Déchirement des Nations,* ed. Jacques Rupnik (Paris: Editions du Seuil, 1995), 188; my translation.

35 Ibid., 190.

36 Around fifty intellectuals gathered for a three-day meeting (September 25–27, 1989) in Cairo. The debate was published in book form as *Al-hiwar al-qawmi a-dini* (The nationalist/religious dialogue) (Beirut: Center for Arab Unity, 1989).

37 Salamé, "Le nationalisme arabe," 206.

38 Ibid., 189.

39 Ibid., 209; my translation. Fouad Ajami puts it thus: "The secularist impulse took a savage beating in the Arab world of the 1980s. A circle was closed: Christian Arabs had played a leading role in the development of Arab nationalism. They had begun their work in the final years of the nineteenth century, when liberal nationalism rode triumphant. They were the tribunes and pamphleteers of Arab nationalism. A century later, the Christian Arab communities had become marginalized." With even more characteristic flair, Ajami describes Islamization as "the determined traditionalization of culture" mobilized against the "mimicry" of "Levantization." See Ajami, *The Arab Predicament: Arab Political Thought and Practice since 1967* (1981; rpt. Cambridge: Cambridge University Press, 1992), 246, 213.

40 Hobsbawm, *Nations and Nationalism,* 150–52, 160–62. I am, of course, arguing that an Arab nation has never existed in the first place for it to be (re)united. Treaties and economic exchange may facilitate rapprochements but will not eliminate local specificities. The same is true for the Islamic nation. There have been peoples united by a common faith, but not all Muslims were the subjects of one ruler, not even at the height of the Abbasid or Ottoman periods. Moreover, the few enduring political models, such as Morocco and, more recently, Saudi Arabia, cannot easily be reproduced elsewhere. See Field, *Inside the Arab World,* 185, 192.

41 Especially after the Gulf War. Even Maghreb unity, to the disappointment of older Arab nationalists, has turned out to be largely a myth.

Tunisia, Algeria, and Morocco emphasized Arabism in the 1960s and 1970s, "but in the early 1990s people are recognizing that they belong to several places. They are part of the Arab world, but also part of Africa, of the Mediterranean basin and, they say, of Europe. The Tunisians and Algerians in particular are not happy with this complicated, ill-defined identity—the Moroccans are more satisfied with being simply Moroccan—but the change in emphasis away from Arabism may have the long-term practical benefit of discouraging dreaming and encouraging regional co-operation." See Field, *Inside the Arab World,* 394–95. By the time of this writing, the push to establish a viable Maghrebian union is still facing serious obstacles.

42 In the religious-nationalist meeting mentioned above, Sheikh Mohamed al-Ghazali, a well known *'alim,* defined himself as an "Egyptian man Arabized through Islam." One participant reminded the audience that some of the major heroes of Islamic history, such as Salahuddin al-Ayubi (Saladin), were not ethnically Arab; another participant simply stated that there has been no Arabness without Islam. See *Al-hiwar al-qawmi a-dini,* 118, 126, 129.

43 See, for instance, Fred Halliday, "The Politics of Islamic Fundamentalism: Iran, Tunisia, and the Challenge to the Secular State," in *Islam, Globalization, Postmodernity,* ed. Akbar S. Ahmed and Hastings Donnan (New York: Routledge, 1994), 91.

44 The ideological and cultural boycotting of Christian lands was almost total in the precolonial period. Europeans traveling or residing in coastal towns in Morocco frequently reported on the general hatred of Muslims for the "Nazarenes." Most Muslims, even celebrated travelers such as Ibn Battuta, deliberately avoided travel in Christian lands. As late as the mid–nineteenth century, Moroccan *'ulama* were still debating whether it was advisable for Muslims to travel in Europe. See Susan Gilson Miller, ed. and trans., *Disorienting Encounters: Travels of a Moroccan Scholar in France in 1845–1846: The Voyage of Muhammad As-Saffar* (Berkeley: University of California Press, 1992), 11–12 n. 25. Bernard Lewis discussed the obstacles that may have prevented Muslims from knowing Europe at length in his *Muslim Discovery of Europe.* Contemporary Islamists have no trouble traveling in Christian lands and very often enjoy good relations with devout Christians. Their fundamentalism is therefore not entirely scriptural but a response to modern displacements.

45 Fawzy Mansour, *The Arab World: Nation, State, and Democracy,* intro. Samir Amin (London: Zed, 1992), 46; Amin, "Culture and Ideology in the Contemporary Arab World," 15–16.

46 Abdellah Laroui, *The Crisis of the Arab Intellectual: Traditionalism or Historicism?* (Berkeley: University of California Press, 1976), 156.

47 Von Laue, *World Revolution of Westernization*, 129–30, 209–35. Hitler and Stalin are classic examples. It is interesting to note that once these figures appear in European or Western history, they are quickly designated as aberrations and, in fact, assigned Oriental traits. In Western iconography, villains almost inevitably look threateningly dark (whether it be the Jew, Hitler, or the Muslim). For an interesting analysis, see Jürger Link, "Fanatics, Fundamentalists, Lunatics, and Drug Traffickers—The New Southern Enemy Image," *Cultural Critique*, no. 19 (fall 1991): 67–95. Link's article is especially relevant to the discussion of Orientalism below.

48 Serge Latouche, *L'Occidentalisation du Monde: Essai sur la signification, la portée et les limites de l'uniformisation planétaire* (Paris: Editions La Découverte, 1989), 63, 24–25.

49 Ibid., 24–25. Industrialization, technicalization, and development are value systems that simply cannot be purchased. See Latouche, *L'Occidentalisation du Monde*, 73, 63–65; and Von Laue, *World Revolution of Westernization*, 314–15. "Ethnocide" is defined by Latouche as a form of extreme deculturation (65).

50 Boullata, *Trends and Issues in Contemporary Arab Thought*, 105.

51 Hodgson, *Venture of Islam*, 3: 238–39.

52 European dress is inconvenient for prayer, and the Latinization of languages inserts radical ruptures in the Islamic heritage. Arabic letters, however, survived as charms and talismans in Turkey (see Hodgson, *Venture of Islam*, 3: 244, 269).

53 Ibid., 384; my emphasis. This situation still obtains today: *Time* magazine's prognosis assumes the continuation of imperialism into the next millennium.

54 Ibrahim M. Abu-Rabiʿ, *Intellectual Origins of the Islamic Resurgence in the Modern Arab World* (Albany: State University of New York Press, 1996), 43, 49, 50–51, 249.

55 See the case of the Saudi *ʾalim* and orator, al-Zaʾyr in Talal Asad, *Genealogies of Religion: Discipline and Reasons of Power in Christianity and Islam* (Baltimore, Md.: Johns Hopkins University Press, 1993), 220–21.

56 Latouche, *L'Occidentalisation du Monde*, 77.

57 See Laroui, *Islam et modernité*, 56, 58–59.

58 The eminent anthropologist Talal Asad argues that secular nation-states are far more totalitarian than "anything to be found in Islamic history" (13). As the following passage from Robert Musil's novel

The Man without Qualities (vol. 1) chillingly illustrates, the modern nation-state reaches into every corner and detail of social life, and leaves nothing outside its regulatory mechanism: "The fact is, living permanently in a well-ordered State has an out-and-out spectral aspect: one cannot step into the street or drink a glass of water or get into a tram without touching the perfectly balanced levers of a gigantic apparatus of laws and relations, setting them in motion or letting them maintain one in the peace and quiet of one's existence. One hardly knows any of these levers, which extend deep into the inner workings and on the other side are lost in a network the entire constitution of which has never been disentangled by any living being. Hence one denies their existence, just as the common man denies the existence of the air, insisting that it is mere emptiness" (quoted in Talal Asad, *The Idea of an Anthropology of Islam* [Washington, D.C.: Georgetown University, Center for Contemporary Arab Studies, 1986], 21 n. 23). Owen Chadwick has also pointed out the same paradox of demanding "natural rights" from a state apparatus that had destroyed traditional protections and left the individual—strong in his pursuit of self-interest—naked in front of its regimented power. See Chadwick, *Secularization of the European Mind in the Nineteenth Century*, 25–26.

59 Laroui, *Islam et modernité*, 63; my translation. For a similar argument, see Lewis, *Multiple Identities of the Middle East*, 98–99.

60 Laroui, *Islam et modernité*, 63. Talal Asad suggests that the sectarian wars of the sixteenth and seventeenth centuries in Europe led to the privatization of belief, thereby strengthening the state. Religion would then be constructed "as a new historical object: anchored in personal experience, expressible as belief-statements, dependent on private institutions, and practiced in one's spare time." See *Genealogies of Religion*, 206–7. One can conclude that the implosion of the religiously bonded community opens up new spaces for the state, which then opportunistically fills up the gaps with its own system of controls.

61 See Taha, *Second Message of Islam*, 112, 129.

62 See Mansour, *Arab World*, 51; and Samir Amin's introduction, "Contribution to a Debate: The World Capitalist System and Previous Systems" in Mansour, *Arab World*, 17.

63 The cultures of both the West and Islam cannot be properly understood, at least sociologically, without taking the impact of modern imperialism on these cultures into account. One way to do this is through what Edward Said has called "contrapuntal" reading in his book *Culture and Imperialism*.

64 Asad, *The Idea of an Anthropology of Islam*, 4–5.

65 See Asad, *Genealogies of Religion*, 19–23, 200–201.

66 Said wrote, "Almost without exception, every Orientalist began his career as a philologist." See Said, *Orientalism*, 98.

67 Bernard Lewis, *Semites and Anti-Semites: An Inquiry into Conflict and Prejudice* (New York: Norton, 1986), 43–45, 83, 94–95.

68 Although anthropology began to supplant the Noah's curse myth in Genesis by the eighteenth century, the Genesis genealogical narrative survived until the nineteenth century, if not beyond. It is probably significant to note that the Dreyfus affair divided "Arabs" into two religious camps: while Muslims sympathized with Dreyfus, Christian Arabs adopted anti-Dreyfusian and anti-Semitic positions. See Lewis, *Semites and Anti-Semites*, 26–28, 42–43, 89, 133–34.

69 Fred Halliday, *Islam and the Myth of Confrontation: Religion and Politics in the Middle East* (London: I. B. Tauris, 1996), 187–93.

70 Akbar Ahmed, *Postmodernism and Islam*, 182.

71 Laroui, *Crisis of the Arab Intellectual*, 44, 52, 72, 160–62.

72 Aziz Al-Azmeh, *Islams and Modernities* (London: Verso, 1993), 125–31.

73 See Bryan S. Turner, *Orientalism, Postmodernism, and Globalism* (London: Routledge, 1994), 39–40.

74 Ibid., 7, 9; Al-Azmeh, *Islams and Modernities*, 139–40.

75 Halliday, *Islam and the Myth of Confrontation*, 210–15, 201.

76 Laroui, *Islam et modernité*, 155–57, 167–68; Abdellah Labdaoui, *Les Nouveaux Intellectuels Arabes* (Paris: Editions L'Harmattan, 1993), 248–56.

77 Fazlur Rahman, *Islam and Modernity: Transformation of an Intellectual Tradition* (Chicago: University of Chicago Press, 1982), 146.

78 Leonard Binder, *Islamic Liberalism: A Critique of Development Ideologies* (Chicago: University of Chicago Press, 1988), 78–84.

79 The literature on this subject is already too voluminous. For a good example of how capitalist cultures are harmful, see Jerry Mander, *In the Absence of the Sacred: The Failure of Technology and the Survival of the Indian Nations* (San Francisco: Sierra Club Books, 1992); and Richard Douthwaite, *The Growth Illusion: How Economic Growth Has Enriched the Few, Impoverished the Many, and Endangered the Planet* (Tulsa, Okla.: Council Oak Books, 1993).

80 Douthwaite, *Growth Illusion*, 315, 150, 321. For a full account of Samir Amin's theory, see *Delinking: Toward a Polycentric World*, trans. Michael Wolfers (London: Zed, 1990).

81 See Cornelius Castoriadis, *Philosophy, Politics, Autonomy*, ed. David Ames Curtis (New York: Oxford University Press, 1991), 183–85. Chapter 8 ("Reflections on 'Rationality' and 'Development'") is an excellent

discussion of the ideology of development. The long quote is from page 185.

82 Because the Greeks excluded "extrahuman authority" from the process of history making, they were able "to create democracy and philosophy." At least, until the later era of the Stoics, "adoration of the *fait accompli* is unknown and impossible as an attitude of the mind." This democratic project of autonomy "emerges when explicit and unlimited interrogation explodes on the scene." The Greek ideal of uncompromising critique of everything is, of course, far removed from the contemporary intellectual and political predisposition to assume that Western capitalism is the end of history. See Castoriadis, *Philosophy, Politics, Autonomy*, 4, 8, 9–12, 163. See also chapter 5, "The Greek *Polis* and the Creation of Democracy" for an illuminating discussion of the original meaning of the term.

83 Burgat, *Islamic Movement in North Africa*, 65.

84 See the survey on "Islam and the West" in *Economist*, 6 August 1994, 1–18.

3. The North as Apocalypse

1 Driss Chraibi, *The Simple Past*, trans. Hugh A. Harter (Washington, D.C.: Three Continents Press, 1990), 56. Originally published as *Le Passé simple* (1983).

2 See Thomas Spear, "Politics and Literature: An Interview with Tahar Ben Jelloun," *Yale French Studies* 83 (1993): 30–31.

3 James Markham, "Arab Novelist Falls in Love with French," *New York Times*, 25 November 1987.

4 Mahdi El Mandjra, *Nord/Sud: Prélude à l'ère Postcoloniale* (Casablanca: Les Editions Toubkal, 1992), 138, 128.

5 See Louis Brenner, "Muslim Representations of Unity and Difference in the African Discourse," in *Muslim Identity and Social Change in Sub-Saharan Africa*, ed. Louis Brenner (Bloomington: University of Indiana Press, 1993), 16–17.

6 Roland Oliver, *The African Experience: Major Themes in African History from Earliest Times to the Present* (New York: IconEditions, 1992), 201–2. In another context, Roland Oliver and J. D. Fage are unequivocal about the spread of Islam prior to European colonialism, especially when discussing the eastern part of the continent: "Had there been no direct intervention of European power, the influence of the Muslims would have consolidated itself not only on the east coast and in the northern

Sudan but in the southern Sudan also, and in many parts of East Africa and Zaire. To some extent this would have been the result of deliberate colonization by alien ruling groups, but to some extent too commercial contacts and political influence would have led to the Islamization of local institutions, as they had done in much of the Sudan in earlier times. It is doubtful whether Christian missions, starting as late as they did, would have been in time to forestall an Islamic expansion once Muslims had political power firmly in their hands. Had full-scale European intervention been delayed fifty years, not merely the northern third of Africa but the southern two-thirds would have belonged culturally to the world of Islam." See Roland Oliver and J. D. Fage, *A Short History of Africa,* 6th ed. (New York: Penguin, 1988), 157.

7 Rodney, *How Europe Underdeveloped Africa,* 240, 255–59.

8 Basil Davidson, *The Black Man's Burden: Africa and the Curse of the Nation-State* (New York: Times Books, 1992), 10.

9 Ibid., 76–77.

10 Basil Davidson, *The Search for Africa: History, Culture, Politics* (New York: Times Books, 1992), 27, 31, 36, 56.

11 A. G. Hopkins, *Economic History of West Africa* (New York: Columbia University Press, 1973), 64–65. Mervyn Hiskett also wrote that by the year 1400 "it would probably have been impossible to conduct business between the Sudan, North Africa and Egypt without substantial reliance upon the commercial practice of the *Shari'a.*" See Mervyn Hiskett, *The Course of Islam in Africa* (Edinburgh: Edinburgh University Press, 1994), 100. Slaves constituted a significant portion of the trade.

12 See Muhyiddeen Saber, "Al-'alaqat athaqafiyya bayna ifriqya wal 'arab" (Cultural relations between Africa and the Arabs), in *Al-'arabu wa ifriqya* (The Arabs and Africa) (Beirut: Center for Arab Unity Studies, 1984), 497–504; Azzeddine Omar Musa, "Al-islam wa ifriqya" (Islam and Africa), in *Al-'arabu wa ifriqya,* 71. Because of some confusion regarding definitions, I am not associating the Arabic language with Arab ethnicity. Arabic was, before the emergence of modern nationalism, a sacred script for all Muslim peoples, not the basis of identity. There is some evidence, which has yet to be fully explored, of Arab racist attitudes toward blacks both in the modern and early Islamic periods. Because slavery is not explicitly prohibited by the Qur'an, and free Muslims cannot be enslaved, Muslims recruited slaves from conquered peoples and raided non-Muslim lands for the capture of slaves. For example, the sudden outburst of the Ottoman slave trade in Africa during the nineteenth century is partly explained by the loss of other

traditional sources in Europe. Despite the cruelties and dehumanizing effects of slavery and the nontransatlantic slave trade, "Islamic law, in contrast to ancient and colonial systems, accords the slave a certain legal status and assigns obligations as well as rights to the slave owner. The manumission of slaves, though recommended as a meritorious act, is not required, and the institution of slavery not only is recognized but is elaborately regulated by *Shari'a* law. Perhaps for this very reason the position of the domestic slave in Muslim society was in most respects better than in either classical antiquity or the nineteenth-century Americas." Sometimes the situation of the slave in Muslim society was even better "than that of the free poor." The prohibition of the Muslim enslavement of black Muslims was sometimes violated and justified by the dubious claim that the slaves were idolators, but most jurists were categorically opposed to the enslavement of any Muslim, black or white. Ahmad ibn Khalid al-Nasiri, the nineteenth-century Moroccan historian, condemned such practices as "one of the greatest abominations against religion, because the black people are Muslim people, with the same rights and duties as ourselves." See Bernard Lewis, *Race and Slavery in the Middle East: An Historical Enquiry* (New York: Oxford University Press, 1990), 78, 58; and Murray Gordon, *Slavery in the Arab World* (New York: New Amsterdam Books, 1992).

13 Hiskett, *Course of Islam in Africa,* 178, 181.

14 Saber, "Cultural Relations between Africa and the Arabs," 499–500; Yussef Fadhl Hassan, "Al-judhur a-tarikhiyya lil-'alaqaat al-'arabiyya al-ifriqiyya" (The historical roots of Arab-African relations), in *Al-'arabu wa ifriqya,* 44–45.

15 David Robinson, "An Approach to Islam in West African History," in *Faces of Islam in African Literature,* ed. Kenneth W. Harrow (Portsmouth, N.H.: Heinemann, 1991), 119.

16 Cheikh Hamidou Kane, *Ambiguous Adventure,* trans. Katherine Woods (Portsmouth, N.H.: Heinemann, 1972); Tayeb Salih, *Season of Migration to the North,* trans. Denys Johnson-Davies (1969; rpt. Portsmouth, N.H.: Heinemann, 1976); Ken Bugul [Mariétou M'Baye], *The Abandoned Baobab: The Autobiography of a Senegalese Woman,* trans. Marjolijn de Jager (Brooklyn, N.Y.: Lawrence Hills Books, 1991). The idea of modernity goes back to the Christian Middle Ages, but it was only after the seventeenth century, when secular notions of time and progress began to replace older millennial beliefs, that modernity came to mean a complete break with time. Newness and change, which had been condemned before (the Renaissance is an attempt to return to a golden antiquity), were now desirable. The notion was crystallized in the

second half of the eighteenth century, during the Age of Reason. The modernist cultural movement was a self-generated ambivalent response to a modernity that relied on excessive Reason and the oppressive scientific rationalities of bourgeois cultures. See Kumar, *From Post-Industrial to Post-Modern Society,* 66–100. Kwame Anthony Appiah describes modernity (achieved through a Western-inspired literacy) as a strategy of separating the educated elites from their ancestors. This, in turn, leads to self-commodification, a process that clears the way for one's insertion into the culture of the marketplace. See his *In My Father's House: Africa in the Philosophy of Culture* (New York: Oxford University Press, 1992), 133, 142–43, 145–46. Abdulwahab al Masseri has made a similar argument in relation to secularism.

17 Ngũgĩ, *Decolonising the Mind,* 15, 17.

18 For poignant examples, see Ayi Kwei Armah, *The Beautyful Ones Are Not Born Yet* (1969; rpt. Portsmouth, N.H.: Heinemann, 1988); and Chinua Achebe, *Anthills of the Savannah* (New York: Anchor Books, 1988).

19 George Lang, "Through a Prism Darkly: 'Orientalism' in European-Language African Writing," in Harrow, *Faces of Islam in African Literature,* 304–5.

20 One general characterization of Tahar ben Jelloun's (which, to some extent, he shares with Driss Chraibi) is his protest against the dehumanizing effects of Islamic orthodoxy and widespread corruption at home and the endemic racism against North Africans in France.

21 Pierre-Louis, despite his Christian name, is the descendant of a Muslim family in the old kingdom of Mali. When his great-grandfather was enslaved, he dropped his Muslim last name of Kati "so as not to dishonor it" and simply kept Pierre-Louis (130).

22 This predicament has been transformed and even celebrated as "hybridity" and "homelessness." The basic foundations of the large corpus of postmodern theory is predicated on the notion that the world is forever fragmented into small, localized, and easily perishable truths. That this may be the case should not obscure the incontrovertible fact that theorizing displacement does not render the global capitalist apparatus harmless.

23 Fanon, *Wretched of the Earth,* 218.

24 Robinson, "Approach to Islam in West African History," 121.

25 See Chidi Amuta, *The Theory of African Literature: Implications for Practical Criticism* (London: Zed Books, 1989), 84.

26 Said, *Culture and Imperialism,* 332.

27 Saree S. Makdisi, "The Empire Renarrated: Season of Migration to the

North and the Reinvention of the Present," *Critical Inquiry* 18 (summer 1992): 804–20.

28 Edward Said, with his vast knowledge of the Western humanistic tradition, reads the novel as a "rewriting of Conrad's *Heart of Darkness.*" See "Criticism / Self-Criticism," *Lingua Franca,* February–March 1992, 37–43. That Mustafa Sa'eed goes through a process of "individuation," or "self-realization," that broadens his consciousness and leads him "to realize the bipolar potentialities of the self" is discussed by Muhammed Siddiq in "The Process of Individuation in Al-Tayyeb Salih's Novel Season of Migration to the North," *Journal of Arabic Literature* 9 (1978): 67–104.

29 Mona Takieddine-Amyuni, "Tayeb Salih's *Season of Migration to the North*: An Interpretation," *Arab Studies Quarterly* 2 (winter 1980): 10.

30 Some of my reading has already been alluded to by M. Peled, including Mustafa Sa'eed's ruthless manipulation of the myth of the African in order to extract a sort of unfulfilling and, in the long term, self-destructive revenge from the Europeans. However, I find his suggestion that "the [ultimately traumatic] encounter with Western women constitutes the essence of the cultural experience of the young Arab in the West" to be particularly illuminating. "Perhaps the trauma is so severe," Peled adds, "because in Arab-Muslim system of values the position of the woman and her relations with the opposite sex have always been considered as the 'center of gravity' of the social fabric. The fundamentally different relationship between the sexes in the West tends to be seen and interpreted by the visitor from the East as highly promiscuous, offering too many temptations and pitfalls" (Peled, "Portrait of an Intellectual," *Middle Eastern Studies* 13 [May 1977]: 220–21). These pitfalls, in the end, affect both men and women, as the case of Ken Bugul illustrates.

31 Gibreel Farishta, the controversial character in Salman Rushdie's *The Satanic Verses* who dreams up the blasphemous scenes about the Prophet Mohamed, experiences England in similar ways—a cold, ordered country whose women are ultimately fatal. His woman, Allie, is "the bringer of tribulation, creatrix of strife, of soreness of the heart! Siren, temptress, fiend in human form! That snowlike body with its pale, pale hair: how she had used it to fog his soul, and how hard he had found it, in the weakness of his flesh, to resist" (321). There are other parallels here that could lead to an illuminating comparative study.

32 Takieddine-Amyuni, "Tayeb Salih's *Season of Migration to the North*: An Interpretation," 1. According to Takieddine-Amyuni, *Season of Mi-*

gration is "the epitome in fiction of the three-stage dialectical inter-action between East and West, Black and White, Muslim and Christian" (2). That is, the novel encapsulates most of the crises born out of the colonial experience.

33 In addition to meaning season, the Arabic word *mawsim* in the original Arabic title also refers to the monsoon winds that, historically, linked the East African coast to the Persian Gulf and India. In this case, the title of the novel reinforces the irresistibility of the North and illustrates the rearranged poles of attraction in the colonial period. On the etymology of the term *monsoon,* see Gordon, *Slavery in the Arab World,* 12; and the *Oxford English Dictionary,* vol. 6 (1933), 630.

34 In *Heirs to the Past,* Driss Chraibi describes the shocking disappointment upon discovering the real Europe, not the mythical, carefully cultivated one through academic curricula in the colonies, as the "violence of susceptibility." The colonially educated, exiled protagonist willingness to be colonized for the benefit of participating in the high, civilized European culture preached in colonial schools turns out to be based on deception. " 'I've slammed all the doors of my past because I'm heading towards Europe and Western civilization, and where is that civilization then, show it to me, show me one drop of it, I'm ready to believe I'll believe anything. Show yourselves, you civilizers in whom your books have caused me to believe. You colonized my country, and you say I believe you that you went there to bring enlightenment, a better standard of living, missionaries the lot of you, or almost. Here I am—I've come to see you in your own homes. Come forth. Come out of your houses and yourselves so that I can see you. And welcome me, oh welcome me' " (Chraibi, *Heirs to the Past,* trans. Len Orzen [Portsmouth, N.H.: Heinemann, 1971], 15, 16. The novel was first published in French as *Succession Ouverte* [1962]).

35 See Mildred Mortimer, *Journeys through the French African Novel* (Portsmouth, N.H.: Heinemann, 1990), 168.

36 For a good, insightful, and humanistic interpretation of Marx's early writings, see Erich Fromm, *Marx's Concept of Man* (New York: Continuum, 1961).

37 Mbye B. Cham, "Islam in Senegalese Literature and Film," in Harrow, *Faces of Islam in African Literature,* 169.

38 "*L'Aventure Ambiguë* is the first major work of African fiction to construct an explicit defense of African Islamic life and faith against the European ideological and cultural menace" (Kenneth W. Harrow, "Camara Laye, Cheikh Hamidou Kane, and Tayeb Salih: Three Sufi Authors," in Harrow, *Faces of Islam in African Literature,* 286).

39 See Lang, "Through a Prism Darkly," 302.

40 Quoted in Mortimer, *Journeys through the French African Novel,* 64.

41 Spencer Trimingham, *Influence of Islam upon Africa,* 2d ed. (London: Longman, 1980), 106.

42 Davidson, *Black Man's Burden,* 92, 94.

43 Ngũgĩ, *Moving the Center,* 172–73.

44 Quoted in Ngũgĩ, *Decolonising the Mind,* 97

45 The papers and interventions are published in *Al-'arabu wa Ifriqya.*

46 Brenner, "Muslim Representation of Unity and Difference in the African Discourse," 12.

47 See "Enquête sur la déferlante Islamiste," *L'Evenement du Jeudi,* 25 November–1 December 1993, 32–58. On the growth of Islamism in the Ivory Coast and the whole of Africa, see Francis Kpatindé, "Le croissant et la bannière," *Jeune Afrique,* 27 October–9 November 1994, 18–23; and Marc Yared, "Les Islamistes à l'assaut de l'Afrique noire," *Jeune Afrique économie,* November 1994, 100–109. An equally alarmist article in English titled "March of Islam in Africa" appeared in the British-based magazine *New African,* December 1994, 11–13. But while Islam is contested in the Western media, Paul Johnson, a Western intellectual, is calling for recolonization as a solution to African troubles. See Paul Johnson, "Colonialism's Back—and Not a Moment Too Soon," *New York Times Magazine,* 18 April 1993, 22, 43–44.

48 Marc Yared's article in *Jeune Afrique économie* is the most detailed and comprehensive magazine report I have seen so far. Although the title ("Les Islamistes à l'assaut de l'Afrique noire") is clearly alarmist and even suggests that an unsuspecting African population is being aggressively attacked by Muslim fundamentalists, the article, in typical schizophrenic fashion, does mention that growing Islamic movements in Senegal and Nigeria, for instance, are indigenous movements, "largement enracinés dans les traditions nationales, peu influençables par les courants venus du monde arabe" (106). In Sudan, Islamic resistance to Westernization is far from being a new phenomenon. "The mahdist revolution (1882–85), one the great cataclysms in modern Islamic history, swept the colonial regime of the Egyptians away and established what was the first ostensibly theocratic state in the Sudan (1885–98)." See R. S. O'Fahey, "Islamic Hegemonies in the Sudan: Sufism, Mahdism and Islamism," in Brenner, *Muslim Identity and Social Change in Sub-Saharan Africa,* 30. Similarly, when the Islamic group Mustarshidine wal Mustarshidat staged violent protests against the government of Abdou Diaf in the wake of France's unilateral devaluation of the West African franc (CFA) on January 11, 1994,

they were reenacting an old and indigenous form of protest, especially since the more secular political groups proved to be, once again, utterly ineffective. For an analysis of the consequences of the devaluation of the CFA and solutions to West Africa's economic predicament, see Sanou MBaye's two articles, "L'Afrique noire happé par le marché mondial," *Le Monde diplomatique,* March 1994, 24–25; and "Souhaitable union des économies africaines," *Le Monde diplomatique,* September 1995, 12. For the Islamic response to this event in Senegal, see Géraldine Faes, "SOS détresse," *Jeune Afrique,* 24 February–2 March 1994, 14–17.

49 For a good study of this process, see Stefan Reichmuth, "Islamic Learning and Its Interaction with 'Western' Education in Ilorin, Nigeria," in Brenner, *Muslim Identity and Social Change in Sub-Saharan Africa,* 179–97.

50 Fanon, *Wretched of the Earth,* 315.

51 Camara Laye, *The Radiance of the King,* trans. James Kirkup (New York: Vintage, 1989). The novel was initially published in French in 1955, one year after the publication of his autobiographical novel, *The Dark Child,* written when Laye was working in a car factory in France. Here the author recounts the whole disruptive process ushered in by French colonial education in equally moving detail. See *The Dark Child: The Autobiography of an African Boy,* trans. James Kirkup and Ernest Jones (New York: Hill and Wang, 1954).

52 See Adele King, *The Writings of Camara Laye* (London: Heinemann, 1980), 40, 44; Gerald Moore, *Twelve African Writers* (Bloomington: Indiana University Press, 1980), 90; Harrow, "Camara Laye, Cheikh Hamidou Kane, and Tayeb Salih," 262–78.

4. Women's Freedom in Muslim Spaces

1 Burgat, *Islamic Movement in North Africa,* 101–4.

2 Leila Ahmed, "Women and the Advent of Islam," *Signs: Journal of Women in Culture and Society* 11 (summer 1986): 677.

3 Whenever I use the word *Arab,* I do so only to reflect the original designations in my references. Epistemological confusions are one of the pitfalls of studying Islamic societies today.

4 Marnia Lazreg, "Feminism and Difference: The Perils of Writing as a Woman on Women in Algeria," *Feminist Studies* 14 (spring 1988): 85, 88, 89, 95.

5 I use the word *imperialism* here consciously, although expressions such

as *neocolonialism, postcolonialism,* and others have been used frequently in recent literature. The usefulness of the term *imperialism* was the topic of a roundtable forum at the December 1992 meeting of the American Historical Association; the papers are published in *Radical History* (fall 1993): 7–84. Terms such as *postimperialism* have been suggested but, in the final analysis, *imperialism* continues to describe adequately the underlying structures of present global and human relations.

6 See Ignacy Sachs, "Contre l'exclusion, l'ardente obligation du co-développement planétaire," *Le Monde diplomatique,* November 1995, 12–13.

7 Tahar ben Jelloun, *The Sand Child,* trans. Alan Sheridan (New York: Ballantine, 1989); and *The Sacred Night,* trans. Alan Sheridan (New York: Ballantine, 1991).

8 John D. Erickson, "Veiled Woman and Veiled Narrative in Tahar ben Jelloun's *The Sandchild,*" *boundary 2* 20 (spring 1993): 48, 59.

9 Tahar ben Jelloun, *Les yeux baissés* (Paris: Seuil, 1991).

10 Thanks to the work of Billie Melman, we now know that the negative connotations associated with "Orientalism" are mostly the result of particular Western masculinist perceptions of the Orient. European women travelers who had an intimate—not imagined—knowledge of women's lives were able to "de-hegemonise" the Orient through the exclusively feminine genre of "harem literature." For them, "the *orientale,* as a fixed category of promiscuous feminine sensuality, was supplanted by 'oriental women', whose *sameness* to middle-class Western women was repeatedly emphasised." See Billie Melman, *Women's Orients: English Women and the Middle East, 1718–1918* (Ann Arbor: University of Michigan Press, 1992), 311–12. In fact, English travelers and authors of harem literature may very well have been the first to detect the insidious effects of Orientalism. Julia Sophia Pardoe, author of *The City and the Sultan and the Domestic Manners of the Turks in 1836* (1837), a classic of harem literature, defined Orientalism in very much the same terms as we know it today: "The European mind has become so imbued with ideas of Oriental mysteriousness, mysticism and magnificence, and it has been so long accustomed to pillow its faith on the marvels and metaphors of tourists, that it is to be doubted whether it will willingly cast off its old associations, and suffer itself to be undeceived" (quoted in Melman, *Women's Orients,* 99).

11 See, for example, Margaret Randall's critique of socialist revolutionary movements' failure to allow for an autonomous feminist agenda in her book *Gathering Rage* (New York: Monthly Review Press, 1992). Randall

argues that the fate of socialism ultimately depends on how women are treated in epochs of revolution and beyond. "I believe that in each of the revolutionary experiments the failure to develop an indigenous feminist discourse and a vital feminist agenda impeded the consolidation that would push an otherwise more humane society forward" (160).

12 Magida Salman, "Arab Women," *Khamsin* 6: 28–29.

13 I am using the concept of "bourgeois democracy," although Marx is not known to have used this expression and, in fact, favored universal suffrage—wherever possible—as a strategic move to wrest power from the capitalist ruling class. Indeed, Marxian socialists believed in this strategy until Lenin problematized it in his polemical argument with Kautsy. But Marx was fully aware that the grand freedoms granted by the bourgeoisie are, in the final analysis, heavily circumscribed by legal trappings, such as the often appended proviso of "exceptions made by law," or the prohibitive expense of making oneself heard. In "The Constitution of the French Republic Adopted November 4, 1848," published in 1851, Marx denounced the nullifying effect of legal and economic systems on freedom in bourgeois societies: "This trick of granting full liberty, of laying down the finest principles, and leaving their application, the *details,* to be decided by subsequent laws, the Austrian and Prussian middle-classes have borrowed from their French prototypes. . . . The middle class can be democratic in *words,* but will not be so in deeds—they will recognize the truth of a principle, but never carry it into practice" (quoted in Richard N. Hunt, *The Political Ideas of Marx and Engels,* vol. 2, *Classical Marxism, 1850–1895* [Pittsburgh: University of Pittsburgh Press, 1984], 171). Before the collapse of the Soviet Union, many scholars, probably sobered by the Soviet nightmarish experiment, continued to argue for "reformism" within the democratic system as a useful strategy toward achieving socialism. See Ralph Miliband, *Marxism and Politics* (Oxford: Oxford University Press, 1977); and for a brief history of the polemic surrounding the Marxist view of democracy, see the entry "democracy" in Tom Bottomore, ed., *A Dictionary of Marxist Thought,* 2d rev. ed. (Oxford: Blackwell, 1991), 133–34. But now in the post-Soviet era, the question of whether capitalism is compatible with popular democracy is posed with a heightened sense of urgency, especially as corporate capitalism has reduced public freedoms, even in the most advanced industrialized economies, to hollow statements propagated by an increasingly privatized media. In these circumstances, the erosion of human rights should be of equal concern to U.S. intellectuals who choose to focus

on Third World countries and ignore the "Brazilianization" of their own society. While the managerial techniques of "lean management" have increased the profit margins of corporations and stockholders, economic precariousness continues unabated and is further aggravating social imbalances in the United States. See Simon Head, "The New Ruthless Economy," *New York Review of Books*, 29 February 1996, 47–52.

14 See Fatima Mernissi, *Beyond the Veil: Male-Female Dynamics in a Modern Muslim Society*, rev. ed. (Bloomington: Indiana University Press, 1992).

15 Mernissi, *La peur-modernité*, 80–83, 110–12.

16 Fatima Mernissi, *Le harem politique: Le Prophète et les femmes* (Paris: Albin Michel, 1987).

17 See Fatima Mernissi, *Sultanes Oubliées: Femmes chefs d'État en Islam* (Casablanca: Editions le Fennec, 1990).

18 Mervat Hatem, "Class and Patriarchy as Competing Paradigms for the Study of Middle Eastern Women," *Society for Comparative Studies of Society and History* 29 (October 1987): 816–18.

19 Fatima Mernissi, *Women's Rebellion and Islamic Memory* (London: Zed, 1996), 92.

20 Ibid., 119.

21 See Gudrun Krämer, "Islamist Notions of Democracy," *Middle East Report* 23 (July–August 1993): 2–8.

22 There is a tacit understanding among Marxists that, although the Islamic struggle against imperialism needs to be supported, the reactionary tendencies of the petite bourgeoisie (the main support base of Islamic revivalist movements today) must be rigorously critiqued. See Phil Marshall, "Islamic Fundamentalism—Oppression and Revolution," *International Socialism* 40 (autumn 1988): 1–51. Although I believe that no emancipatory system can be complete without a thorough understanding of capitalism, I must stress that Islam is a broadly defined philosophy of life rather than the set of narrowly defined principles proposed by many militants. With the exception of a few rules in the Qur'an, one can negotiate any ideology within the wide and amorphous parameters of the faith. In the medieval period, Islam "permitted many schools of thought, great freedom of thought, and tremendous development of philosophical and scientific thinking." See Rodinson, *Marxism and the Muslim World*, 66.

23 Nawal El Saadawi, *The Hidden Face of Eve: Women in the Arab World* (London: Zed, 1980).

24 See also Mernissi, *Beyond the Veil*, 172–73.

25 Evelyne Accad, by contrast, singles out macho Mediterranean Arabs and (especially Marxist) feminists who subsume sexual pleasure under the overriding imperative of class struggle and cultural liberation as a culprit in the suppression of women's emancipation in the Arab world. For Accad, a healthier attitude toward sexuality (love, pleasure) will temper other passions and bring civil war in Lebanon to an end. Thus a liberated sexuality should be treated as fundamental in the national-ist struggle of the Lebanese—and other Arab—peoples. See Evelyne Accad, "Sexuality and Sexual Politics," in *Third World Women and the Politics of Feminism,* ed. Chandra T. Mohanty et al. (Bloomington: Indiana University Press, 1991), 237–60. Strange as this theory may seem (for the fate of Lebanon was and still is entangled in regional and global contestations for hegemony and sovereignty), the equation of feminism with a Western-style mode of existence has been the most conspicuous public assumption in some North African countries.

26 Claire Dwyer has discussed "the fetishisation of the veil as the signifier of both Oriental women and of the Orient" in her astute study of photographic representations of Islam. She notes the West's fascination with the veil and demonstrates how it has come to "represent a whole constellation of meanings over time—mystery, exoticism, forbiddeness [*sic*], sensuality, sexuality, backwardness, resistance, domination, pas-sivity, religious fundamentalism." See Claire Dwyer, " 'Ninja Women': The Representation of Muslim Women in the West," *Intertwine* (Jour-nal of the Association of International Students at Syracuse University) (1991–92): 8–13. This all-signifying motif, inherited from an enduring legacy of Orientalism, is also an apt metaphor both for the West's perpetual attempt to undress Muslims and make them available to its gaze and for Muslims' equally obdurate resistance to such crude efforts. Lazreg states that "the persistence of the veil as a symbol that essentially stands for women illustrates the difficulty researchers have in dealing with a reality with which they are unfamiliar" ("Feminism and Differ-ence," 85). Even Fatima Mernissi has been convinced, despite her pro-testations, by French and German editors to put the word *harem* in the title of her books to enhance their marketability. It's almost as if the West wants to hold onto an image of an archaic Islam that has been radically transformed by modernity. Otherwise, how is one to explain the fact that the ratio of women to men college professors in Iran was higher than Germany's in 1986 (19 percent and 17 percent, respectively) or that the same ratio in Egypt in 1986 (28 percent) was higher than that of the United States in 1980 (24 percent) and France in 1987 (23 percent)? See Mernissi, *La peur-modernité,* 206–7, 209 n. 10.

27 See Wiebke Walther, *Women in Islam*, trans. C. S. V. Salt (Princeton, N.J.: Markus Weiner Publishing, 1993), 69–70.

28 Leila Ahmed, *Women and Gender in Islam: Historical Roots of a Modern Debate* (New Haven, Conn.: Yale University Press, 1992), 63.

29 Walther, *Women in Islam*, 6–7, 60–61.

30 Ahmed, *Women and Gender in Islam*, 66.

31 Walther, *Women in Islam*, 51.

32 Ibid., 94.

33 Ahmed, *Women and Gender in Islam*, 88.

34 See Mernissi, *Soultanes Oubliées*, 135.

35 Afsaneh Najmabadi, "Veiled Discourses—Unveiled Bodies," *Feminist Studies* 19 (fall 1993): 487–518.

36 Walther, *Women in Islam*, 144–49.

37 Quoted in Melman, *Women's Orients*, 87.

38 Melman, *Women's Orients*, 106–7.

39 See Afaf Lutfi al-Sayyid Marsot, "Entrepreneurial Women in Egypt," in *Feminism and Islam: Legal and Literary Perspectives*, ed. Mai Yamani (New York: New York University Press, 1996), 39–44.

40 Najmabadi, "Veiled Discourses—Unveiled Bodies," 487–504, 507–12.

41 Walther, *Women in Islam*, 40.

42 Ahmed, *Women and Gender in Islam*, 163–64.

43 Ibid., 164.

44 Farzaneh Milani, *Veils and Words: The Emerging Voices of Iranian Women Writers* (Syracuse, N.Y.: Syracuse University Press, 1992), 28, 35.

45 Afsaneh Najmabadi, "Hazards of Modernity and Morality: Women, State, and Ideology in Contemporary Iran" in *Women, Islam, and the State*, ed. Deniz Kandiyoti (Philadelphia: Temple University Press, 1991), 59, 60, 63.

46 Afsaneh Najmabadi, "Iran's Turn to Islam: From Modernism to a Moral Order," *Middle East Journal* 41 (spring 1987): 202–17.

47 Quoted in Deniz Kandiyoti's introduction to *Women, Islam, and the State*, 7.

48 See Milani, *Veils and Words*, esp. 19–45.

49 See Ahmed, *Women and Gender in Islam*, esp. chap. 9.

50 Ibid., 195.

51 Ahmed, *Women and Gender in Islam*, 244, 225. Professional Muslim women in Turkey have been fighting the ban against wearing headscarves at work. The fact that the Turkish Bar Association's 1985 dress code prohibits headscarves means that secularism has a superficial hold on Turkish society and can be maintained only by decree. See Celeste Bohlen, "Turkish Lawyers Are at Center of a Battle over Mus-

lim Head Coverings for Women," *New York Times,* 12 November 1995, sec. 4.

52 Nawal El Saadawi, "Dissidence and Creativity," *Women: A Cultural Review* 4 (summer 1995): 4.

53 Abdulwahab al Masseri, "The Imperialist Epistemological Vision," *American Journal of Islamic Social Scientists* 11 (fall 1994): 403.

54 Esposito, *Islamic Threat,* 15–16, 22–23.

55 The hypervigilant Turkish military goes as far as charging people for suggesting that they may have allegiances other than to the state's secular ideology. See Stephen Kinzer, "Turkey Secularists Take Their Battle into Court," *New York Times,* 5 April 1998, sec. 1.

56 The cosmopolitan Islamicate society is the successor to a variety of cultures and high civilizations that had existed at the strategic heart of the "Oikoumene"—the Nile-to-Oxus region, which, by the end of the Axial age, had become culturally a rather distinct area. Hellenestic, Indic, Irano-Semitic, and, later, Roman and Sassanid traditions converged to give the birthplace of the early Islamic empires, already at the heart of a large mercantile nexus, a very urban outlook. See Hodgson, *Venture of Islam,* 1: 103–45.

57 Ali Mazrui calls them "camel-and-date" economies. See Mazrui, *Cultural Forces in World Politics* (Portsmouth, N.H.: Heinemann, 1990), 72.

58 For a good example of the strange attempt to match all scientific discoveries with the Qur'an, see Pervez Hoodboy, *Islam and Science: Religious Orthodoxy and the Battle for Rationality* (London: Zed, 1991).

59 John Esposito, *Women in Muslim Family Law* (Syracuse: Syracuse University Press, 1982), 116, 108, 124, 133.

60 Ibid., 134.

61 Mernissi, *La peur-modernité,* 205. The precarious situation of women in the family law codes of the Maghreb and Turkey cannot always, however, be attributed to Islamically based discriminatory practices. Sometimes, the position of women in these countries is determined by the larger Mediterranean ethos of machismo and the cult of honor. In fact, the Tunisian Code of Personal Status enacted in 1956 was not only the most modern in the Arab world, but its divorce provisions "were ahead of many contemporaneous divorce laws in Western countries." But again, granting more liberties for women is sometimes part of the government's plan to use women as a showcase of modernization and resist the threat of fundamentalism. See Ann Elizabeth Mayer, "Reform of Personal Status Laws in North Africa: A Problem of Islamic or Mediterranean Laws?" *Middle East Journal* 49 (summer 1995): 434.

62 The U.S. government uses the National Endowment for Democracy,

an "independent, non-governmental foundation which receives a grant from Congress every year" to promote democratization overseas. Official sponsorship of such a venture (it is estimated that the Clinton administration spent more than $725 million on "democracy-related programs" in fiscal 1995) reveals the extent to which "democracy" is ideologically deployed to serve national interests. See David Samuels, "At Play in the Fields of Oppression," *Harper's*, May 1995, 47–54. But despite its rhetorical commitment to democracy, the United States is, in fact, wary of the democratization of Middle Eastern societies, since such a process cannot be guaranteed to serve U.S. vital interests in the region. "The worry is that anti-American, militantly Islamic regimes might replace the durably autocratic but pro-American governments of Egypt, Saudi Arabia, and many gulf states." See Judith Miller, "At Hour of Triumph, Democracy Recedes as the Global Ideal," *New York Times*, 18 February 1996, sec. 4.

63 Ann Elizabeth Mayer, *Islam and Human Rights: Tradition and Politics*, 2d ed. (Boulder, Colo.: Westview, 1995), 94. Mayer's study included the Iranian Constitution of 1979, the Universal Islamic Declaration of Human Rights, the Azhar Draft Islamic Constitution, the Cairo Declaration, the Saudi Basic Law, certain policies of the Sudanese government, and other writings by influential intellectuals such as the Iranian Sufi Sultanhussein Tabardeh and the Pakistani scholar Mawdudi.

64 See Barry Hindess, "Marxism and Parliamentary Democracy," in *Marxism and Democracy*, ed. Alan Hunt (London: Lawrence and Wishart, 1980), 52.

65 Quoted in Hunt, *Political Ideas of Marx and Engels*, 165.

66 Suad Joseph, "Gender and Civil Society," *Middle East Report* 23 (July–August 1993): 22–26.

67 Mayer, *Islam and Human Rights*, 38.

68 Mahmood Monshipouri, "Islamic Thinking and the Internationalization of Human Rights," *Muslim World* 84 (July–October 1994): 217.

69 Al Masseri, "Imperialist Epistemological Vision," 412–13.

70 Monshipouri, "Islamic Thinking and the Internationalization of Human Rights," 225, 237, 238.

71 Ibid., 218.

72 Taha writes: "An individual can never achieve absolute individual freedom as long as he is divided within himself, with one part at war with the other. He must restore unity to his being, so that he may be at peace with himself, before he can attempt to be at peace with others. One cannot give what he does not have. One can be at peace with himself when the conscious is not in conflict and opposition with the uncon-

scious." And such a state, he explains, can only be achieved through the agency of Islam (110–11). In *Gathering Rage,* Margaret Randall comes to a similar conclusion: "Authentic power comes from a fully developed sense of self, possible only when both individual and collective memory is retrieved" (171).

73 Christain de Brie, "Champ libre au modèle libéral et démocratique," *Le Monde diplomatique,* November 1991, 22–23; Mohamed Khamlishi, "Al-'arabu, al-'ilmaniya wa huququ al-insan" (Arabs, secularism, and human rights), *Anoual* (Moroccan newspaper), 11–14 August 1993, 7.

74 See the two articles by Alan Riding in the *New York Times*: "The West Gets Some Tough Questions," 20 June 1993, sec. 4; and "Rights Forum Ends in a Call for a Greater Role by UN," 26 June 1993.

75 At the time of the conference in Vienna, the United States had not ratified the Covenant on Economic, Social, and Cultural Rights and was thus seen as having double standards. See Beth Stephens, "Hypocrisy on Rights," *New York Times,* 24 June 1993.

76 Joseph, "Gender and Civil Society," 26.

77 See Dorothy Smith, *The Everyday as Problematic: A Feminist Sociology* (Boston: Northeastern University Press, 1987), 3. " 'Relations of ruling' is a concept that grasps power, organization, direction, and regulation as more pervasively structured than can be expressed in traditional concepts provided by the discourses of power. I have come to see a specific interrelation between the dynamic advance of the distinctive forms of organizing and ruling contemporary capitalist society and the patriarchal forms of our contemporary experience."

78 See Nayereh Tohidi, "Gender and Islamic Fundamentalism," in Mohanty et al., *Third World Women and the Politics of Feminism,* 251–67.

79 Joseph, "Gender and Civil Society," 23.

80 Bernard Lewis has shown that this concept of the "father" is essentially a Christian one. See Bernard Lewis, *The Political Language of Islam* (Princeton, N.J.: Princeton University Press, 1984), 64–70. See also Yahya Sadowsky, "The New Orientalism and the Democracy Debate," *Middle East Report* 23 (July–August 1993): 14–21.

81 Adam Seligman, *The Idea of Civil Society* (1992; rpt. Princeton, N.J.: Princeton University Press, 1995), 200, 205.

82 Joseph, "Gender and Civil Society," 24.

83 See Valentine M. Moghadam, ed., introduction to *Gender and National Identity: Women and Politics in Muslim Societies* (London: Zed, 1994), 3, 9.

84 Cherifa Bouatta, "Feminine Militancy: Moudjadidates during and after the Algerian War," in Moghadam, *Gender and National Identity,* 18–

39; Doria Cherifati-Merabitine, "Algeria at a Crossroads: National Liberation, Islamization and Women," in Moghadam, *Gender and National Identity*, 40–62. *Moudjahidates*, the term used to describe women freedom fighters in Algeria, "is representative of the schizophrenic imagination afflicting secular nationalists in the Arab world. As I indicated in chapter 2, the "usurpation" and "illicit secularization" of religious referents (such as *umma*) reveal the extent to which secular projects are hopelessly imprisoned in a Qur'anic vocabulary and make it quite clear that modernist ideologies have failed significantly to alter prerevolutionary cultural patterns in postcolonial Algeria, notwithstanding the modernist rhetoric of the elites. See Lahourai Addi, "De la démocratie en Algérie," *Le Monde diplomatique*, October 1989, 9; Thierry Michalon, "L'Algérie des cousins," *Le Monde diplomatique*, November 1994, 16–17. Again, this should not be surprising, since it was through Islam that the Bedouin culture of Arabia was both spread and superseded. And though Arabism existed as a sentiment before 1914, it was through the confrontation with the Turks (the Arabs' Other) that Arab nationalism was born and consolidated. The reversal to a superficially constructed ethnicity was inspired by the European concept of nation.

85 See Cherifati-Merabitine, "Algeria at a Crossroads."

86 By 1987 Algerian women "constituted only 3.3 percent of the paid work force. The average woman had eight children." It was clear to her that the Algerian Francophone males were paying only "lip service" to women's rights. See Judith Miller, "Women Regain a Kind of Security in Islam's Embrace," *New York Times*, 27 December 1992, sec. 4.

87 Esposito, *Women in Muslim Family Law*, 102.

88 Asghar Ali Engineer, *The Rights of Women in Islam* (New York: St. Martin's Press, 1992), 9.

89 Taha, *Second Message of Islam*, 21. This argument is significantly different from the one recently advanced by As'ad AbuKhalil, who claims that the inferiority of women is unequivocally stated in the Qur'an and the *hadith*, and that it cannot be dispensed with either by conservative clerics or by women revisionists. AbuKhalil places Mernissi in this apologetic school and argues finally that Islam is incompatible with both democracy and gender equality. Although AbuKhalil argues for lifting "the hegemony of Muslim laws," he wants to see these replaced by secular status laws. See As'ad AbuKhalil, "Toward the Study of Women and Politics in the Arab World: The Debate and the Reality," *Feminist Issues* 13 (spring 1993): 3–22; AbuKhalil, "A Viable Partnership: Islam, Democracy, and the Arab World," in *Altered States: A*

Reader in the New World Order, ed. Phyllis Bennis and Michel Mou-
shabek (New York: Olive Branch Press, 1993), 239–45.

90 Taha, *Second Message of Islam*, 39, 52–53, 28, 153.

91 Abdullahi Ahmed An-Na'im, *Toward an Islamic Reformation: Civil
Liberties, Human Rights, and International Law* (Syracuse, N.Y.: Syracuse University Press, 1990), xv, 14, 6–8, 72, 162–64.

92 David Rieff calls Islam the last credible force of resistance left to the
superfluous globalism of American culture. See David Rieff, "A
Global Culture?" *World Policy Journal* 10 (winter 1993–94): 77.

93 See Said, *Covering Islam*, 161.

94 Chandra Talpade Mohanty, "Under Western Eyes: Feminist Scholarship and Colonial Discourses" in Mohanty et al., *Third World Women
and the Politics of Feminism*, 53–54.

95 Mohanty, "Under Western Eyes," 58, 71–74.

96 Lazreg, "Feminism and Difference," 101.

97 Ahmed, *Women and Gender in Islam*, 88, 66.

98 Magali Morsy, *Les femmes du Prophète* (Paris: Mercure de France,
1989), 19–20. Morsy's book is a useful study of the Prophet's wives.
Leila Ahmed posits the thesis that the comparative freedom enjoyed
by the first generation of Muslim women reflects the persistence of
Jahiliyan mores in early Islam. This freedom, as Leila Ahmed has
shown, was eventually eroded, as clerical Islam began to cast a stifling
and gloomy shadow on the fate of women.

99 Morsy, *Les femmes du Prophète*, 163–64.

100 See Ali Banuazizi, "Iran's Revolutionary Impasse: Political Factional-
ism and Societal Resistance," *Middle East Report* 24 (November–
December 1994): 7; Fariba Adelkhah, "L'Offensive des intellectuals en
Iran," *Le Monde diplomatique*, January 1995, 20; Robin Wright, "Shak-
ing the Foundation of Islam," *Portland Press Herald*, 30 January 1995;
Azaden Kian, "Des femmes iranniennes contre le clergé," *Le Monde
diplomatique*, November 1996, 8; Ziba Mir-Hosseini, "Stretching the
Limits: A Feminist Reading of the *Shari'a* in Post-Khomeini Iran," in
Yamani, *Feminism and Islam*, 285–319. Both Banuazizi and Kian describe the dynamic intellectual climate in Iran, which, in many ways, is
superior to that of the days before the Islamic revolution. Even unor-
thodox, if not quite radical, religious ideas are now widely discussed.
Iranian films, "increasingly admired at international film festivals,"
are also severely critical of the government despite the puritanical code
they are subjected to. See Geraldine Brooks, "In Iran, Quiet Films Can
Speak Volumes," *New York Times*, 28 January 1996, sec. 2.

101 Nayereh Tohidi, "Modernity, Islamization, and Women in Iran," in Moghadam, *Gender and National Identity*, 142.

102 Mir-Hosseini, "Stretching the Limits," 316.

103 For a good report on the struggle for Islamic legitimacy and the condition of women in contemporary Iran, see Eric Rouleau, "En Iran, islam contre islam," *Le Monde diplomatique*, June 1999, 20–21. For an overview of Muslim women's attempt to articulate a progressive agenda within Islam, see Yamani, *Feminism and Islam*. Such contestations are happening against a background of unprecedented education levels in Iranian history, and so the reform movement must be seen as some measure of (ironic) success for the Islamic regime. See Robin Wright, "We Invite the Hostages to Return," *New Yorker*, 8 November 1999, 38–47.

104 Leila Abouzeid, *Year of the Elephant: A Moroccan Woman's Journey toward Independence,* trans. Barbara Parmenter (Austin: University of Texas, Center for Middle East Studies, 1989), 1–70.

Conclusion: *Indispensable Polycentricity*

1 Castoriadis, *Philosophy, Politics, Autonomy,* 37.

2 Ibid., 34–36. "Because the being of a social-historical entity is not purely (not even essentially) 'intelligible' or reducible to 'intelligible' elements, it is in principle impossible to recover, after it is destroyed, the *eidos* it embodies and realizes. It is not only the glory that was Athens or Rome that has vanished. It is the whole world of meanings, of affects, and of intentions—of social imaginary significations—created by these societies and holding them together that cannot be recovered, but only approximated with the greatest difficulty" (35). The "social imaginary," an approximate translation of the French *l'imaginaire*, is "the symbolic domains of social myth, ideology, common sense through which people live, communicate, and define the meanings and significance (*significations*) in a society." See Martin O'Connor and Rosemary Arnoux, trans., introduction to *In the Wake of the Affluent Society: An Exploration of Post-Development*, by Serge Latouche (London: Zed, 1993), 1.

3 Blaut, *Colonizer's Model of the World*, 1–49.

4 Mercantilism—or what Blaut calls the protocapitalist phase—persisted and enabled tributary relations to endure well into capitalist phase in the periphery, even as they were inexorably drawn into the vortex of

the capitalist market. See Wolf, *Europe and the People without History*, 305–7.

5 Whether the slave system is a form of capitalist exploitation or not is irrelevant.

6 Amin, *Eurocentrism*, 24. Of course, the most devastating argument proving the racist motives behind the rewriting or the resituating of Greece in the modern period remains Martin Bernal's monumental study, *Black Athena: The Afroasiatic Roots of Classical Civilization*, 2 vols. (New Brunswick, N.J.: Rutgers University Press, 1987–1991).

7 Hobsbawm, *Age of Extremes*, 225–37.

8 Annemarie Schimmel, *Islam: An Introduction* (Albany: State University of New York Press, 1992), 1.

9 Greider, *One World, Ready or Not: The Manic Logic of Global Capitalism* (New York: Simon and Schuster, 1997), 15.

10 See Tim Weiner, "U.S. Spy Agencies Find Scant Peril on Horizon," *New York Times*, 29 January 1998, New England edition.

11 Though I am relying, in this chapter, on recently published studies of the global economy, Ernest Mandel, relying on Karl Marx, had long diagnosed the contradictions and dangers of late capitalism. As early as 1972, when his book, *Late Capitalism*, was published in German, Mandel stated that the intensification of "capital export" and automation "can achieve only a limited success, and both will reproduce even more acute social contradictions" in the long term. One brilliant insight of Mandel was his prediction that "capital" will eventually resist full automation, since its logical outcome would be the reduction of surplus-value. "For reasons of its own self-preservation, capital could never afford to transform all workers into scientists, just as it could never afford to transform all material production into full automation." The contradictions of capitalism increase parasitism, waste, and the dangers facing the planet. "The inherent inability of late capitalism to generalize the vast possibilities of the third technological revolution or of automation constitutes as potent an expression of this tendency of its squandering of forces of production by turning them into forces of destruction: permanent arms build-up, hunger in the semi-colonies (whose average labour productivity has been restricted to a level entirely unrelated to what is technically and scientifically feasible today), contamination of the atmosphere and waters, disruption of the ecological equilibrium, and so on—the features of imperialism or late capitalism traditionally most denounced by socialists." See Mandel, *Late Capitalism* (London: Verso, 1978), 182–83, 207–8, 214.

12 Barnet and Cavanagh, *Global Dreams*, 425.

13 Ken Silverstein, "Millions for Viagra, Pennies for Diseases of the Poor," *The Nation*, 19 July 1999, 13–19; "Kofi Annan's Astonishing Facts!" *New York Times*, 27 September 1998, sec. 4. See also Barbara Crossette, "Most Consuming More, and the Rich Much More," *New York Times*, 13 September 1998, sec. 1.

14 "Since 1970, the world's forests have declined from 4.4 square miles per 1,000 people to 2.8 square miles per 1,000 people. In addition, a quarter of the world's fish stocks have been depleted or are in danger of being depleted and another 44 percent are being fished at their biological limit" (Crossette, "Most Consuming More, and the Rich Much More").

15 Hobsbawm, *Age of Extremes*, 584–85.

16 "Kofi Annan's Astonishing Facts!"

17 Winin Pereira, *Inhuman Rights: The Western System and Global Human Rights Abuse* (Mapusa, Goa, India: Other Indian Press, 1997).

18 Heiner Bielefeldt, "Muslim Voices in the Human Rights Debate," *Human Rights Quarterly* 17 (1995): 590.

19 Latouche, *In the Wake of the Affluent Society*, 93; see also 25, 73–74, 81, 97.

20 See Koren, *When Corporations Rule the World*, 325–28; Greider, *One World, Ready or Not*, 469.

21 See Fanon, *Wretched of the Earth*, 311–16; A. M. Babu, postscript to Rodney, *How Europe Underdeveloped Africa*, 283–88; Douthwaite, *Growth Illusion*, 319–23; Koren, *When Corporations Rule the World*, 257.

22 Amin, *Eurocentrism*, 111, 116.

23 Amin, *Delinking*, 187–88.

24 Christian Smith, *The Emergence of Liberation Theology: Radical Religion and Social Movement Theory* (Chicago: University of Chicago Press, 1991), 27, 36–39, 43; Leonardo Boff and Clodovis Boff, *Introducing Liberation Theology*, trans. Paul Burns (Maryknoll, N.Y.: Orbis, 1988), 3–4, 28–30, 48–49.

25 Pope Pius XI's *Quadragesimo Anno* (1931) is quoted in Smith, *Emergence of Liberation Theology*, 85.

26 Smith, *Emergence of Liberation Theology*, 124–26.

27 See Boff and Boff, *Introducing Liberation Theology*, 88. In his latest encyclicals and tours, Pope John Paul II has consistently championed the rights of the dispossessed and condemned the traumatizing and antihuman ethos of unrestrained capitalism. On the eve of the new millennium, the pope stated in an apostolic letter that "for too many people, freedom remains a word without meaning." See Alessandra Stanley, "Pope Is Returning to Mexico with New Target: Capitalism," *New York Times*, 22 January 1999, New England edition.

28 See John Joseph Marsden, *Marxian and Christian Utopianism: Toward a Socialist Political Theology* (New York: Monthly Review Press, 1991), 138.

29 Ibid., 139–40.

30 See Karl Marx and Fredrick Engels, *Selected Correspondence, 1846–1895*, trans. Donna Torr (New York: International Publishers, 1942), 475.

31 Marsden, *Marxian and Christian Utopianism*, 169–70.

32 L. S. Stavrianos, *Lifelines from Our Past: A New World History* (Armonk, N.Y.: M. E. Sharpe, 1992), 231.

33 Sohail H. Hashimi, "International Society and Its Islamic Malcontents," *Fletcher Forum of World Affairs* 20 (winter-spring 1996): 17.

34 See Nicholas D. Kristoff, "Asians Worry That U.S. Aid Is a New Colonialism," *New York Times*, 17 February 1998, New England edition; Seth Mydans, "Indonesia Begins the Rescue and Consolidation of Banks," *New York Times*, 20 January 1998, New England edition. A dramatic and almost choreographed photograph of white-robed women in prayer accompanies this business article. As I noted in the introduction, the regime was later brought down and a new president elected.

35 See Gary Gardner and Brian Halweil, "Nourishing the Underfed and Overfed," in *State of the World 2000*, ed. Lester R. Brown et al. (New York: Norton, 2000), 59–78. The authors also point out that "liposuction is now the leading form of cosmetic surgery in the United States, at 400,000 operations a year" (76). Assessing such a bewildering landscape of starved bodies in the midst of "unprecedented global prosperity," the authors conclude that "poorly nourished people are a sign of development gone awry" (78).

36 John Maynard Keynes, "Economic Possibilities for Our Grandchildren," in *Essays in Persuasion* (New York: Norton, 1963), 369–70.

37 Hodgson, *Venture of Islam*, 3: 429, 433.

38 John Gray, *Endgames: Questions in Late Modern Political Thought* (Cambridge: Polity Press, 1997), 182–83.

39 Terry Eagleton, *Exiles and Emigrés: Studies in Modern Literature* (New York: Schocken, 1970), 10 n. 1. Quoted in Hartman, *Fateful Question of Culture*, 225–26.

40 Harvey Cox, "The Market as God," *Atlantic*, March 1999, 18–23.

Index

Anouar Majid is Associate Professor of English
at the University of New England.

Library of Congress Cataloging-in-Publication Data

Majid, Anouar, 1960–
Unveiling traditions : postcolonial Islam in a polycentric
world / Anouar Majid.
p. cm.
Includes index.
ISBN 0-8223-2629-9 (cloth : alk. paper)—
ISBN 0-8223-2623-X (alk. paper)
1. Islam—20th century. 2. Capitalism—Religious aspects—
Islam. 3. Islam—Economic aspects. 4. Europe—Relations—
Islamic countries. 5. Islamic countries—Relations—Europe.
6. Islam and world politics. 7. Islamic countries—Politics and
government. I. Title.
BP163.M342 2000
306′.0917′671—dc21   00-037553